*How to Raise
Good Catholic Children*

Mary Reed Newland

How to Raise
Good Catholic
Children

SOPHIA INSTITUTE PRESS®
Manchester, New Hampshire

How to Raise Good Catholic Children was originally published in 1954 by
P. J. Kenedy and Sons under the title *We and Our Children*. This 2004
edition by Sophia Institute Press® includes minor editorial revisions to
correct infelicities in grammar and to update or omit dated material.
New chapter titles and subheadings have also been added.

Sophia Institute Press®
Box 5284, Manchester, NH 03108
1-800-888-9344
www.sophiainstitute.com
Nihil obstat: Rev. Andrew A. Martin, *Censor Librorum*
Imprimatur: Christopher J. Weldon
Bishop of Springfield, Massachusetts, August 13, 1954

Library of Congress Cataloging-in-Publication Data

Newland, Mary Reed.
 [We and our children]
 How to raise good Catholic children / Mary Reed Newland.
  p. cm.
 Originally published: We and our children. New York : P. J.
Kenedy and Sons, 1954.
  ISBN 1-928832-86-5 (pbk. : alk. paper)
  1. Christian education — Home training. 2. Catholic
children — Religious life. 3. Christian education of children.
4. Catholic Church — Education. I. Title.
  BV1590.N4 2004
  248.8'45'088282 — dc22   2003027846

05 06 07 08 10 9 8 7 6 5 4 3 2

To our Lady —
for her birthday

Contents

How to Raise
Good Catholic Children

Chapter 1

Introduce your child to God

Not long ago, I heard someone who has worked long and hard in apostolic causes described as "deeply spiritual — *but,* like the saints, so impractical." That contradiction sums up as nicely and neatly as possible the confusion of most moderns — some Catholics among them — with respect to man's end, the things that are God's, and the spiritual life. Highly impractical . . .

It was an odd remark coming from someone who, if he were asked, would reply in the next breath that man is made to know and love and serve God on this earth and be happy with Him forever in Heaven. If we must face the fact that death is inevitable (and we certainly must) and that eternity begins right on its heels, then to imitate the saints is not unpractical, but quite as practical as it is possible to be. After all, the saints are the only ones we know for sure have arrived at the "forever in Heaven." And when you realize that the spiritual life thrives in proportion as we cultivate the life of God in our soul, then to attempt a spirituality like the saints' is the only kind of living that makes any sense.

The saints, contrary creatures, lived as though the soul were all, and as an afterthought gave a nod now and then to the body. To their own bodies, that is; they poured out endless charity on the bodies of others. Not that they despised their own bodies — no saint despises the work of God's hands — but they understood them well: their corruptibility, their weakness, their nuisance value, all inherited through Original Sin. So, rather than depend on their short-lived and highly fallible flesh, they turned their entire attention to the soul.

Peculiarly enough, once the saints concentrated on the soul, it followed that the body fell in line, subdued and obedient, and their comings and goings in this world were marked with remarkable perspicacity and acumen. They got more work done, undertook and accomplished more impossible things, acquired more friends and influenced more people than whole regiments of worldlings steeped in the rules for success.

⌒

Teach your child to love God

It's amusing to observe the contradictions apparent in the comparison of materialism versus spirituality, but it's not amusing for long — because there's more involved than a game. Each man caught in the embrace of materialism is a soul in danger of hellfire, and each soul is infinitely precious to God. For those of us who are parents, the challenge is terrible indeed. We have placed in our care for a few short years precious immortal souls who belong to God, whose destiny is an eternity in and with God, and who depend entirely upon us for the formation of a way of life that will lead them surely to God. And woe to us if we fail in this charge.

Who would blame a child who runs headlong into the path of an onrushing truck if his parents have failed to warn him of the perils of trucks? And who would blame a child who fires a loaded gun, killing his friend, if his parents have failed to warn him of the perils of guns? Then who shall blame a child whose soul turns eagerly to the noise and distraction of worldliness, if his parents have failed to show him that love and peace and beauty are found only in God?

"It were better for him if a millstone were hung about his neck and he were cast into the sea, than that he should cause one of these little ones to sin."[1] That is Christ, speaking of scandal. And the scandal of the neglected souls of children is manifest all about, in their confusion and delinquency, and of children grown up to adulthood in their godlessness and immorality.

"He who abides with me, and I in him, he bears much fruit; for without me you can do nothing."[2] That is Christ, too, speaking of the spiritual life. No need to argue more about imitating saints, nor look any further for a reason we should start now, in their earliest years, to show our children why, and, as best we can, how one sets about trying to be a saint.

There's no difference in terms of time in souls. A child's soul is not, although we may think of it that way, a "child soul." Sin, not years, makes the differences in souls, and the only variation between the spiritual life for a child and for a grown-up is the means of communication. Although children are taught with simpler words and ways, the end of the teaching is the same. And if this seems too good to be true, and far too easy, remember, "Whosoever does not accept the kingdom of God as a little child will not enter into it."[3]

So it all begins with loving God, and learning how He loves us. That he is loved by God is very easy for a child to believe. He's

[1] Cf. Mark 9:41-42. The biblical quotations in this book are taken from the Douay-Rheims edition of the Old and New Testaments. Where applicable, quotations have been cross-referenced with the differing names and enumeration in the Revised Standard Version, using the following symbol: (RSV =).

[2] Cf. John 15:5.

[3] Cf. Mark 10:15.

How to Raise Good Catholic Children

hungry to be loved, and it's a hunger God planted in him. His reaction to the knowledge of God's love is perfect faith. It's no accident, nor is it a matter of taking advantage of his emptiness of knowledge. The virtue of faith is his at the moment of Baptism, infused into his soul by the Holy Spirit. What we see happening in our children when we introduce the revelation that there is a God and He loves them is inevitable. It's the first movement in them of the divine virtue of faith responding to the word of God. It slips into the life of a child so easily, without fanfare or excitement, that we hardly notice that it has happened.

He's very little, and one day it's time to tell him. We pat him dry, after his bath, and kneeling there, loving the marvel of his neat little body, we say, "Stephen, do you know who made you?"

"Who made me?"

"God made you, Stephen."

"Oh." And he stops, and thinks, and confirms it. "God made Stephen."

And the gift of faith is at work. If one can say that God waits for things, then God has waited for this since forever. It is the beginning of why Stephen is here. "To know God . . ." And he trots down the hall to his crib, a different child that night because now he knows who made him. Many wise men may know many more things than Stephen, but may not know who made them.

When you tuck him in and say, "Do you know why God made you, Stephen?" he will hardly ever answer, "No." But almost always, "Why?" And you tell him, "Because He loves you." And Stephen knows the most important thing in all the world.

I asked a little boy of two and a half, "Why did God make you?" and he gave me such a look — *didn't I know?*

"Because He wants me!" And he laughed and laughed. Such a joy, to know one is wanted.

8

This is *security*, the first and last and only real security. And we must make it so real for our children that they will look out at the world from the snug safety of God's love. They must know that He loves them as though they were His only love, and that they need not fear the dividing of His love because it's indivisible. It is like the flame of a candle, which will light another candle, and another, and another, and still burn as before. Nowhere is there more love than this. This is *all* love, it never changes, and they may turn to it from the middle of sin or sanctity and always find asylum.

A little boy of four told me, in great excitement, "You know what? God didn't make me like you make a house. You know how He made me? He just *thinked,* and there I was. Like this . . ." And he stood very still and blinked his eyes once, the best way he knew to express in physical terms how God made him. Just to think, and make a little boy. What could be more wonderful?

For a child to learn that he is loved and wanted is pure delight, but to root it deep in his soul takes care and practice, and we must teach him to delight in it often.

"God made you, dear, ages before He put you on this earth. You were in the mind of God so long ago that even Mother cannot tell you when it was. Always He knew you, always He wanted you, and because He knows all things, He knew when was the perfect time for you to come so you could do what He has planned for you."

It's easy to take these beginnings for granted, but if we would stop to consider them as acts of great supernatural significance, we would learn much faster to appreciate the vast potential waiting to be developed in the souls of the smallest children. Children believe with simplicity because, along with the other gifts of the Holy Spirit at Baptism, they possess the gift of wisdom, so different from the book-learning we think synonymous with wisdom. Father Walter Farrell, in his *Companion to the Summa,* says that to question the simplicity of God's omnipotence, His ability to create a man or a universe out of nothing, is as ridiculous as to hold that a man may not move through a fog without punching it with his fist. This child's acceptance of the most staggering acts of creation is precisely the acceptance that Christ said will qualify us for Heaven. Understanding the meaning of grace, and faith, and revelation, and their supernatural effects in the uncluttered souls of children, it is utter absurdity to hold that "in all fairness," a child should be left untaught until he is old enough to decide what to believe for himself. It's not only an absurdity, but a consummate mockery of the Holy Spirit.

Still, to be honest, one must admit that the word *God* is really only a word, so far, and what children love is not the word, but the love. I suppose one could substitute any word for the word *God* and they would love being loved this way just as much. So we must make Someone, not just a something, of God. And quite without realizing it, we have arrived at the beginning of catechism.

It's a bit of a jolt to start thinking in terms of catechism so long before one absolutely must. Poor catechism, maligned and mossy with dreary associations. But if we apply ourselves seriously to teaching our children the spiritual life, one of the greatest challenges is the dare to turn catechism into the happiest of all their studies. It should be. It could be.

Perhaps the reason it hasn't been so far is that we mistake it for an end, not a means. It is as though, reading the recipe for a cake on a printed page, we should decide that it's all very dull and never bother putting it together and making the cake. There's a great difference between reading the directions and eating the cake. The bone-dry definitions in the catechism are as essential as the recipe for the cake, but if we put them together with imagination and enthusiasm, and add love and experience, then set them afire with the teaching of Christ, His stories, His life, the Old Testament as well as the New, and the lives of the saints, we can make the study of catechism a tremendous adventure.

~

Begin with the Creation

The first lessons in any catechism are about God and creation. If you read the story of creation to your children out of Genesis, and translate it into their own words, and linger lovingly over all the projections of it that are a part of their own lives, their first glance at that same lesson in the book finds them already knowing the answers. "Who made the world?" In the first chapter of the first book of the Old Testament is the story of how God made the world. This is how it goes:

Out of nothing God made this great, complicated world. First, He made the light, and then the space (which is called *firmament* in most translations), that emptiness between earth and the highest stars. Already there is something that has enormous meaning for small boys whose cereal boxes screech of spaceships and trips to the moon. One would think, these days, that scientists or cartoonists or scriptwriters created space. Well, they didn't. God did. For all their hip-de-do about trips to the moon, there would be none, even in the funny papers, if God hadn't made space.

Then He gathered together all the waters under the space and called them seas, and what was left was dry land, and that He called earth. And when it was done, He looked at it lovingly and said, "It is good."[4]

Then He made all the green growing things on the earth, and then — lovely invention — He made the stars. Next the sun, and

[4] Gen. 1:10.

the moon, and then the fish in the seas and the birds in the air. After He made the fish and the birds, He blessed them, so that they would have the power to lay eggs and raise families and one day there would be our phoebe, in her funny mud nest over the door — the bold, saucy phoebe, who built her nest where the light should be, and now we can't put a light over our front door. God even knew that and saw us stumbling around in the dark with a flashlight, all because of a phoebe. Our phoebe was in the mind of God that day when He blessed the very first phoebe so that she could start her family and be many times over a grandmother to our phoebe.

Now children begin to see a great deal more about the God who loves them so much. Not only did He know them that long ago, but He also planned things for them, so their world would be full of fun and beauty.

After the fishes and the birds, God made the animals, and of course He knew the first lady goat who would be many times over a grandmother to our goats. He thought, "I shall design a goat, of course, with chin whiskers and a voice that sounds like cloth tearing, because my children will want to have some goats." So Nanny and Helen were known, too, even then. How much God knows! It would be quite impossible to fool Him.

Then came the best part of all. After all the world was made, and the sky and the stars and the sun and the moon were in place, and there were green growing things, with rivers and seas and land where birds flew and animals and fishes lived, then (and have them look for themselves, and see that the words are there on the page exactly as you read them), He said, "Let us make man to our image and likeness."[5] God the Father, and God the Son, and God

---

[5] Gen. 1:26.

the Holy Spirit all made man together out of the slime of the earth and breathed their own foreverness into him, and loved him. And here is their first knowledge of the soul.

"What do you suppose it means: 'They made man in Their image and likeness'?"

No one knows; so they wait to hear what it means.

"It doesn't mean we look like God, because this happened in the very beginning, long before the Son of God came down to earth to take the form of a human baby. And it couldn't mean that He made us out of the same stuff as Himself, because God isn't made out of stuff: God is a spirit, without a body. He never changes, but we change. So it couldn't be that we're like Him in our body, which changes every year and grows bigger and older all the time.

"It's the *foreverness* that He breathed into man that is like Him, the part of us that never dies, as God never dies. We are like Him deep inside, where our love comes from. That is the part of us we call our soul, and we cannot see it, or touch it, because, like God, it is a spirit."

Just recently a mother asked me, "But do you really mean to say you can teach a four-year-old that he has a soul, and expect him to understand it?"

Yes, I do, because I've seen it happen. A four-year-old does not *doubt*. It may be hard for him to visualize it, but he accepts it simply because you tell him. And there is this we forget, because we are grown and the years of first faith are so far behind: children have a sense of their *being* very early in life. It isn't just the physical sensation that goes with having a body that can feel hot, cold, hunger, and weariness. It's a real sense of their soul.

I can remember distinctly as a child stopping in midair, as it were, and realizing "I am." I'm sure I didn't put it that way, but that's what it amounted to.

How to Raise Good Catholic Children

My own children have tried to tell me about it in various ways: "Mother, sometimes I get the funniest feeling — about me, and if I'm awake, or am I dreaming, or is this whole world real, or just me?"

Children may be clumsy with words, but that part of them which is eternal makes itself known in flashes of puzzlement like this, and we ought not to be surprised when it does. We ought to expect that such a staggering thing as an imperishable soul, filled with God, would be able to beat through the consciousness of flesh now and then and make us stop and wonder. Doubtless, four-year-olds do not often stop to register awareness of their souls, but their acceptance of them is the same act of faith as their acceptance of God.

⁀

A father's roles make a good analogy for the Trinity

One difficulty needs to be resolved, usually, before the reading of Genesis and the Creation is far along, and that is the divine *us* in "Let us make man to our image and likeness." It comes straight at children in the beginning of catechism, so we can't just skip over it because the Trinity is a mystery. I'm sure that when St. Patrick explained it with his shamrock, it was as clear as it's possible for the Trinity to be; and I'm equally sure that it was St. Patrick, and not the shamrock, that did the trick, because, as a child listening to others explain it with a shamrock, I was left completely cold. The three-in-one was all that registered, and since there was a furniture polish by that name, the whole lesson stayed right there on the same level with the furniture polish.

Another way of explaining it is with the three forms of water: water, ice, and steam; but steam is over the heads of most children, so that lets the three forms of water out.

After much thinking and struggling, we have hit on a way, inadequate at best, of trying to explain three Persons in one God by comparing it to the children's own human father. At home, among the children, he's known as Daddy, and his role is that of father. At work, among his fellow workers, he's known as Mr. Newland, and his role is that of wage earner. To Mother, he's known as Bill, and his role is husband. He is the same man, but he has three different roles to play.

Very roughly, it draws a parallel to the three dispensations, as theologians call them, of the Persons of the Trinity. God the Father we think of as Creator. God the Son we think of as Redeemer. God the Holy Spirit we think of as Divine Love. Very little children will not even ask for more than an explanation of who are the "We." And they will accept your explanation of Father, Son, and Holy Spirit as they do their knowledge of God, His love, and their souls. But at five or six, they want a little more, and until we happen on something better, we have found that the parallel in their own father's three roles explains it as well as it can be explained.

≈

Emphasize the presence of
the Trinity in your child's soul

Now, back to Genesis and the story of Creation (which includes so much more of the catechism than we ever dreamed). Having arched the centuries from God's knowledge of our phoebe, so alive in her nest today, and her many-times-removed grandmother on that day of the creation of birds, they can see quite easily that the creation of Adam and Eve has a special meaning in relation to themselves. When you read, "Let us make man to our image and likeness," there *they* are. And when you come to the place where God tells Adam that the whole earth and all that is in it is his to enjoy and rule over, their cup is full, and little girls and little boys can stand very still and look around them at the world and say in utter truth and simplicity, "He made the world for me."

But growing up is not always a happy thing. It is often very thorny for a child because he can't possibly understand the vast human weaknesses that underlie the behavior of the adults around him, and as a result, he is easily hurt by the very people who love him most. Unlike God's love, ours blows hot and cold, subject to all the worries and pressures of family affairs. It's easy to imagine the damage done to such little ones when the mother or father they love brushes them aside in the heat of domestic high tension. Without an adequate knowledge of God's love, the bottom drops out of everything. A merely vague indication that He's somewhere about and loves them is small comfort when they're really hurt and heartsick.

I learned this in a way I shall never forget. After a nasty display of temper, prompted by something I can't even remember now, I found Monica, then six, watching me with concern. When I asked her what she was thinking, she said, somewhat timidly, "You said I mustn't be naughty if I want to be a saint, so I was asking God to help you not be cross, so you can be a saint."

That I had trampled all over her with my peevishness was a matter of deep shame, but above that, there was profound gratitude that, driven into solitude, she shared her solitude with God. How terrible, the loneliness of a child without God at such a time. There are people in mental hospitals today because they never learned to share solitude and loneliness with God when they were children.

Thus, a child's faith in God must be sharply drawn. It must be so concrete that he can all but put out his hands and touch it. And the secret of its reality is the indwelling of the Holy Trinity.

"God loves you so, dear, that it was *not* enough for Him to send you down to earth and then stand far away in Heaven and watch you. He cannot bear to be parted from you. So when you were baptized, at that very moment, Heaven opened and, faster than the wind, God the Father, God the Son, and God the Holy Spirit came rushing down to make their home in your soul. No one can ever make Them leave but you. Only if you should commit a serious sin would They have to go. You must stop many times during the day and think about Them, turn to Them in your very own soul, tell Them you love Them, and ask Them to help you love Them more."

This is what spiritual directors recommend to their penitents when they say, "Acknowledge daily the indwelling of the Holy Trinity." One does not have to wait until he's grown to begin — not if he is taught when he is little. Then God doesn't have to wait years, in silence and longing, for the invitation to move and kindle the love, to draw His creature inward to life in Him. "Abide in me, and I in you."

~

Form in your child a habit of holiness

It isn't difficult to find opportunities for acknowledging the indwelling of the Trinity. For all it may sound affected when reduced to words on paper, it's easy to find times when a child is alone with you, perhaps drying the dishes, making the beds, out in the garden with you planting the beans, when you can kneel down to his size and whisper, "Let's be very still for a minute and think about the Holy Trinity in our souls, and let us love God very much." This is a very reasonable suggestion to a child, and if he has been taught, he will kneel and without any affectation say, "Holy Trinity, living in my soul, I love You very much. Please help me to love You more."

And he will return to planting his beans. It's such a little act, hardly enough to stir the surface of a minute, but it's the one thing the Trinity awaits. God is bound by our own free wills; we must permit Him to move us, or He cannot.

But like the more mundane things — washing hands, brushing teeth, learning to say "please" and "thank you" — this will become a habit only if there is constant repetition. And there must be constant repetition, because the spiritual life is built upon this silent love of God. This is the beginning of silence, and simplicity, and contemplation. This is the first tiny step toward union. This *must* be if there is to be any spiritual life at all.

God does the work, but He must have the opportunity. We can't possibly reveal all His secrets to our children. We can't illuminate their souls beyond the point of a kind of charting. Grace does the illuminating, and through grace, they will discover the joy of a life lived in union with God. We work with grace toward this union when we teach our children to be still, to listen, to wait, to love.

We're living at a time when love has been so defiled that to use the word in its Christian sense is to invite misunderstanding. People don't get what we're driving at when we talk of loving one another: it sounds much too unrestrained and, frankly, rather queer. It has one meaning only, for most of the world, and that's physical passion, with no understanding whatsoever that physical love is beautiful only when it imitates God's love. So it's terribly urgent that we reveal to our children what love really is, *who* Love is, because they must love Him wildly if they are to protect themselves against the time when passion moves in and masquerades as beauty. Physical passion is only one small fragment reflecting God's love; and unless children recognize love as the source of serenity and peace and grace, they will be quite defenseless before the fragment that pretends to be the whole.

God will be loved by our children as much as we have permitted Him to be loved. In a strange way, He's at our mercy, and so are they. In His love, He has brought them forth out of us, but He must wait for us to make Him known to them.

And it's God's love — not brains, or brawn, or talent — that is the common denominator for all men. A man is wise or a fool, safe or in danger, in proportion to his response to God's love. If we're tempted to doubt this, the lives of the child saints prove it over and over again. Maria Goretti was poor, uneducated, the essence of simplicity. Heroic virtue, for her, was born of the love of God taught to her by a tired, overburdened mother to whom the intricacies of theological argument were as much a mystery as the geography of the moon. But God and His love were not. They were as daily bread. Guided by the graces He sends to all mothers, she fed her child the best way she knew how. Obviously it could not have been better.

When they questioned this mother at her daughter's canonization: "How does one go about raising a child who will be a saint?" her answer was simple. There was no secret available to her, she said, that is not available to all mothers. She merely taught her all she knew about God and His love, and His delight in a soul untouched by sin. If an uneducated peasant woman can do it in the middle of a world reeking with hideous sin, we have little excuse for not doing it ourselves.

Simplicity of soul is one of the prerequisites of sanctity, and it's one of the things our children already possess. We must be very careful not to contribute to the great cluttering up. We must make a heroic effort to rid our lives of all but one motive, that "impractical" spirituality of the saints, a life in union with God. If this is the undercurrent of our existence, we can expect the spiritual training of our children to bear fruit. Without it, what they learn of God as children will be easily shoved aside when the world begins to make its noise in their ears. We inherited Heaven at the Cross, and a way of life that should lead us all to sublime heights. Our obligation as parents is heavy: we must raise children who are in love with God.

Chapter 2

Teach your child to pray

Praying is pretty personal. After all, it's conversation with God, and conversation with someone you love ought to be entirely personal — warm and intimate, full of secrets and praises and declarations of love.

Praying ought to be fun, too, most of the time, because it's our one chance to talk as much as we like and know that we don't bore, that we will be heard, and that everything we say draws us closer to God — which is what He wants and the reason for praying in the first place.

The trouble is that many people think of prayer more as a recitation than as a conversation, and all their lives they speak to God with words that other people have put together for them. They're beautiful words, beautifully put together, and they give great praise. But it's a big mistake to think that only formal prayers are proper when we speak to the Father who made us, who knows us better than we know ourselves and would like us to come simply, like children, and say what we want to say in our own words.

Once there was a girl who told her confessor, "Father, I try to say the Rosary every night when I'm in bed, but get so involved talking to God that, before I know it, I've fallen asleep. Do you think I'm deliberately allowing myself to be distracted?"

Her confessor laughed. "If you were God," he said, "would you rather have someone talk to you in his own words, or in someone else's? By all means, say your Rosary some other time, but continue your conversations with God, and do stop confusing distraction with mental prayer."

This is the understanding of prayer we can give our children in their earliest years, long before they learn recited prayers, and in this way we give them a pattern of approach to God in prayer that will suit not only their childhood, but all the years of their lives. Even when they begin to learn formal prayers, in the beginning they have no real understanding of them, and it's a rather bleak start to one's life of prayer to think it must consist of a lot of phrases learned by heart but not understood, which one repeats at certain times because Mother says you must.

The Our Father is the perfect pattern for prayer because when the Apostles asked our Lord how they should pray, He gave this prayer to them. The Mass contains the same pattern, and both make clear the four aspects of our relation to God: penitent, seeker, beloved, and gratefully blessed. If our children learn to pray each of these roles, they will have learned the rudiments of all prayer, without which the saints say no progress is possible in the spiritual life.

It would be presumptuous for me to tell someone else how he should pray or what words he should use, because the words one person would choose are rarely the words another would choose, and each person's way is shaped and colored by his tastes, personality, and all the many small differences that make him who he is and not someone else.

Following, just for the sake of illustration, is how we have taught our children to pray. Children can begin to pray like this when they're three and a half or four.

Examination of conscience

The first thing, after "Dear Blessed Jesus," or whatever children like to call Him best, is their examination of conscience, because it's easier to settle down to a really good talk with God after we get our sins out of the way. This is why the Mass starts with the penitential rite.

The important thing about a child's examination of conscience is that he be assured that his parents will not scold him if he reveals some carefully concealed guilt of the day. His sins are sins against God, not his parents, and he will not hesitate to drag out the most jealously guarded secrets if he's certain his parents understand that he's confessing to God, not to them, and that they will resist the temptation to lecture.

For instance, in the summertime we have a problem called "dirt in the hair." Every night the children turn up at bedtime with their heads gritty with topsoil. The culprit is conspicuous, if at all, only by his silence — until he examines his conscience. "I poured dirt on everybody's head because I felt like it." The immediate reaction of any normally weary mother facing a lineup of shampoos is at least mild rage, but in the face of such a confession freely made, the only permissible comment is, "Are you *really* sorry?" to lead the self-accused to a sincere act of contrition.

"I am sorry, and *please help me not to do it again.*" Here they learn to guard against presumption. The inclination is to vow solemnly that they will never do it again (O happy day!), but sanctity does not come that easily. Unless they beg for the grace to reform, they are apt to do it again and again.

Some days are quite good, and they will charge into night prayers loudly with, "I was very good today, God!" With presumption again in mind, it is better to say something like, "I tried to be good today, but if I did anything to offend You, I am sorry. Please help me never to offend You again."

Not all children are shouters at prayers, but we have had some who were, and their attempts to make themselves heard way off in Heaven certainly robbed their prayers, while not of sincerity, at least of privacy. Learning that God is near, is here, is everywhere, and can hear even the whispered prayers and secret thoughts, is a wonderful discovery for shouters and non-shouters alike and, incidentally, covers one whole lesson in the catechism: *Where is God? If God is everywhere, why don't we see Him? Does God see us? Does God know all things? Can God do all things? Is God just, holy, and merciful?*

The answers to all these questions can be learned in the course of the many interruptions to night prayers. "How can He hear me if I don't even see Him? When did He come in? Did He come in the door? Can He come through the wall? Could He see a mouse in the wall? A mosquito on the ceiling? If I just think my prayers, can He hear them?"

If the question about God's being just, holy, and merciful seems a bit difficult, it fits in when we explain that confessing the sins of the day is something entirely between them and God, and is the reason — when correction and punishment are a mother's and father's concern elsewhere — they do not belong at night prayers. One sins against God, who can already see the sin, and see the sorrow for it, and will reward a sincere confession with forgiveness and the grace to do better next time.

⤙

Intentions

Next come the petitions. "God blessing" is a sweet part of every child's prayers, but it's a question whether they understand what it really means. It helps if they have a definite favor to ask with the blessings: "God bless my mother and father, and help them with their work. God bless my granny, and help her knee to get better," and so on. Then the rest of the family and friends, sometimes grouping them for the sake of brevity. And when the lists of intentions have grown so long that it would take until dawn to name them, one can say, "All those for whom we have promised, proposed, and ought to pray."

Let us not burden ourselves or our children with the idea that our prayers are divided like so many slices of bread and applied in diminishing amounts in proportion to the number of people we would pray for. St. Thérèse embraced the entire universe with her prayer and left it to the mysterious ways of God to apply her love wholly and intensely for everyone on earth.

Children must not feel that because of their littleness, their prayers lack power. Because of their stunning purity and their childlike love, their prayers are probably far more powerful than our own. We should encourage them to pray boldly and should point out all they can accomplish by uniting their prayers to Christ's prayers for all men. This gives them the soundest, most mature, and most inspiring reason for acquiring habits of prayer. Of course, they must know that their first obligation is to save their own souls, but people often find that their most inspiring motive for living and praying heroically is the need of others, all of which is intimately bound to the saving of their own souls.

Once explained, children do not find it hard to believe that God is able to "keep a list" of intentions and benefactors to be prayed for, and as long as they return from time to time to renew the intentions, there is no great danger of growing slipshod.

Then we add, "everyone who has been so good to us, everyone in the world, all the souls in Purgatory, and please help the Russian people to find God." This last poses a lot of questions, and the easiest way to explain is by telling the story of Fatima, how our Lady asked especially for prayers for Russia.

All these requests for "everyone" play an important part in forming a child's understanding of his part in the Mystical Body of Christ — in the Church. Gradually he will begin to see himself as a member, to see that on him also, as well as on the grown-ups, religious, and the Holy Father, rests the burden of continuing the work of the Redemption, saving the souls of all men and restoring the world to Christ.

Next, "Please help us all to be saints."

I remember hearing someone tell that, asked in Confession if she didn't want to be a saint, she replied, "Oh no, Father. I'll be grateful if I manage to get to Purgatory." But God *wants* us to be saints, which is quite a different thing from saying we think we're saints. When He has troubled to make it clear, "Be perfect as your heavenly Father is perfect,"[6] and when He has left the Body of His Son and a wealth of revelation, prayer, sacraments, and grace at our disposal, it's a perverse kind of humility that prompts us to aspire to no more than Purgatory.

Children want to be saints. It's part of knowing God and loving Him, and wanting to be with Him in Heaven. We cheat them when we forget to teach them to ask daily for the grace to be saints.

⚬

Loving and thanking God

Spiritual and temporal needs over with, children can turn to the joy that is simply loving God. "I love You, Blessed Jesus, and I

[6] Cf. Matt. 5:48.

love Your Blessed Mother." This must be the part He listens for the hardest. It's really all He asks, because if love is there and a right disposition, with grace the rest will follow. So we encourage children to say it over and over until their whole idea of God is bound inseparably to their love for Him.

After the loving comes the thanking; one follows the other with ease. "And thank You for . . ." each night a different blessing, from babies and books to lollipops and circuses — anything and everything — so that they will see that their world is full of blessings straight from the hand of God.

Gradually, as they grow older, the form of their prayers will change. If they attend parochial school and Sister recommends certain practices, we should help to put these into effect. They will learn formal prayers, prayers proper to each liturgical season, the family Rosary, the Stations of the Cross, Mass preparations, and much more. But the approach of their prayers remains unchanged, the contrition, asking, praising, and thanksgiving are in all these, and if they understand, above all, that prayer is talking to God, the knowledge will never leave them.

Knowing all this, however, is still no guarantee that children will always *want* to pray. Would that all *grown-ups* always wanted to pray. But they don't, and their own perversity is not always the reason.

Many times God allows it to be hard to pray, simply to school us in applying our wills, to teach us that the value of prayer does not depend on the amount of emotion we can whip up. So when "Time for prayers" is greeted with moans and groans, it's time to explain that saying prayers when you least want to, simply because you love God and have a kind of dry respect and a sense of obedience, is to gain the greatest merit for them. Many times the saints had trouble getting excited about prayers, but they said them, because prayers were due and their value had nothing to do with how eagerly they went about saying them.

"But with so many people in the world praying, I get the feeling God can't really be listening to me."

Here we can remind our children of how our Lord said that God counts even the hairs on our heads, and all the sparrows that fall. It's hard to understand, but we need not understand; we need only *believe* that every word and sigh and flick of an eyelash is watched and weighed and counted, and every word is heard as though we were the only one praying.

The morning offering can be a simple form of gathering up the day and all it will hold and giving it to God. Our children say, "I offer You this day as a prayer of love and thanksgiving, and thank You for keeping me safe through the night. Please help me to be pure and good, and keep me safe from harm. Please help us all with our work." They can offer it for one or many intentions, or simply give it to Jesus and Mary and ask them to apply its merits as they wish. The "safe through the night" isn't meant to imply that dying in the night would be the horror of horrors, but to remind them of God's watchfulness while we sleep and to teach that, if we have survived the night, obviously God's will for us includes another day of work and play and prayer to be lived as best we can.

When the older children started catechism classes (we have no parochial schools in our town), Sister taught them the traditional Morning Offering; so now they like to say that. But whatever form of offering they use, the important thing is to think of it like the net that strained with many fishes but still did not break. It will hold all the good a child can say and think and do in his entire day and give him a wonderful sense of having used every minute. Many times I have heard one or another of our children (who are really no more pious than other children) say, "There, now wiping the dishes is part of my prayers because I made my Morning Offering."

⤳

Work can be prayer

And that brings us to work as a form of prayer, and helping children understand that work done for the love of God is as tangible an act of love as if they were to run to Him with an embrace.

In the beginning, learning to make our bed, dry the dishes, and polish shoes is fun and a kind of play at being grown up, but soon the novelty wears off, and the chores that started out being fun can lose their glamour and become unpleasant drudgery. If they are prayer, however, it can be different. Not that tasks we hate doing are suddenly transformed into occasions of great spiritual joy; but there's a great difference between doing them because you're told you must, and doing them because they can be applied to the sufferings of some other child somewhere, who has no bed to make, who must spend his nights curled up in a hole, shivering, starved, unhappy, and with no one to care for him.

Then there's a good reason to try to make our bed with care instead of pulling up the covers to hide the rumples underneath. Then smoothing the sheets, and squaring the corners, and plumping the pillows can be small ceremonies of love from a small girl who does them because Christ can use them as balm for one of His suffering members. And one of the loveliest things about teaching children that work is prayer is that mothers can't help having it rub off on them. These diapers that are changed daily, these meals that are cooked again and again, these floors that are scrubbed today only to get dirty tomorrow — these are as truly prayer in a mother's vocation as the watches and prayers of the religious are in theirs.

*Encourage your child
to offer up his sufferings*

There is suffering, too, in the lives of children, and it is eloquent prayer. Mere stoicism has no part in the training of a Christian. Too often it's the death knell to humility. But suffering
embraced and offered to the suffering Christ, even with howls and
tears, is a mighty weapon.

The road to Calvary was one long, unending bruise, and it
helps a child to remember when he's hurt that Jesus was hurt like
this, and much more, and this pain in a mysterious way can be
poured on His wounds and will help make up for the pain He had
to bear. Every mother in the world kisses the bumps and bruises of
her young to "make them well." We can give them something
much more tangible to do with their hurts than merely bring them
to be kissed. We can comfort and calm and then direct them in
the use of the pain, and it's surprising how willingly they will learn
the lesson of pain and its value.

"Offer it up, dear; give it to Jesus to help comfort Him for the
pain of the nails in His poor hands and feet." Faced as he is with a
lifetime of recurring suffering (in one way or another), we give a
child the only wholesome weapon to be used when we teach him
to take his own pain in his own two hands and apply it freely, as he
does work and play and prayer, to the comforting of Christ and His
work in His Church.

Many times, parents will turn to scolding the "naughty chair"
or the "bad table" in an effort to ease the pain and insult of a child
who comes to grief through his own carelessness. In the process,
they feed little desires for vengeance; they give him no recourse
but senseless, continuing rebellion against anything and everything that crosses him.

One time, a man who lives in our town was working on his car with no success, growing more and more angry because the cursed (and I do mean cursed) car would not start. In a rage, finally, he threw his wrench at it, broke a part, and instead of a tricky repair job, he had added to his woes the problem of thumbing a ride to a service station to buy a new part, thumbing a ride back, and starting from scratch to install the new part. Perhaps his explosion was only the fault of an ungovernable temper, but perhaps — who knows? — it had its beginning long ago in childhood when the only solace for a barked shin was, "Naughty chair to hurt the baby. Kick it back, sonny, kick it back."

Living in a fallen world, our children are bound to be hurt, both physically and spiritually. We will save them years of wasted opportunities if we teach them that, along with everything else, pain is part of their prayer.

Play can be prayer

Play is prayer, too, although we all seem to think God wants only the whiny gifts and none of the shiny ones. If a queen is crowned and people dance in the streets, the queen says she's honored. But we have the idea that play, if it has any relation to God at all, is at best "time out" from serving Him with daily prayers and duties.

We have borrowed from St. Paul for our grace before meals, to help remind the children that the joys in life are prayers, too: "Whether we eat or sleep, whether we work or play, may it all be for the honor and glory of God."[7] Many times a day, a mother may remind her children to offer their play as part of their prayer. Trips

[7] Cf. 1 Cor. 10:31.

33

into the house for drinks of water, mittens, coats on, coats off —
all are opportunities to be reminded. "Having fun?" It's what all
mothers say. They can add, "Be sure to offer your fun to God, because He loves being prayed to with fun." It will help plant deep in
their hearts the instinct for holy fun, for sensing that amusement
that isn't wholesome cannot be offered, and is therefore not fitting
play if it doesn't make fitting prayer.

Last of all, we can teach our children to practice mental prayer.
Understood too little, mental prayer is simply "lifting the heart and
the mind to God." And for children with an understanding that
prayer is talking to God, it's no more difficult than daydreaming.

We have a kind of game to play at night that is really mental
prayer, but which the children call "What shall I think about before I go to sleep?"

"Why don't you pretend you're walking down a street in Nazareth, and you come to a little house with a blue door. You knock at
the door, and when it opens, there is the most beautiful lady in the
world. The Blessed Mother! And she says, 'Why, Jamie! I was just
thinking of you. Do come in, and have a glass of milk and some
cookies, and we'll have a good talk. Tell me all about your day. All
the things that bothered you, and all the things that were fun.
And afterward, you may go out to the carpenter shop in the back.
Jesus and Joseph are out there making me a birthday present, but
they won't tell me what it is. Maybe they will tell you, and let you
help. And then you can go to the well with Jesus and get the water,
and help Him milk the goat, and pick the peas for supper."

From there on, they manage by themselves (I know only because they tell me). Sometimes they go up into the hills with Jesus
to explore, or sometimes they take their lunch in little backpacks
and eat it by a brook. Sometimes they discover that it's a boat He's
making for His Mother, and they take it to the brook to see if it

will sail. Sometimes they stay in the shop, and Joseph helps them make a jalopy.

And sometimes, best thing of all, they build a tree house, and the Blessed Mother makes sandwiches, and they scramble into the tree and eat them, roosting high in the sky with the Lord of the world.

Jesus is just their age, and likes to do just the things they like to do, and with help and suggestions and encouragement every night, He can become "really and truly my very best friend." To wander the last corridor to sleep with all the persons of the fairytales, with Thumbelina and Peter Pan is fun, but at best only entertainment; but to walk the streets of His town, sit with His mother, and work with His stepfather, to talk and eat and play with the boy Christ — this is fun that fans their love, is rich in grace, and teaches them a habit that is real and serious mental prayer.

There's nothing good the day can hold that cannot be prayer. Helping children to pray, not only with their lips and their hearts, but with their work and play and hurts and dreaming — everything in their lives — this is teaching them to "pray always."[8]

---

[8] 1 Thess. 5:17.

Chapter 3

*Encourage your child
to love the world rightly*

No one can *teach* you detachment. It's something you must learn by yourself. And learning it is very hard, because perfect detachment is final death to self. It's being so caught up in God that, like a star that has no light but the light it reflects from the sun, life has no other meaning but as a reflection of the honor and glory of God.

But that isn't what most people think of when you say *detachment*. They think it means being disinterested and aloof, walking on the clouds, feeding on airy nothings and paying no attention to what's on the ground, and they decide that people who talk about detachment belong lumped together in a combination of the absentminded, the poetic, or those rare and peculiar creatures, the contemplative religious.

This just isn't true. The more people grow in Christian detachment, the more they're concerned about all things and all other people — but these things and these people in relation to God. St. Paul said, having arrived, "Now I live, not I, but Christ lives in me."[9] That is detachment.

But to propose detachment for children looks like asking the impossible. It isn't. Pope Pius XII said, "In the kingdom of grace, there are no children; all are adults." And when you understand

[9] Cf. Gal. 2:20.

that detachment is the end of all this knowledge and love of God we're trying to give our children, we ought to hope that it will be inevitable.

Dom John Chapman wrote that we receive first the knowledge of God and the Faith, then we make it solid in us by the use of our reason (thinking about it and, with the help of parents and teachers, using it in daily life), and then: "By grace, this becomes a *passion.*" So detachment is there, waiting at the end of it all.

Of course, children don't become easily detached, but neither do grown-ups; so that doesn't mean a thing. Because it's a thing you have to learn painfully, it takes a long time. But we can help our children form a detached vision, or at least set them on the path; and it starts with the simple things that fill the world around them, building up to all the human relationships, both at home and in society.

Show your child
how nature reveals God

Sky, trees, sun, all of nature was created by God and serves Him perfectly, giving Him great glory. But nature study by itself teaches only an assortment of interesting facts. It can teach much more, if we would use it to teach as our Lord did and help our children to see the world as proof of God and His greatness and generosity.

For instance, one time our Lord said:

Consider the ravens, for they sow not, neither do they reap, neither have they storehouse nor barn, and God feedeth them. How much are you more valuable than they![10]

[10]Luke 12:24.

Encourage your child to love the world rightly

He was talking to grown-ups at the time, telling them to be so detached that the sight of a flock of crows would remind them to trust their Father in Heaven.

We have crows all over our pasture and woods in the summertime, and the children love to think of Christ watching just such flights, hearing the same sounds of cawing when He told his listeners to think of crows like this. If you live in the city and complain, "But we have only sparrows in the city," well, He said the same thing about sparrows. Weren't two sparrows sold for only a penny? He asked. And yet not one fell to the ground without God's first giving permission. "Fear not, therefore; you are of more value than many sparrows."[11]

We do not have to tax our ingenuity in our use of nature to teach our children these first steps toward detachment. We need only to imitate Christ. That is one of the ways He taught most often.

Encouraged to look at the world this way and to wonder at all its beauty and mystery, they begin to see these truths by themselves. Then the ants around an anthill tell them wonderful things, not just about ants, but about the power of God, who could give such tiny insects instincts of order and industry that they follow faithfully and thereby give glory to Him.

A child will come in to report tearfully that kitty has caught a mouse and is eating it on the porch, and it's the beginning of learning the incredible obedience in nature: that it's the nature of kitty to do just that. A mouse will eat the grain (or nibble the bread in the pantry), a cat will eat the mouse, a dog will chase the cat, and on up the scale. It's a fallen world since the first sin in the Garden, and we are all the victims of fallen nature. Animals

[11]Luke 12:7.

have no soul like ours, no reason, no gifts of grace. So they are obedient to their nature by doing the things their instincts tell them
to do. And in their obedience, they praise God.

During deer season in our part of the country, the children are
horror-stricken at the thought of killing deer; even seeing hunters
cross our land to go into the hills makes for much excitement. So
every season, we have to reread the passage in Genesis where God
gave man all the beasts of the earth for his food. Then, explaining
that by hunting, for the purpose of food, the deer population is
kept in check and the orchards that bear our native apples and
peaches are protected from damage by too many deer, they begin
to learn something of the divine economy in nature, the pattern of
victim to prey, and the great dignity of man, to whom God made
all other things subject.

These things may seem trivial, far afield of detachment, but for
children, they're the beginning. But often we miss the opportunity, in our haste to correct them for some attitude we think cruel
or disrespectful, to use such situations to anchor them just a bit
more firmly in their knowledge of God.

For instance, some children discovered a turtle and started
pelting him with stones. When they ran back to report the fun to
the grown-ups, some admonished them not to throw stones at
turtles: "It isn't nice." Others said, "You mustn't throw stones at
turtles. God made the turtle, and he is obeying God perfectly, according to his turtle way. You are far above a turtle. You have a
mind and a soul, many things he has not. When you see a turtle,
see him as something quite wonderful coming from the hand of
God, with a funny little head that goes in and out, and a little
house he carries on his back. And remember that both you and he
were put here by God to do His will and praise Him — the one by
acting like a turtle, the other by acting like a boy."

Encourage your child to love the world rightly

This sounds like the kind of thing that might go in one ear and out the other, especially coming in the middle of an afternoon of noisy play. But days later, one of the boys at the turtle episode ran to his brothers after discovering a baby rabbit in its nest.

"Did you catch it?"

"No, it's God's. I just kneeled down and looked at it."

Every mouse, every bird, every ant and grub can be an occasion for a small reflection, and these poured together like grains of sand slowly, surely, help to anchor a child in God.

~

Sin, not God,
causes nature's harshness

Someone posed this problem, however. If you go too far with all this, wouldn't a child conclude that he must stand still and let a wild beast devour him because the beast is God's? But we're always permitted to defend ourselves. God gave Adam the animals and told him to "rule over them." So we're their masters, and they were made to serve us. If some of the saints, in perfect detachment, could walk with serenity into the jaws of wild beasts, we can only wonder at their abandonment and pray that we, too, may one day trust as they did. Lacking such trust (and it's a rare and wonderful gift), it's never a sin to kill a mad dog, or a poisonous snake, or even — and children will bring it up — swat a fly or kill a mosquito.

"Well, I wish they'd never committed Original Sin, and these darned mosquitoes wouldn't bite." And Jamie, scratching madly, begins to understand something of the nature of a fallen world when he applies it to mosquito bites.

St. Paul's letter to the Romans helps a great deal to explain to children about the world and its longing to be restored to harmony (although it has to be retold in words they understand). In it he wrote:

> Creation was made subject to vanity, not by its own will, but by reason of Him that made it subject, in hope, because creation itself also shall be delivered from its slavery to corruption, into the freedom of the glory of the sons of God. For we know that all creation groans and travails in pain until now.[12]

Even the storms and tornadoes and earthquakes that seem so cruel and mysterious are the result of the Fall. And St. Paul says that this would not have happened if God hadn't made nature share in the punishment for man's sin. But in its way, nature, too, hopes for the day when harmony will be restored and it will be perfect again.

This is very comforting to a child who listens to hurricane warnings on the radio and asks, "Will there be a hurricane because God wants to show us His power?" He is not a cruel God. He is perfect and just. But He warned Adam not to disobey. It was Adam's sin that set in motion the cruelty in nature, and if Jesus had not consented to become man and share these misfortunes with us, we would never know what to do with them. He turned punishment inside out for us, and gave us a way to use the sufferings we endure, from mosquito bites all the way up to hurricanes. We can pour them into the well of His own suffering and help Him redeem the world.

And of course this is the only answer to natural disorders and afflictions that makes any sense. Many children learn it, while many "wise" men do not.

[12]Cf. Rom. 8:20-22.

Encourage your child to love the world rightly

⌒

Use the right words

Children are always amazed to discover that Adam named the animals, and they love reading about it in Genesis.

> And the Lord . . . brought them to Adam to see what he would call them, for whatsoever Adam called any living creature, the same is its name. And Adam called all the beasts by their names, and all the fowls of the air, and all the cattle of the field. . . .[13]

It was, I imagine, the world's first parade (the second one was that great embarkation into the Ark). So, after a trip to the zoo or the circus, or an afternoon with a pile of old *National Geographics*, it's fun to ponder Adam sounding out names for the beasts. *Hippopotamus* is so right for the hippo — because, of course, she is so hippy. Then to discover that Adam's word for her was nowhere near what it is in our language, it certainly shows the concern of Divine Providence about even names for animals that make sense. No one who was not inspired could have chosen *hyena* for the hyena. Then, when you remind them that St. Paul sent greetings in one of his letters to "Phoebe," there's nothing to conclude but that the first girl named Phoebe was really named after a bird.

Geology is another means to help children develop a sense of wonder over God's way with the universe; and it's as close by as the stones in the backyard, a hammer and chisel, and a book from the library. The slates in garden paths, or on the roofs of buildings, are dried flakes of what was once mud, baked for thousands of years in the hot sun. The colored streaks inside stones all have names and stories, and the stones themselves are the shape they are from

---

[13]Gen. 2:19-20.

45

thousands of tons of water running over them and smoothing them, or being chipped off giant cliffs, or once hot molten fluid, having cooled and hardened. How marvelous it is to begin to understand that the earth, the mountains, the islands, and the seas are all guardians of His mysteries, and yet we're more precious to Him than all of these.

Small children can anticipate one whole lesson in the catechism, long before they're old enough to go to school, by playing a game called "Finding the things God made." On a walk, or looking out the window down into the street, they pick out things that come to us straight from His hand, such as sky and trees and clouds and sun, birds and dogs and cats, and contrast them with things man has made with the gifts God has given him, such as cars and baseballs and clotheslines and street lights. We can help them form their first understanding about the right use of these gifts by considering (when they are a little older) how wrong it is, for instance, to cut down forests of trees to make into paper, then use the paper to print comic books which not only frighten children with their horrors, but teach them how to commit crimes and disobey God.

Considering God as the source of all things, it's easier to learn how to use words correctly, and reserve the superlatives for the things that are superlative. I was startled to hear one small boy patiently explaining to a visitor who said she "loved hamburgers," that "You can't love hamburgers. You can only love God, and people, animals, too — but not hamburgers." Nor should one "adore" movie stars, or think new hats are "divine."

I've heard people demur at this sort of thing, because it leaves nothing to be enjoyed for the sake of itself, they say. Everything has a moral attached to it, they say, and this is dull. This is *not* dull. And it's particularly not dull for children. If we have grown world-weary and bored and are beyond the point of wonder, then more's the pity, because the world is full of wonder, and it all makes sense when you understand that first there is God. Children are secure and at home, in fact very comfortable, in a world that is furnished by their Father in Heaven. The bad things in it are bad for a reason. The good things are good for a reason, and only people who do not have the right conception of God think that to connect Him with everything is to be utterly boring.

Somewhere (*Orthodoxy*, perhaps?), Chesterton remarks that only people who believe in God could believe in fairies. Because, of course, God could make fairies. St. John the Baptist said that He could raise up children of Abraham out of the stones, if He wished.

Perhaps to write all these things down makes them sound dull, but when you communicate them to children, you don't do it by writing them down. You don't create artificial situations for the preaching of sermons. You simply live with them, and they present the opportunities to you. And because they're so quick to learn and love and wonder, you could also write much more — about the things *they* say, and these would sound entirely hopeless on paper, because what children say is almost untranslatable on paper. It's more than their words. It's the face on them, and the excitement of them, the great triumph of having discovered for themselves the meaning of things you've taught them. Call it what you want — a form of security, gathering knowledge, helping them acquire a diversity of interests — little by little it's the knitting of the fabric of detachment, seeing all things against a background of God.

＞

Train your children to see Christ in others

This detachment in respect to nature offers no very big problem. It's in the complicated relations with humans that problems arise. And if we teach the way to detachment in relation to nature by helping children see all things against a background of God, we teach them detachment in relation to people by helping them see all men as other Christs.

It need not, indeed should not, be a matter of preaching a sermon every hour on the hour, but it's good to remember that these problems have to be treated some way, and if not this way, some way that is less good. The alternative is a far vaguer conception of goodness for the sake of being nice. And don't tell me this formless niceness that people hold up to one another as the measure for behavior is more convincing than Christ. At times it may be easier to live with, but the easier it is to live with, the less effect it usually has, and it's apt to end up being mightily confusing and meaning nothing. Some people think that birth control is nice. And some think euthanasia is nice.

We can start children off on the lifelong struggle to live reverently with their fellowman by teaching them how to see Christ in one another. This is not hard, because our Lord explained it so simply Himself: "Whatsoever you do to these, the least of my brethren, you do unto me."[14]

It is also very evident in the story of St. Paul thrown from his horse on the way to Damascus. Our Lord had ascended into Heaven. Paul had never known Him. And yet, when he lay there whimpering in the dust, blind and frightened, the voice he heard said to him: "Saul, Saul, why persecutest thou *me*?"[15] What else can it mean than that we are to see Christ in all men? *He* wasn't personally hiding in Damascus. Paul had no confusion in *his* mind about whom he was after.

[14]Cf. Matt. 25:40.
[15]Acts 9:4.

We can explain this to our children, and they're delighted to discover it. But the process of getting it straight in their heads leads into some strange and winding ways. For instance, there was the time John was helping Peter get into his sneakers. As it happened, Peter was fresh from a long talk with his mother about seeing Christ in his brothers. What with the fat feet and the limp sneakers, the red hair and the bad temper, they were getting nowhere fast. Finally John yelled, "Get your feet in!"

And Peter said, smiling smugly, "Remember, I'm Baby Jesus."

Providentially his mother was within earshot, or I shudder to think of Peter growing up identifying himself so intimately with deity. So we had to get it explained again; and after a deep breath and a good try, John helped Peter into his sneakers *as though* he were helping Baby Jesus, and Peter cooperated the way Baby Jesus would have cooperated.

But these things are really ironed out very easily, and children do get it straight. Although, like everything else, they need constant reminding, it's a far more direct way to go after kind, patient, loving ministrations between brother and brother, brother and sister, our children and the neighbors', than the old worn-out, "Now, be nice."

Then there are hurt feelings, which can be much more effectively handled through Christ than with mere purring sympathy. For instance, one day Monica was getting off the bus with a group of children, when one of them kicked her scuffed shoes and sneered, "Ugh! What shoes!"

To be publicly scorned by the neighborhood fashion plate was a bitter blow. She came home close to tears and poured out her woe over the bread and butter. So we got to talking about our Lord, and how He had walked many miles either barefoot or in dusty, and probably badly scuffed, sandals. One has that to share with Him when she has to wear beat-up shoes until it's time for her to have new ones, and it will help her understand a bit how things were with Him — because, of course, people made fun of Him, too.

There was the time the soldiers scourged Him and then put the crown of thorns on His head and the purple robe over His shoulders, handed Him a reed for a scepter, and then mocked Him, bowing and scraping and saluting Him as king. It was all a joke; they never realized that all the time He was their King, silent and loving them, and offering His suffering for them in the hope that one day grace would help them understand, and be sorry.

"Instead of hating someone who makes fun of you, you can remember what you learned: 'Whatsoever you do to these, the least of my brethren, you do unto me.' And then you see that they hurt our Lord even more than you by their unkindness. And here's a thought: perhaps God permitted it to happen because this child doesn't know how to love, and it will remind you to pray for her and ask Him to teach her how to love Him, too."

Sooner or later it occurs to them to ask, "But how can you see Christ in really *bad* people?" And this, it's true, is very hard. But we can see the price Christ puts on bad people right there on the crucifix hanging on the kitchen wall. So we cannot hate them, even when we fear them and hate the things they do. Our Lord took particular pains to teach from the Cross how we are to feel about the "bad people": "Father, forgive them, for they know not what they do."[16]

Now and then, children will bring this up when they see some news broadcast or headline concerning people who have acted wickedly. Because they have no firsthand knowledge of these people, they accept quite easily the explanation that they must pray

[16]Luke 23:34.

for them with love because they are precious to God and, as long as they are alive, might still one day be saints. It has happened to men just as bad.

But when it is someone real, someone who, perhaps, has humiliated them in front of the schoolroom, or has bullied them cruelly in neighborhood play, *there* is the challenge. With such a one, they cannot drum up any emotion of loving, any very real pity, or even much understanding, and the only wholesome way to go about healing a fear or a hurt of that sort is by remembering the price Christ paid for *these* "bad ones." He loves them, so He can help us to learn to love them too, and if we can help our children forgive them by even the driest act of the will, and pray for the grace to love, it will come — even though it will be long and hard and seem to be impossible.

The end of all this, one day, is that death to self which our Lord said must take place if we are to live in Him, and He in us. In the meantime, it's the preparation of a soul that can look around itself at the world and the people in it and evaluate it all with God as the measure. It's the key to all the tense relationships within households where too many live in too small a space, where older people must bear the difficult noise and distraction of youngsters, and where youngsters must bear the carping and irritation of the much older. It can be a lifeline for a child suffering at the hands of a sarcastic teacher, a persecuting neighbor, or a difficult bus driver.

A little boy we know learned to conquer his fear of teasing by each day accepting it silently as Christ did His tormentors', praying for those who teased him. To help him endure, he marked each day's victory over fear and self-pity with a counter in a jar. One day he put no counter in the jar. When his mother asked him why, he said, somewhat surprised, "But they don't tease me anymore." Working at his problem spiritually, he had leveled the valley of his fear and, ceasing to react to the teasing, he had removed the motive for it. When the others found they could no longer irritate him, it was no fun to try.

This is the most practical approach to all sorts of trying problems in human relations. It's the beginning of the end of self-pity, frustration, pessimism, and all the things we must rid ourselves of if we're going to try to be saints.

There are heavy burdens for children to bear if they are to take part in restoring the world to Christ, burdens that demand great faith and charity. They will have to practice fortitude, patience, chastity, kindness, justice, mercy — all the virtues carried to a heroic degree. Only if they lose themselves in God will they ever be able to do it, and losing oneself in God is detachment.

Chapter 4

*Train your child
in good behavior*

Struggling with behavior problems is like darning socks — or rather, the way darning socks used to be. You'd work and work at it until the holes were finally closed, and then one wearing — and, more holes! That kept up until finally the sock was more darn than sock and you'd whine a little to yourself, wondering who appreciated it anyway. If only they'd stay darned! But they never did, and you were forever starting all over again.

But because God uses the most trivial things to point out the way to perfection, once in a while in the middle of a whine you'd understand that even if no one else saw how much work you put into it, God did. And every snip and stitch was holy in His sight, because you were working away at the vocation that, for you, was the way to Heaven. This could be called "detachment in darning": to darn socks for the love of God.

We have to develop this same kind of detachment if we are to lead our children to detachment in their behavior. They will learn it and apply it with ease to all the beauty and order and blessedness of nature, but it's infinitely more difficult, and painfully slow, learning to apply it to themselves. It means learning the same lessons over and over again.

Modern mothers have been relying on psychology books to interpret child behavior for so long now that if all the psychology books were burned to a crisp, few mothers could relax with the conviction that God's love, the maternal instinct, and divine grace could take their place.

I'm not minimizing the work of child psychologists. They've taught us many new insights into the needs and behavior of our children. But God can teach us even more, because children's willfulness, their disobedience, and their tantrums speak just as eloquently for their own search for God and perfection as our sins do for ours.

What we all — little or big — want is God; if we do not realize it, however, we choose many ignoble things in His place. And if we want to teach children to be good with a goodness that's lasting, we must teach them to be good for the love of God.

❧

Emphasize the importance of truth

To deny that God is the remedy for a child's lying is to forget that Christ said, "I am the Truth."[17] It is quite probable that there are more immediate reasons, but there's only one perfect cure, and that is love of Christ. Children are not born liars. They don't bother to lie when they're tiny because they haven't learned yet the pattern of crime and punishment. But after they have, they decide to try ducking the punishment by pretending they have committed no crime. On the surface, it's a perfectly logical thing to do. Any mother who has a child who has never told a lie must thank God for giving her child unusual graces.

However, all is not lost if a child does lie. It only means that he is showing the effects of Original Sin. Our job is to give him a motive for *not* lying that will override the motives *for* lying.

---

[17] John 14:6.

Telling him it isn't nice won't do it. By the time he's in the first grade, he'll discover that it isn't always honesty that is rewarded, but carefulness. And the older he gets, the more he's able to look about the world and discover that the rules for success do not include a complete devotion to truth.

We can tell him that lying is a sin, which he certainly must realize; indeed, for children who have made their First Communion, it's a matter for Confession. To hold that fear of sin is a bad thing for a child is nonsense. The fruits of sin are death to the soul, and it depends on how you look at the soul just where you intend to start setting up a few healthy frustrations. You can give way to the philosophy of complete freedom and permit your child to run wild in the name of the passive approach, and he may end up in eternity with a frustration for which there is no cure. Nevertheless, just chatting about sin won't accomplish much if he has nothing against which to measure sin.

The story of Moses receiving the Ten Commandments on Mount Sinai is a dramatic framework in which to anchor the idea of sin, and reading children the nineteenth and twentieth chapters of Exodus — in their own words — will help to make not only the Commandments but the catechism lessons on the Commandments far more vivid and dramatic than dry references to them as things to be learned and obeyed. Lying is a sin against the Eighth Commandment: "Thou shalt not bear false witness against thy neighbor."

A picture of a soul in the state of grace helps, too. It's told of St. Catherine of Siena that she fell to her knees before a vision of such light and beauty that she thought it was God. And when an angel said to her, "Arise, Catherine, for it is God alone thou shalt adore," she asked what it was she saw. The angel replied that it was only the sight of a soul in the state of grace.

How to Raise Good Catholic Children

If we have taught our children that the Holy Trinity resides in their souls as long as they commit no serious sin, we must make it clear that venial sin does destroy some of the splendor, and although the Trinity remains, out of merciful pity for our weakness, God is not so sublimely happy as before. It's my experience that, of all the things one says to a child who is tempted to lie, "Please, dear, don't do anything that will destroy the beauty of your soul" has the most telling effect. That is, if he understands something of the beauty of the soul.

The positive reasons for being good are, however, far more rewarding than the negative, and the positive reason for not lying is Jesus' statement, "I am the Truth." When He stood before Pilate, He said, "Everyone that is of truth heareth my voice."[18] The small voice of conscience that warns us to tell the truth in times of temptation is like the voice of our Lord in us, begging us to be one with Him.

"You must try to remember, dear, when you're tempted to lie, that Jesus is present, waiting to see if you will be with Him or against Him. He not only said He is the Truth, but He also said the Devil is the father of lies. So there is a great choice to be made. A lie doesn't just pop into your head. The Devil whispers it there. He hates our Lord and wants you to hate Him, too. When you think it would be better to lie than receive the blame for something wrong you've done, try to stop first, and think how much you love our Lord. If you're afraid to tell the truth, then inside yourself tell Him you're afraid. Ask Him, quickly, 'Please help me to tell the truth.' He'll send you the grace in the wink of an eye if only you'll ask, and your soul will be stronger for telling the truth because you'll have done a very brave thing."

[18]John 18:37.

Does it work? I wish I could say, "Yes, they'll never tell a lie again." But it's such a big idea, and children do not retain a lesson, word for word, after being told just once. The emotional urgency is very strong when it comes to telling a lie. It isn't the same mood at all as night prayers, when a child is fairly recollected and thinking of God. It usually follows some calamity, and with his heart pounding in his breast the temptation comes and almost overpowers him. He's frightened, or he wouldn't toy with the idea in the first place. And we must try to remember this.

It's best never to ask a child (if we can keep our heads), "Did you do it?" especially if we know that the temptation to lie is especially strong in this child. Given only a matter of seconds to reply, he's quite likely to seek frantic cover in a lie. Demanding such a quick answer is unfair. And although it isn't good to hint that we will distrust his answer even before he gives it, for children who find telling the truth difficult there's a measure of security to be told, "Now, before I ask you, I want you to know I understand how hard it is sometimes to tell the truth. If you did this thing that you know was naughty, there must be some kind of right punishment for it. But to add a lie would only make it twice as bad. Stop and ask God to help you tell the truth, and then if you must have a punishment, it can be your penance, your way of telling Him you're sorry."

I know one little boy who had great difficulty with lies. He learned to calm down and get over his first panic when he was given five minutes to go alone to his room and kneel down and say a Hail Mary to ask for the grace to tell the truth. This is not just a mechanical trick to free a child of his tension. Hail Marys are effective — and why shouldn't they be? Mary is the Mediatrix of all grace; if human mothers are concerned about teaching their children truthfulness, how much more so the Mother of God?

So often, however, the situation that precipitates a lie has everyone off balance, mother as well as child; and only because I have made the mistake myself do I presume to warn other mothers against the "I want the truth" approach. God wants the truth, whether from a small child or a grown man; to allow it to rest simply on a mother's demand for the truth leaves the field wide open for lying under other circumstances.

We're raising children who will soon be men and women, who will have to contain within them the soundest reasons of all for telling the truth, no matter what the personal cost. It's obvious from the daily news reports that even personal honor has no meaning to many people anymore, that perjury is as easy as breathing, and if no one finds out, what does it matter?

But even personal honor is not a good enough reason. Pride in one's truthfulness is as risky for the soul as cleverness at lying, and it's a form of self-love with which the Devil can eventually have a field day. If we can teach our children to tell the truth for the love of God, we can know for certain that each temptation resisted binds them closer to Christ and that through Him they will gradually develop a hunger for the truth.

Relating punishment to penance helps to lift it out of the category of "getting it" because Mother is mad. It helps a mother or father, too, to remember the reason for punishment for anyone, for anything. Fundamentally it is because we have offended God. If we start punishing children or men or societies because we're mad, we'll end up annihilating them. Unless we really want our children to conclude that we're mean little dictators, we must learn to instruct and chastise them from God's point of view.

I must confess this is very hard, not so much the instruction as the chastising — and if suffering all the remorse that follows the too-harsh punishment of a child has any value for parents, it is seeing all over again their own weakness and how, if they are to teach effectively at all, they must learn detachment well enough to be able to separate their own irritations and anger from the cause, and not use punishments as a personal sop for their disappointment with their children.

Of course, when you know that a child has done something wrong, it's being coy to ask him if he did. It's better to let him see that you know. Asking is only throwing temptation in his way. As for children who spin tales, all mothers recognize these tales when they hear them; and when children are very little, they love to have us pretend to believe them.

Like Stephen's mythical "friends." His friends do all the horrid things he's not supposed to do. He feels very virtuous to be able to regale us with hair-raising accounts of how some of his friends eat, talk back to their mothers, stamp their feet, and throw stones through windows. I am sure it's very healthy for Stephen to have such horrible friends and to feel so superior to them. At least it makes eating nicely much more rewarding when he's able to drain off his secret desire to get in there with both hands by clucking over his friends. But then Stephen is only three and some months, and no one, not even he, is really fooled.

Another lad who is older can spin a yarn that is really out of this world. He once had a teacher who rubbed him the wrong way, and he came home with wild tales about things she said to him. None of it belonged in the class of serious lies. It was his own private way of getting sympathy and "getting even." And he nearly got me into difficulty one time by reporting that she had publicly criticized him for not having his hair shampooed often enough (could be). I was all set to bike down and give her a small piece of my mind on the subject of humiliating children in front of the class.

How to Raise Good Catholic Children

But God is good. Before my temperature rose too high, He sent a small grace that suggested I take a chance on guessing that it was an invention. I said, "You really made that up, didn't you?" He looked a little sheepish, and then said yes. We had a long talk about making up stories, and how sometimes it seems like a good thing to do, and how it isn't really a bad thing to do unless, of course, you make up something like this, which puts someone else in a very bad light. Then it could be terrible. Now that he was older, he ought to try to remember that it's best to identify the stories as "stories" and be more careful not to give everyone the impression that he doesn't care about the truth. When we finally got down to business and shampooed his hair, I decided Teacher would have been well justified if she had made some remarks about it. It was June, and he was pretty grimy, and maybe the whole thing started in the first place because, poor darling, he was longing for a shampoo.

Anyway, if you persevere, the teaching about lying works eventually. With some children, it works right away, but the fact that a child does have difficulty with lying is no reason to abandon hope. One who will not lie may find that some other virtue is hard. Our job is to explain it patiently and often, theirs is to ask for the grace, and God will do most of the work.

Monica was telling me about a wrangle at school that involved lying. A Catholic child and a Protestant child were having an argument over religion. The Catholic child said that Catholics do not lie. The Protestant child said they do; only Protestants do not lie.

"What did you say?"

"Oh, I said both Catholics and Protestants will lie if only they will listen to the Devil telling them to lie."

So that's that.

Now, all this will be so much noise if we're not examples of impeccable truthfulness ourselves. Children are not easy to fool, and if we're given to elaborate promises that we don't qualify ("If it's possible, I will . . ." "I'll try very hard to . . ." "We'll see, dear, maybe we can . . ." and so forth) and don't keep, they'll do exactly as they see us do, and we can take all the credit for it. This involves all kinds of things, such as what to tell them about Santa Claus and the Easter Bunny, where babies come from, and all the rest. And whether they like to admit it or not, the elaborate fictions parents invent about these things amount, in the end, to nothing more or less than lies.

⇌

Teach your child to love obedience

Obedience is another problem that demands honesty from parents as well as from children. It's practically impossible to explain obedience to a very small child. He has to learn it through restrictions and moderate punishments. But along about four (and a wild age it is), he's capable of considering obedience as a real, although intangible, virtue.

The ideal way of introducing him to the idea of obedience is the story of the Boy Christ in the Temple. It's perfect because it was an occasion when Jesus was not doing something that was *wrong*, but something contrary to the wishes of Mary and Joseph. Then, if we relate it to the Fourth Commandment, "Honor thy father and thy mother," we can show him how, even to Jesus, who was God, the commandment applied. His perfect obedience in returning to Nazareth to be "subject to them"[19] is something to ponder, and we can tell the story in terms of their own lives — deciding

---

[19]Luke 2:51.

what chores He probably helped with, what His town was like, His routine (like ours) of work, meals, prayer, play, and rest. And when we read St. Luke's words, "And Jesus advanced in wisdom, and age, and grace, with God and men,"[20] we can help them to see that obedience is not just rules to obey, but the way to wisdom and grace.

Like everything else, however, it has to be repeated and repeated. One of the big troubles is that we're always demanding obedience now and not then. Our own inconsistency is often more confusing and blameworthy than children's willfulness, and if we are entirely honest, we have to admit that many times we abuse obedience by demanding it in things where it is not entirely reasonable.

It's good to remember why we want them to be obedient. We're used to thinking of it in terms of living in a society where there are laws to be respected, with obedience at home as training for obedience in the world. But we don't really want to teach them these things just so that they will stay out of jail! We want them to *love* obedience, because in obedience to duly constituted authority, they're obeying God, from whom comes all authority. And obedience in all things is the way to peace. It's one of the least understood of all the virtues (especially in adult life), one of the least loved, and I think it's the most beautiful — because it covers everything, and perfect obedience can grow only out of love.

When our children are in a nice, quiet mood and we're talking about things in general and get around to saints, one of the things they love most to hear is how St. Thérèse loved obedience so perfectly that if she were writing when the bell rang, she would put her pen down and go, not even stopping to dot an *i*. And for a

[20]Luke 2:52.

while — say, a few hours — we have utterly lovely obedience in our house because everyone is imitating Thérèse.

Obedience is not usually so lovely, however. It's dull, no fun, and very, very hard. This is as it should be. We aren't going to grow strong by doing things that are easy. So we can remind children that even Jesus, in the Garden of Gethsemane, wept and sweat blood at the thought of the obedience asked of Him. And He asked His Father to take away the hard thing He was supposed to do. But then He said, "Not my will, but Thine,"[21] because more than all other things, He loved doing the will of His Father. Later, when the story of His Passion and death was written in the Gospels, it was written: "He was obedient unto the end."[22]

So if there has been disobedience, there must be a punishment, and like the Lord High Executioner, we must try to make the punishment fit the crime. Depriving children of privileges is about the best way, because it gives them time to reflect about what they might have been doing if they hadn't been disobedient. And when it's time to punish, there must be the understanding that the punishment is retribution made to God as well as to parents. It helps to have it explained.

"You see, dear, mothers and fathers have to be obedient to God's will, too. It would be easier, sometimes, to let you do what you want. Much more pleasant for you and less trouble for us. But God has given you to us for a while on earth, and because He wants you to be a saint, we must try to teach you all the things that will help you be a saint. Obedience is one of them. When you're big, you'll have people you'll have to teach — maybe children, maybe other grown-ups. How will you teach them obedience if

[21]Luke 22:42.
[22]Cf. Phil. 2:8.

you don't know what it is yourself? How will we ever be saints if we are disobedient?

"Every time you obey, it makes it that much easier to obey the next time, because your soul is forming the habit and you're using the graces God sends to help you with obedience. You can learn to love obedience if only you will work at it and pray about it. Remember the obedience of our Lord when He was only twelve, quite near your own age. Pray to Him, and ask Him to help you. *He* can teach you to love obedience."

Our John is much given to lamenting in the middle of a punishment, "Now things aren't nice anymore. Everything's spoiled." Precisely. It started with Original Sin, and everything but *everything,* was spoiled, beginning with man's sanctifying grace all the way through the order in nature. Disobedience has only one function: to spoil everything.

There is a difference between disobedience and "not paying attention," and it's very easy to fall into this trap and hand out punishment when it really isn't due. Disobedience is a form of rebellion. Not paying attention is a very human weakness (which, I grant you, needs correction, but doesn't belong in this class).

There is a story told of Susanna Wesley that helps us remember this. She had asked one of her many children again and again to do something, and the child, absorbed in something else, failed to do it. When she asked again, her husband said to her, "Susanna, I have heard you ask that child to do that nineteen times already. How is it you have the patience to ask him the twentieth?"

And she replied, "But at last he has done it; so you see, if I had not asked the nineteen times, he would not have done it the twentieth." It takes that discernment to tell the difference between disobedience and inattention, and that kind of patience. No wonder Susanna Wesley was famous for being a good mother.

Then there are temper tantrums. Not all children have them, although all lose their tempers from time to time. What we're concerned with here is children given to consistent displays of temper (a subject on which I'm an authority). Many times a temper tantrum is just another way of trying to obtain attention, and for the very young, the best method is to ignore them. Usually leaving them alone to carry on without an audience is more effective than trying to reason. But if it continues (and there are children who come dangerously close to harming themselves in a fit of temper, banging their heads on the floor, and so forth), a firm hand is called for.

⁀

Resort to spanking only when necessary

In these days of debating over whether to spank or not to spank, it's an intrepid soul who comes right out and says, "Spank." That's me. I've heard all the arguments pro and con, and I still believe there are some misdemeanors that are never so well disposed of as with a good spank. No doubt the term *corporal punishment* was invented by people who disapprove of it, for it sounds worse than it usually is. It sounds like beating, which is far different from spanking, and it bullies people into thinking they ought not "believe in it" even when they do.

The most violent opposition I've ever encountered on the score of spanking has come from people who eventually admit that they have no children. I suppose there are some parents who have never spanked, but I've met but one — and what her child needed most of all was a good spanking. A child in a temper tantrum will find that his pointless fury is shattered by a spank when nothing else will touch it, and a good cry about the spanking will gradually relax him, and his anger will drain off. Spanking is dangerous when your own temper is so out of control that you don't trust yourself, and in that case, I personally have to resort to the "sit on a chair" technique and go off to the other end of the house to groan and pray.

We have found that spankings are more quickly forgotten than any other kind of punishment. They suffice at the moment (assuming they're administered with some control) as a punishment for the crime of the moment, and a child forgets them. A child who does something he knows is extremely naughty, after having been taught, warned, and reasoned with, actually expects to be punished for it, or his parents lose stature in his eyes. It isn't uncommon to discover that the insecurity of children whose parents' indifference was their only reaction to their bad behavior lies in their desire to have some limits set beyond which they're not permitted to go.

Continued coolness between me and a punished child has come more often after some calculated deprivation than after a spanking which, once over, is over. If we try hard not to spank unless it is really due, and never to spank in public (or chastise in any way, if possible, because humiliation leaves more scars on children than anything else), almost every time, when the tears are dry and the sting gone from the blushing bottom, they'll come and put their arms around you and say, "I'm sorry." Then it's easy to have a cozy chat and explain that mothers and fathers really don't like to spank, and only have to when boys insist on being naughty even though they know enough not to.

Maybe it doesn't prove anything, but I know I was spanked in my childhood, yet I can't remember a single instance of it. I can remember other punishments, being sent to my room, not being allowed to go with the others, being kept in the yard, but never one spanking comes back to haunt me.

⌇

Help your child to master his temper

As a child grows older and reaches the point where he can deliberate and consider certain of his weaknesses objectively, it helps him to be given some simple means of dealing with them. The effectiveness of this depends largely on the rest of the family. We have had, as I say, some pretty grim tempers in our family. One boy in particular was given to such magnificent displays that when the rest were sitting around with nothing to do, they were not above "egging him on" until he finally blew up. It was a form of rainy-day entertainment for a while. This sort of thing will not do, obviously, and we had to make it clear to them that they were as responsible as he if they deliberately tried to make him angry. But it was their brother who needed help most.

As a very small child, he was the kind who, denied something, reprimanded for something, couldn't get his sweater off, his shoe on, would throw a horrendous fit and also the shoe. Now, not all children will do this. Some will come and ask for help. Others will just whine. Others will wander off without their shoes. But not N. And we were properly discouraged.

Whenever we would reprimand him for a display of temper, he would shriek, "All right, then I don't love you anymore!"

After it was all over and forgotten, he would line up with the rest for hugs and kisses at bedtime, and it was when he was calm and old enough (between three and four) that we began to get somewhere with him. Why did he, of all people, want to be hugged and kissed?

"Because I love you."

"But you said you didn't."

"Oh yes, I do."

"Well, why did you say you didn't?"

"I don't know. I didn't mean it."

And this is where you move in.

"If you didn't mean it, you really shouldn't have said it. How do you suppose your guardian angel feels, standing around and watching you hop up and down and scream that you don't love your mother? And how about Blessed Jesus inside your soul? You know you don't do these things just in front of me. Our Lady sees them, all our angels, the Holy Trinity, probably everyone in Heaven. You know something? You have a pretty bad temper, and it makes you do things you don't want to do, and say things you don't want to say. Now, tonight, when you say your prayers, think about it, and ask God to help you keep your temper. Tell Him what you did today, and ask Him to forgive you for losing your temper."

So he started including the struggle with his temper in his daily prayers, and when it was clear a storm was brewing, we tried to help him before he got lost in it. "Be careful now. You'll be losing your temper if you don't watch out. Don't say something you don't really mean."

And having decided that he really did love us, mad or not, he substituted, "All right, then I'm going someplace else to live!"

Now, all children say this, and all sorts of advice is given about it. Some of the experts caution us never to pretend to take them up on it; it leaves them fearing you really don't care if they do leave. We have one child who, when he threatens to leave, we instinctively respond with, "Oh, come, you don't mean that. You know you don't want to go off and live somewhere else." But this peppery boy seemed to call for a real showdown. (And the best reason I can give for this is simply maternal instinct.) So one raw November day, after threatening for weeks, we said: All right, if he really wanted to, he could leave. He got his things on, and we packed some toys in a bag (one must save face, of course; so he was very cheerful about the whole thing), and off he went in the teeth of a gale. After about forty minutes of roaming around in the yard, he was banging on the door to come in.

"But you said you wanted to go away."

"Now I don't."

"Then why did you say you did?"

"I don't know. I didn't mean it."

Pretty silly. He admitted it. Losing his temper this time nearly did him out of a lot of dearly loved creature comforts.

The next threat was a considerable surprise when he screamed from the middle of a rage, "All right, then I'll hit myself on the head with a hammer!" This because a hammer was on a chair nearby. Everybody howled. He's one boy who is not given to the enjoyment of physical pain, and of course we hastily removed the hammer. Poor lamb. I've never seen such embarrassment as his that night at prayers when, examining his conscience, he muttered, "I got mad and said I'd hit myself on the head with a hammer."

The following fury hit an all-time high in nonsense with: "All right, then I'll cut the ends off my shoelaces!" And we proposed he do exactly that — only remember, he'd have to slop around with his shoes untied ever after. He retreated in grand confusion.

All this was drawn out for very long, but trying to help a bad-tempered child is tedious business. He was slowly learning to walk softly with his "mads," and came the day when he ran in from digging holes in the driveway to announce, "Hey, I threw my bad temper away."

His temper, need I say, has not been entirely thrown away, but it isn't especially outstanding anymore, and what there is of it will probably be forever. One doesn't get rid of a temper as one does a diseased appendix. But he has had enough experience in his few years of growing to know that praying does help and that there's such a thing as learning to try to control a weakness.

It's a great step to be able to be detached enough to admit you have such a weakness. A more perfect detachment will come when, older, he begins to understand that temper in the raw can be transformed into the kind of dynamic drive that helped the saints defy the Devil. It has a use.

One of the great blessings is to know that the saints had these same weaknesses as we, and children love to hang on hard to some saint who had a bad temper, told lies, and stumbled into the same kinds of trouble. St. Peter qualified for just about everything we have trouble with in our family, and to know that he was made head of the Church, instead of St. John, whose love was so flaw-less, is a great comfort to all.

There's another form of temper tantrums: brutality with other children. Hitting, kicking, biting, spitting, and all the rest are quick, vicious tantrums, and the same approach works with the same slow effect. Here, however, there is the business of apology added to the struggle.

Spiritual directors tell their penitents that, during aridity, to make the body go through the postures and attitudes of reverence will help the act of the will and drag the emotions and imagina-tion in line. This works, too, with children and their apologizing. A child who mutters "I'm sorry" because his mother is standing in back of him waiting to hear it doesn't learn a thing from it and probably isn't very sorry. But if he has a minute or two to talk it over with his mother, to return to consider Christ, whom he must see in his playmates, and then faces his victim and says, "I'm sorry I pounded you, and I won't do it again. Please will you for-give me?" — the fact that he has had to say out loud, "I pounded you" makes it quite clear why he's apologizing, and the "Please will you forgive" is the only way to ask forgiveness. A sincere act of contrition has to have that element of "please" in it, or saying "I'm sorry" is nothing more than expediency. Usually the astonished victim has to be prodded into saying, "Yes, I forgive you," but once the routine is established, not only in a family but in a neighborhood, grudges disappear more quickly, and it will have a gradual effect of weatherproofing the common affection.

We've added one more detail to this, although not a public one, and that's an act of contrition. The whole neighborhood doesn't have to know that So-and-so is in the house saying an act of contrition, but it ought to be part of the aftermath of any brawl. Children will even learn to say it without prompting (that's the truth). One of my sons lifted my sagging spirit one day by returning from his act of contrition to say: "I said something else, too. I said, 'Please gimme me some grace.'"

This will nourish you for days. If we can just hang on and keep at it, and if children will just learn to ask for, please, some grace, we won't have to fret too much over the snail's pace of progress. The thing that counts most is that there is Someone who can make it all work out eventually, and He is busy all the time giving grace.

Chapter 5

*Make your
child feel secure*

According to a Polish folktale, Death was once an old woman, and she was sent by God to call the widowed mother of seven little children. The children lamented and pleaded so urgently that at last Death was moved to question God about it. Must she take the mother of the children?

God sent her to the Lord Jesus, and the Lord Jesus sent her to the bottom of the sea to fetch a stone as round as a loaf of bread. She found the stone and brought it back to Him, and He bade her bite it in two. She bit and bit, until her teeth ached; and finally she bit it in two, and there inside was a little worm.

The Lord Jesus spoke once more to Death: "Now, you see? I have remembered this little worm inside the stone at the bottom of the sea. Do you think I would forget the orphans? Go, make haste, and take their mother."

Security is as simple as that. It's found in God alone. When you look it up (thinking that surely there's some more tangible definition), it's defined as "freedom from danger or risk, from care or apprehension." And all a man has cannot free him entirely from these — not money, or a house, or an education, or good food, or dry shoes, or warm clothes. Not even a mother and a father are really a security. Any or all of them can be lost in the wink of an eye, and all there is left is God.

But God can care for us in spite of these things. *He is our security*.

⌒

Assure your child that
God will always provide for him

What this chapter proposes is that it's possible to raise children so convinced of their security in God's love that they need not fear what the world may hand them. And the way to such security is complete faith that everything and anything that happens, happens with the knowledge of God and is permitted for some reason He knows, which is for our best good.

We learned about material security the hard way, by being very poor. Nor are we the only family who learned this way. Like others who did not understand how safe God is, we were afraid. We learned because He made us, and if we had not been poor, perhaps we would never have learned. There were incredible lessons.

We learned that when your children have no shoes, and they ask you, "When will we have shoes?" you face a choice of two things. Either you tell a lie, or you tell the truth. To lie is never the answer to anything. To answer that He will send what is needed at the right time is not so easy as it sounds, but even so (even when you're amazed to hear yourself speak with such daring), it is the only truthful answer. It's a tremendous act of faith, even when He has to wrench it out of you, and He rewards even the small acts of faith with the grace to have more faith, and more simple faith.

"Right now," we told them, "God knows you have no shoes. And He sees you on the grass and the driveway, and He sees the stones and sharp little sticks. He's asking a very big thing of you. He's asking you to wait a little longer until He says the time is right for shoes. You're His children, and He loves you and will care for you. Today He's asking you to show your trust in Him by going barefoot, without any shoes."

Some weeks it was pea soup all week, and some days berries. Or no gas, or heat, or stamps. These things are not unusual with the poor, nor will the poor say they don't pinch and hurt. But they hurt only the part of you that doesn't trust, and if learning to trust is bought with such pinchings as these, it's hardly any price at all, because in the end, you discover you're *always cared for*. Then you learn once and for all that it's foolish to be afraid.

Even so, it seems hardly possible that children could live through all this, accept it, and remain unscarred. But children believe that God is loving and caring for them. They are pure, untouched by sin, radiant with grace. Why is it so hard to believe that faith can sustain them? We judge them by ourselves all the time. Filled with fears we have acquired because we lack faith, we assume that children will have the same fears. We even think that if they don't fear, it's because they haven't enough sense to fear. And all the time we forget that Christ said unless we have childlike faith, we won't even get into Heaven! They are the wise. It is we who are foolish.

But God is very patient, even with our foolishness. Every family that has ever been poor has its own private collection of small miracles by which it has at last learned to trust. And there's always a favorite one that becomes a part of family lore, handed down to the untrusting to remind them they must trust. Our favorite miracle was particularly lovely.

It happened on a day when we had no food left but four loaves of bread, which had used up all the supplies in the house. There was nothing to spread on it, but it was bread. It was all that stood between us and being completely bereft. We sat down to supper, and said grace, and when we were about to eat, there was a knock at the door. It was the little girl from across the road with a bundle wrapped in newspaper. Had we eaten yet? No, wouldn't she like to come in?

"No. I can't. But Johnny thought you might like these." And she thrust the bundle into my husband's hands and darted off into the night. When we opened the newspapers, there were four fishes.

Say if you wish that it wasn't even a miracle. All right. He did not multiply our loaves, nor miraculously provide our fishes. But He put them in the brook. He bade them bite the line. He inspired our neighbors to share them. If being as insecure as we were that night is necessary before we see God's hand providing, then praise be! It's the final casting out of all fear.

But even when intuition senses the truth of all this, souls will hold back from so complete a surrender for fear of the pain that might follow. This is too bad, because there's going to be pain no matter what. It can be fruitful and sweet when we surrender with trust. It can be bitter and breed fear when we refuse to trust. A child's way is the best: to love God and know that He loves you.

One alternative is to build a bulwark against fear. Once when I was in the hospital, there was a mother in the bed next to me. Her youngest daughter was visiting for the length of her mother's confinement, but she was unhappy and wanted to come home. Her father explained that she couldn't, not yet, but if she would be patient for a while longer, she could have a reward.

"What reward?"

He couldn't say at the moment. But something she wanted.

"Then I want a bicycle."

But there wasn't money for the bicycle.

"Oh, yes, there is. In the bank account. Go get it out of the bank account."

The mother groaned. "Now what to do? We've been telling them there's a bank account. You know — so they'd feel secure. But there's no bank account."

How easy it is to sacrifice something good for something senti-mental. That mother was good, and she wanted her children to feel secure, which was good. But God is security, and it's up to us to decide just how much faith we can afford to place in God.

Riches aren't bad in themselves, and it's a mistake to cast asper-sions on those who have no material needs. It's harder for the rich (now someone will say, "Yes, but I'd like to try it for a change") to know God, precisely because they do not need His care the same way the poor need it. For the poor, there's a delicate perception to be formed in their children about riches. Too often a child, absorb-ing his parents' bitterness, will sum it all up with "They think they're better than we are, because they have money." And again we must show them that security does not depend on what you have, but on what you are. We're all the same, the rich and the poor, precious and beloved in the eyes of God, purchased by the blood of Christ. If we differ, it's in degree of love: one is rich or poor, really, in terms of his love. Riches are an accident.

"Do the Joneses have more money than we have? Are we *poor?*"

Childhood is the time for learning that only in one sense is *poor* synonymous with *no money.*

"If you mean, do we have only a little money, why yes, then some people would think we're poor. But we're really very rich in more ways than we're poor. We have God, and we know He loves us. We have the Church to teach us how to save our souls. We have the sacraments, such riches that money can't ever buy. And we have fun together and love each other. Our Lord said (and He *chose* to be poor) that having all the money in the world was noth-ing, if you should lose your soul."

I heard the children talking one day about "being rich." "Well, it depends what you mean," said someone. "Money? Or something like grace?"

We do not have to protect our children from *feeling* poor. With a Christian set of values, they need never feel poor.

⁀

Convince your child of your loyalty to him

But material insecurity is only one of the insecurities. The others are far more subtle. There are terrible emotional insecurities stirred up in children who see their parents habitually disagree. This is no news, nor that great damage is done to a child's character when he discovers that he may take advantage of parental differences and play one parent against the other. This is bad enough, but when it is through his parents that a child must learn about God, and from them see the example of Christlikeness, think of the damage done to faith in both his parents *and* God with his parents' continual contradiction of all that is Christlike in their daily behavior. It's better to submit a thousand times to losing an argument than let children see a parent fail to exhibit the patience and consideration he's trying to teach.

Public confession of faults by parents is more likely to embarrass a child than edify him, but it's another thing to learn to apologize graciously for a bad temper, a too-severe scolding, or just plain grouchiness. Children are not easily fooled, and they see as clearly as anyone the weaknesses in their parents. It helps them to see also that parents consider temper or cross words from themselves the same imperfection they would correct in their children.

Attacking a child's confidence in his parents (by either of them, or others) is very dangerous business. In their early years, children are not at all ready to believe the worst of their parents, even when they see it. Their loyalty is tenacious, and woe to the complainant who would satisfy a grudge by betraying a parent to his children. More often than not, the complainant will suffer by comparison with the silent defendant.

A child from a broken home, listening to her mother berate a neglectful father, used to say to the father, "Don't answer her back. It doesn't do any good."

Simply in the process of growing day by day a little less dependent upon his parents, a child will begin to judge for himself. Then he's able to see loyalty of mother to father, father to mother, and it helps him develop an understanding of that subtle thing called family unity. With the slow decay of family unity, there's apt to be a total casting out of all a child has learned in the bosom of the family. Not only the obvious things, such as respect, consideration, and self-sacrifice, but ultimately perhaps even faith in God, and no one will argue that this is not the greatest scandal of all.

Let your child be messy sometimes

The domestic virtues, exaggerated beyond their importance, can be the cause of deep emotional insecurity. Tidiness, cleanliness, routine — all are valuable and must be cultivated in the family; exaggerated, they can rob a home of all its warmth. Children are not orderly by nature. They are experimenters and explorers, and the world is for them to investigate, with the result that, in their early years, they cannot and will not concentrate for very long on any one thing. This makes for great disorder. But a normal amount of cluttering up is necessary if children are to learn and create and play with any satisfaction, and mothers who suppress it too determinedly for the sake of a tidy house can do great damage. There are men who have never developed the "staying home" habit because their mothers kept their homes too clean to play in, because treasures were labeled trash, and unfinished projects messes, and constant nagging left them so ill at ease playing at home that they were more at home elsewhere.

Disorder can be very trying, especially when children who do surpassingly well at creating their own disorder bring in their talented friends to create even more. Understanding mixed with reasonable requests to help clean up after play pays off in adolescence when the pattern of welcome is set. "Bring your friends home so that we can meet them" is futile advice to a teenager if, during all the years of being a little boy, he has been told to keep his messy friends out of the house.

Children like to be clean. They like the look of it and the feel of it. But they do not care particularly about *staying* clean. This has nothing to do with liking to be dirty. It has everything to do with how children play — and no normal child can play for very long without getting dirty. Healthy play for small children involves playing on the floor, on the grass, in the dirt, and in the water; the inevitable end of it all is getting dirty. Scrubbing up afterward is a small price to pay for energy well spent and for hours of real joy.

Rules about not bringing dirt into the house (by the cupful, not on shoes) are fair and good, and rules about brushing dirt off on the porch before you come in are fair and good, but it is the height of frustration to be told to stop playing "because you're getting dirty." The child who is scolded constantly on this score, dragged in to be washed, changed, and set to something "nice and clean," is doomed to be a perpetual spectator, watching on the sidelines while the rest of men enjoy creative work and play.

Cleanliness for health's sake is another matter. Very few children (none *I* know) seem to think it's important to wash before eating; this simply has to be forced on them. I daresay few develop insecurities from a little brute strength applied here.

They must also learn to wash their hands after going to the bathroom, and it is best if mothers desist from using the clinical reasons and teach this simply as a social nicety. Impressionable children are apt to develop terrible fears about bathroom functions if too much emphasis is put on germs (and this can cause real trouble later on when they learn about their reproductive organs). Unable to understand about germs, learning about them first in the bathroom, then in connection with "dirt," and things on the floor, cats and dogs and money and even the air, the world can soon lose all its loveliness for them and be reduced to nothing but a breeding place for germs. If they should ask why God made germs, we can tell them that, like everything else He created, germs were good before Adam committed Original Sin. It was the sin that destroyed the harmony, and now some germs can do great harm. God gave us heads to learn how to protect ourselves, however, and we can use them, put ourselves in God's care, and refuse to waste time worrying about what *might* happen because of germs.

Brushing teeth, taking baths, washing hair — all the good health habits are an important part of a child's sense of security (although I have seen our children as secure as barnacles, and with the grime so thick it had to be sanded off), not only because they keep him socially acceptable, but also because they are duties of stewardship over a body God has given him. It is when we exaggerate these things out of proportion that they can hurt not only his self-confidence, but also his spiritual values. When impeccable personal habits begin to masquerade as *personal purity*, they can create great moral confusion. Virtue is not synonymous with cleanliness, although it's nice if the virtuous can be clean.

≈

*Show your child how to unite
sickness with Christ's sufferings*

Chronic illness is a very special threat to a child's security, not only for its suffering, but also because it's easy for invalids to feel either totally useless or totally helpless. Uselessness can breed despair, and helplessness can breed a monster of self-pity. This is particularly tragic when we know that suffering played the most noble part of all in our redemption, and suffering that's united to Christ's suffering can be the highest, most mysterious vocation.

Of two families we know whose children suffer the same affliction, one mother comforts her child by reminding him of the afflictions of his friends. This one has braces on his teeth, that one wears glasses, the other can't run very well — and she tries to help him find comfort in the sharing of seeming injustices. It's a little comfort, but not much. It doesn't answer his question, "Why me?"

The other family has taught their son that suffering is powerful prayer. For some reason that God alone knows, He has chosen this boy to share His own suffering from time to time. The boy may, if he will, unite his suffering with Christ's and work with Him to save the souls of men. He can use it for a hundred intentions, for his family, his friends, the missions, the children all over the world who suffer with him. One time I asked him if he used his suffering, and he said very simply, "Oh yes, I always offer it up."

It's the magnificent usefulness of those who *feel* useless.

≈

*Help your child see his
physical flaws in perspective*

Childhood is filled with little problems in security, like being born with a big nose, or too many freckles, like being too fat, or too thin, like being too plain and wishing you were pretty, or having straight hair and wishing it were curly. A thousand things can prey on the confidence of a child and expose him to terrible torments of embarrassment and secret suffering.

Being cheerful is the best cure of all for sensitivity, and when children come to us for comfort in their secret unhappiness, we can help with our own cheerfulness.

"Why, you silly little boy! Here you are, wishing you looked like someone else, and all the time God went to the trouble to make a special one like *you*. With a nose so, and eyes so, and nice, nice freckles (which, of course, He has counted), and red hair that isn't the color of carrots at all, but the color of gold. Have you forgotten who you are? You are *you!* Very lovely in God's sight, and very, very lovable. And if you keep your soul shining and bright, very, *very beautiful*."

Of course, there are things we can do to help. We can help a stout child to control her eating, which, in the unhappily stout, often becomes the only comfort and gradually grows into gluttony. We can help an unattractive child (but are there really any?) to develop all his other gifts, and remind a boy who is, say, self-conscious about his changing, squeaky voice that even Jesus put up with a changing, squeaky voice. We can help them a great deal if we know the stories of the saints, who were all shapes and sizes, funny and lovely to look at, attractive to men and unattractive, and give them these special companions to help them find happiness by learning how to love others and forget themselves.

A boy we know broke off his front tooth and died a thousand deaths wondering how to face his friends. His mother went straight to the heart of suffering and helped him unite his disfigurement with Christ's in the Passion, and in a week's time, he was over his fear and had forgotten his tooth.

A woman we know of worried all her life about a mole above her lip, and finally had it removed. When she did, her friends said among themselves, "But she isn't the same. The mole was part of her." I wonder if it wouldn't have saved her those years of embarrassment if someone had told her how the great Teresa's biographer described her: "On the left side of her face there were three small moles which added to her attractiveness."

A little girl who was always plump offered her suffering lovingly each time she said the Hail Holy Queen, the prayer where we "send up our size." She discovered only when she had read the prayer for the first time (after knowing it by heart for years) what mistake she had innocently made. Today she is a blissfully happy novice, and I wonder if the patiently offered size didn't help as well as all the other prayers she said for the grace to know her vocation.

⁀

Encourage poor students to try hard in school

The Curé d'Ars is a wonderful saint for children who have to struggle with their schoolwork. He had a terrible time in school; by all the standards, he seemed to be quite dumb. But the kind of wisdom that springs from a soul in love with God the Curé never lacked, and there's no one today who would dare call him a blockhead. God counts most how you try, not whether you succeed, and for children who try but still bring home poor report cards, there's strength to be found in praise for honest effort.

A teacher we know was about to give up with a boy who would not study. She had coaxed and appealed and challenged and scolded, and nothing did any good. Then one day she *pretended* he had tried.

"You know, you're doing much better. I knew you could, if you'd try."

From that day on, he began to change. Weeks later, she met his parents, and then she said, "Now I know what was wrong. That child had never been praised for anything. He never even wanted to try."

Herman the Cripple is the friend of all children who are crippled or badly disfigured. "He could not stand, let alone walk; could hardly sit, even in the special chair they made for him; even his fingers were all but too weak and knotted for him to write; even his mouth and palate were deformed, and he could hardly be understood when he spoke." During all his life, Herman was never comfortable, but he was a cheerful soul who spoke of himself as "the least of Christ's poor ones and yes . . . slower than any donkey." Out of all this pain and disfigurement came great glory to God, not only from his industry and determination, for he made astrolabes and clocks and even musical instruments, but from his love — for it's pretty much agreed that Blessed Herman wrote the Hail Holy Queen.

Children do not need to be protected in their afflictions; they need to *know how to use them*. When they are used to draw people closer to God, they cease to be afflictions, and they become blessings.

⤳

Help your child to accept a new sibling

Jealousy is another insecurity, but only when we lose sight of how we are loved by God. Love is not divided with the coming of a new child in the family, only multiplied. One more baby means another brother or sister to *be loved by*, as well as another to love. Helping to care for the baby, doing little chores at bath time and feeding time, thinking of him as "my baby," gradually wear away at the quite normal jealousy of a child who has suddenly lost the spotlight to a new member of the family. But the best cure is to see that the baby is a gift of God's love.

"This is really wonderful, when you think what it means. God knew all the time what a fine boy you are, and how you'd make a fine brother. So He sent you a baby to be a brother to. Brothers are grand things to have. They teach things to babies and take care of them. Our baby is so lucky to have a brother like you."

Most of all, a new baby is like Mary's Baby, and children who still resent his intrusion will often forget immediately if they are helped to see how like the little Jesus he is. "Little hands, and little feet, and a tiny nose, and such a weak little cry. Just think, this is how Baby Jesus was."

Reminding them that God the Father, and the Son, and the Holy Spirit live happily in the soul of the newly baptized baby, just as They do in our own when we are free of serious sin, helps them learn reverence for him, and saying the night prayers beside the new baby helps to sweeten what little resentments are left.

For older children, praise, special and privileged chores, and especially warm and loving appreciation help to quiet jealousy.

"We're so glad God gave us you. Whatever would we do without you? He knew we'd need someone special to help us, someone with your talents, just your kind of person, and the special one He picked for us was *you*."

⤺

Encourage your child
to find courage in God

Danger — real or imagined — can destroy a child's security and make some children physically ill, and it never helps a child to make him do something he's afraid to do. Even the things that cannot be avoided, like entering the hospital or going off to school alone for the first time, can be prepared for with prayer, and grace will come to help.

Our own children suffered a terrible fear of dogs at one time, and the twice-daily walk to the bus and back was running the gamut of fear for them. The dogs they passed never bit them, but they barked so ferociously that certain death was suggested at every turn, and it was only through prayer for faith and trust that they conquered this fear. God knew about the dogs, and He knew about the children. There was nothing to do but pray for the grace to be unafraid. And when you ask God to protect you, you have to try to act unafraid, even if you still are, a little. So they made tremendous acts of faith and started out. And they made tremendous acts of will (and didn't run in front of the dogs). And, of course, because they didn't run, the dogs didn't chase, and in a week they were no longer afraid of dogs. There's a great difference between walking past dogs alone, and walking past dogs with God, and once children have tasted success with such a simple thing as this, they know how to go about battling the fears that will follow.

Life will never be painless for our children, try as we might to spare them. We are foolish to think that we can. And it's wise not to waste time trying. We can bend every energy to giving a child the full measure of God, and in the end, with His help, they can learn to accept and bear, and one day find joy, in whatever assaults their sense of security will have to endure.

Chapter 6

*Teach your child
to love the Rosary*

Let's face it: children do not always like to say the Rosary. A friend of mine, launching her initial attack, countered the protests ("all those prayers at one time!") with, "The Newlands say it every night." The emphatic reply was, "Well, *let* 'em."

It's quite true that the Rosary, for children, is too often nothing but a long-drawn-out affair of kneeling eternally on weary knees and repeating over and over a refrain that has lost all meaning.

Not always, of course. Sometimes they go to it with genuine sweetness and find real satisfaction in the rhythmic chanting, but when something so important as the habit of daily Rosary is concerned (Rosary versus TV at that), it isn't enough to depend on mood alone. Training children to make a lifelong habit of daily Rosary takes all the parents' gifts of persuasion and imagination, and they have to work hard to dress this daily repetition with color and meaning and beauty.

I remember, when I was about eight, kneeling with my mother, my grandmother, and my sisters through interminable Rosaries. One night I decided it was too much and put on what was meant to be a convincing demonstration of Young Child Falls Asleep at Rosary. I drooped and sighed, closed my eyes and fell against my bed, run right into the ground with praying. I waited for some spark of compassion to be aroused in my mother and my grandmother and heard nothing until they were about to leave the room. "Mary," said my mother, "everyone knows you aren't asleep." It was very humiliating, and I never tried it again. Nevertheless, I didn't return to daily Rosary any more enthusiastic than before, only more submissive.

Now, many years later, I find children of my own not above trying the same tricks, and the vivid memory of my own boredom at daily Rosary makes me seek ways of making the Rosary come alive for them.

How the Rosary might have come to be

First of all, why the Rosary anyway? And what is it? How did it begin? Who started saying it, and who says we should say it?

Most people think that the Rosary began with St. Dominic at the time the Blessed Virgin appeared to him to recommend it as a weapon against heresy, but actually it had far simpler beginnings than that. Like many parts of Christian worship, it grew out of a need, the need of simple people who could neither read nor write and had to substitute some form of prayer for the reading of Psalms or the saying of Masses. Centuries ago, when the priests of the monastic orders were saying Masses for the dead, the illiterate lay brothers would recite fifty prayers instead — usually fifty Our Fathers. Keeping track of fifty Our Fathers on your fingers is something of a project; so, in time, they started counting them out with fifty pebbles.

Now, it seems quite possible to me that, having hit on the idea of counting their fifty prayers with pebbles, one day a very old monk, wearing, naturally, a very old habit, might have discovered a hole in his pocket and, alas, some of his fifty pebbles missing.

After struggling with mild scruples, wondering how long they had been missing and if long, how many prayers he had been missing, perhaps it occurred to him that it would be better to count his prayers off with beads on a string instead of pebbles.

Having, perhaps, suggested this to the other brothers, they might have confessed to misgivings about pebbles possibly lost and prayers possibly not said, and all proceeded to make themselves strings of beads on which to count their prayers. From saying fifty Our Fathers to fifty Hail Marys, it was quite logical that they should be inspired to make their beads more beautiful and call the circlet of beads — which suggested a wreath — a *rosarium*, or garland of roses in honor of Mary, the Mystical Rose.

Some rosary beads are carved to look like roses; children love this. They also like to pretend just once, with pebbles from the driveway or the beach or little colored stones from the fish bowl, that they must count their prayers with stones, too, as the monks did so long ago.

Making rosaries with colored beads, or dried seeds, is fun, and it helps clarify in children's minds the number and sequence of prayers and mysteries.

The Creed, said on the Crucifix, comes first because it sums up all a Catholic believes, and it was included for this reason long, long ago. Then an Our Father, the words Jesus used when He taught the Apostles how to pray. Then three Hail Marys, one for faith, one for hope, and one for charity, to ask an increase of these gifts received at the moment of our Baptism. The words of the angel Gabriel and St. Elizabeth compose the first part of the Hail Mary, and the Church has added the words of the second part. Then the Glory Be, to give honor to the Holy Trinity.

Then follow the familiar decades and, after each Glory Be, the little prayer Our Lady of Fatima asked us to include:

How to Raise Good Catholic Children

O my Jesus, forgive us our sins,
save us from the fire of Hell;
draw all souls to Heaven, especially
those most in need of Thy mercy.

At the end, the Hail Holy Queen. You might tell your children that this prayer is supposed to have been written by Blessed Herman the Cripple, whose story is one of the most touching in all the lives of the saints.

≈

Motivate your child to pray the Rosary

Merely knowing how to say the Rosary and what the beads mean is no guarantee that children will love it; so we pray for help before starting: "Please, Blessed Mother, help us to love the Rosary, and help us to say it nicely." Now that we have received the grace to say it nicely, all that remains is to use the grace and say it nicely. With the reminder that if they will attend to business, it will take only fifteen or twenty minutes, the effort doesn't look endless after all.

The most wonderful thing of all about the Rosary is that it's the story of Jesus and Mary. It's the full circle, beginning at the Annunciation and ending in Mary's triumph as Queen of Heaven. It sums up all the Gospels, Christ's life, death, and Resurrection; it's the great feasts of the Church linked together in logical succession, and it's all the liturgical seasons. There's no sorrow or joy, event or situation in our own lives that isn't mirrored in the Rosary; and if we say it — and meditate on it — daily, there are few better ways of living close to the life of Christ.

A word here about the age at which to start the Rosary. Almost every family with a baby who has been watching his elders recite the Rosary from his playpen or high chair will tell you that very early the baby begins to imitate them. If you give him a rosary, he will babble convincingly in the manner of one saying the Rosary — for a few minutes, at least — and then he will break the rosary. So, if the Rosary recitation in your house is reasonably harmonious, then by all means expose the baby.

Three- and four-year-olds will not apply themselves to the Rosary for very long, and when their interest wanders, they will start to play; but being allowed to play near the rest who pray helps to accustom them to the idea that "big" people say the Rosary every night. Since our five-year-old does a very good job at the Rosary, he's expected to say it with the rest, except on nights when he's too tired and is more of a distraction than an addition, in which case he's excused to go to bed. All the rest say it well (the oldest is ten), and very well when they are allowed to take an active part.

After we've broken down the original barrier — boredom — told children of its beginnings, and taught them to pray for the grace to love it, we must teach them how to use it, how to pray, not just say, the Rosary.

~

Help your child to ponder the mysteries of the Rosary
The word *meditate* leaves children cold, even when they understand it. It's not an active word, and children are very active. The Rosary must be an activity for them. There's a game to play while saying the Rosary: "Let's pretend we're there."

"Let's pretend we're there when Gabriel announces to the Virgin Mary that she is to be the Mother of God. We could be very small like a mouse in the corner and watch what happened. Where do you suppose she was when he came? Maybe she was shelling peas on the back porch (like the picture in *The Ageless*

Story), and he knelt beside her in the sun. Or perhaps she was out in her garden under a tree, peeling apples for a pie. Maybe she was standing in her room, looking out the window at the hills and thinking about God. You can pretend her house was like our house, and her yard like our yard; it might have been. Remember, she was very young, only fifteen, very beautiful, and very pure and holy. What did Gabriel say to her when he came?"

"Hail, full of grace, the Lord is with thee. Blessed art thou among women."

"But she was frightened, and didn't understand what he meant. So he said, 'Do not be afraid, Mary, because you have found grace with God!' And he told her she was to have a baby and His name would be Jesus. Then he explained that her Son would be con-ceived by the Holy Spirit (that means God would be His Father), as it says in the Apostles' Creed: 'Conceived by the Holy Spirit, born of the Virgin Mary.' Mary understood and was full of love for God's will, and said, 'Be it done unto me according to thy word.' "

Then the first decade starts with everyone saying together, "The First Joyful Mystery is the Annunciation — that means the announcing that Mary is to be the Mother of God." The other mysteries can be introduced the same way. Reading between times the accounts of these events in the Gospels and the Acts of the Apostles (all except the Assumption and the Coronation) helps them see the Rosary as not only a tribute to Mary, but also a testi-mony to Christ.

⌒

Use drama, games, and art to help your
child remember the mysteries of the Rosary

Children must be themselves, even at the Rosary. After they have learned the mysteries, it helps to keep the Rosary lively if they take turns identifying the mysteries, describing them, and leading a decade. They may depart from tradition, as Jamie did when he described the Third Joyful Mystery as "She had her Baby." But their innovations are reverent, and if they can explain it in their own words, you know that they know it.

Once they know the mysteries, it's fun to dramatize them, and sometimes we do charades instead of merely explaining them. All but the Sorrowful Mysteries make good charades (it would be an indignity to make charades of the Sorrowful Mysteries), and for children who learn best by *doing*, acting out should be used often.

As an example, the Visitation. This is quickly enacted with one child standing in the room and another approaching the door, knocking, and entering. "Elizabeth, dear, are you at home?" Another runs quickly to greet the visitor with, "Blessed art thou among women, and blessed is the Fruit of thy womb." And they embrace.

Twenty Questions, "Who am I?" and "What am I?" are excellent games for teaching the mysteries and ought to be used frequently, especially at such times as when doing dishes, hanging out clothes, and weeding the garden. Suppose you're one of the doves in the Presentation in the Temple; here's a "What am I?"

"Are you a bird?" Yes, a bird.

"A special bird?" Yes, a special bird.

"In a special story?" Yes, a special story.

"About Jesus?" Yes, about Jesus.

"One of the sparrows God watches when it falls?" No, not that.

"The hen — the time Jesus said He would like to gather Jerusalem under His wings like a mother hen?" No, not that.

"In a mystery?" Yes, in a mystery.

"Oh! In the basket, when Blessed Mother went to the Temple? I know — one of the doves in the Fourth Joyful Mystery: the Presentation in the Temple."

Because it's really good fun, they don't realize that they're having a lesson in religion.

Drawing and painting the mysteries is instructive also. One of Monica's most successful attempts with watercolor was an Annunciation with Mary sitting over the mending basket, a cat at her feet, and Gabriel alighting in the corner.

Drawing the mysteries with colored chalk is another way of having fun and learning at the same time. We hung up a blackboard, and across the wall from the blackboard, we mounted a bulletin board of the same size on which paintings and drawings can be mounted. It's one thing to have your pictures admired and then tossed around for the baby to chew. It's quite another to have them mounted where they can be seen. And show me the child who will not stop to explain in great detail what he has painted and why (and if it's a mystery of the Rosary, so much the better), if someone will stop to admire it.

Plasticine and the kind of pottery clay that dries in the oven are cheap and easy to handle; and children who do not know the mysteries will begin to know them when they model, say, Simeon holding the Infant Jesus in his arms and Mary with her basket of doves at the Presentation.

Then there are outdoor things to learn from, too. In our woods in spring, there's always thorn apple growing, a small bush with cruel thorns. The Crowning with Thorns has new meaning after a walk to pick thorn apple, and we return home with stinging scratches to remind us that thorns really hurt, very much. The barberry hedges growing in city parks will have the same effect for city children, and a small branch of locust makes a very poignant reminder of the Third Sorrowful Mystery. One spring, we put our sprig of thorn apple in water, and God did a lovely thing with it for us. He let it sprout little green leaves on Good Friday. This way He taught the children that out of His Son's death on the Cross came new life for all of us.

The Church has a Blessing for Herbs and Flowers that is traditionally bestowed on the Feast of the Assumption, in August, and she encourages families to use this blessing over their flower gardens if they have them, or even the potted plants in the windows of city apartments. Children assisting at this little rite love to hear the legend about the Apostles finding flowers in our Lady's tomb, and remember both the feast and the blessing in connection with the Fourth Glorious Mystery.

The reading for the Mass of the Assumption calls Mary "exalted like a cedar in Libanus, a cypress tree on Mount Sion, a palm tree in Cades, a rose plant in Jericho, a fair olive tree by the water in the streets, a sweet smell like cinnamon and aromatic balm, a sweet odor like the best myrrh."[23] Every mother has cinnamon in her pantry, and many have the sweet smell of cedar in their closets, and children — who learn best by sniffing and touching and tasting and seeing — love the association of her Assumption with such delicious odors. Then even the stick of cinnamon in the applesauce is a reminder of the Assumption.

Scrapbooks illustrating the mysteries are fun, made from religious greeting cards and holy pictures, and they make wonderful gifts for grandmothers and aunts.

And one of the best things of all is to make a magic garden. Made outdoors under a tree, with leaves and grasses, snips of cloth, beads, bits of stone and colored glass, this setting can represent a number of things: Mary's garden for the Annunciation, Elizabeth's doorstep at the Visitation, or the hill outside of Bethany for the Ascension. If there's no outdoors available, a child can make one

---

[23] Cf. Ecclus. 24:17-20 (RSV = Sir. 24:13-15).

in an empty box, with spools and thimbles, matchsticks, a broken mirror, colored paper, buttons — all kinds of things. The empty tomb at the Resurrection, the Upper Room for the Descent of the Holy Spirit upon the Apostles, or the Temple where the Boy Jesus was preaching at the Finding in the Temple — all these take on form and mystery when created in a shoe box. Children's building blocks make wonderful temples, with pillars and steps and mysterious holy places. Friends of ours have their children spend the three hours on Good Friday making Easter gardens in the backyard; and they have been so intent on the three crosses, the empty tomb, and the garden of Joseph of Arimathea that they had spent the entire three hours in silence.

Still another way of remembering is to cut a symbol of a mystery in the top of a pie crust. The nails and crown of thorns, or a manger and a star, a candle with a flame — all these serve the purpose for which slits are needed in pies and at the same time rehearse the small ones in the details of the mysteries.

Postcard reproductions of fine Christian art are cheap and easy to find in art-supply stores, bookstores, or museums; and when friends go off to Europe, we should beg them to bring back postcards of the Christian art they will see. We have a collection that starts with the Christian primitives and goes through Italian, Flemish, German, Spanish, Byzantine, Norman, and Gothic art. There are paintings, frescoes, wood carvings, ceramics, enamels, mosaics, icons, all on postcards, all telling some part of the story of Jesus and Mary. Some appeal to the children, some merely provoke them, but all make for discussion, and many times the children meditate on the mysteries as they say them by choosing a postcard to look at.

City children should visit museums as often as possible to see the exhibits of Christian art. It may seem complicated to get them there and back, but when it's spiritual enrichment as well as cultural, it's worth the effort. There they will see that the mysteries they meditate on each evening have been painted and carved for hundreds of years, to be hung in palaces, on the walls of cathedrals, even in the streets of cities, and the horizons of their reverence will widen farther than ever.

All this, of course, is not meant to make such a production of the Rosary that one cannot do it without a package of postcards in his pocket, a paintbrush in his hand, or a cast for charades at his beck and call. It's the making of a rich store of pictures, colors, figures, sounds, smells, and activities that help the whole family meditate on the meaning of the Rosary and enjoy saying it.

It isn't necessary to kneel each time for the Rosary. Some days, if it isn't said while we work, it isn't said at all. It's a wholesome thing for children to say the Rosary with their chores, while they wipe dishes, help with the ironing, or watch the bread-baking. One family we know always starts their weekend ride in the country by saying the Rosary, that day, in the car. Another friend told me that her mother said it while she hung the clothes, using clothespins to count the prayers on the clothesline. Kneeling should not be omitted entirely, of course (incidentally, you can teach children to make an act of adoration every time they kneel for anything, whether mopping spilled milk, tying the baby's shoes, or whatever).

⌇

Show your child the power of the Rosary
The most elaborate session we've had with the Rosary was the time friends with nine children visited us for the week. Their nine (at the time) and our five (at the time) are a lot of children, and gathering them for the Rosary wasn't always entirely successful.

One day we decided to try it right after lunch, and the moans and groans that greeted this suggestion were properly discouraging. We reminded them of Our Lady's promise at Fatima, of the grace to be won, of the merit stored in Heaven, of the time off in Purgatory, and no one even cared. Then we asked about their intentions. Did any of them have special intentions? That was what got them; everyone took turns listing his personal intentions, the private ones silently, the others aloud. There were the usual things "I want," and the lists of people: all priests, all religious, all bishops, the Holy Father, the soldiers fighting at the time, the refugees, all prisoners, all who would die today, all tempted to commit mortal sin today, the souls in Purgatory, sick friends, friends in financial distress, friends who had helped us, our enemies, our parishes, our families — and, "Please, help us all to be saints."

The Rosary went swiftly and enthusiastically; and when it was finished, we counted the prayers (ten people in all, babies napping and a few having ducked out), and they totaled seven hundred thirty.

"Wow!"

In a new way, they could see the real power of the Rosary. This seems to be the greatest incentive of all for children: showing them how they may use the Rosary, what a power it is in their hands.

Long-term promises are wearying, and Our Lord warned us to beware of fretting too much over tomorrow. "Sufficient for the day . . ."[24] One Rosary at a time, in other words. Then, if a child remarks to you, as one of mine did recently, "You know, Mother, I don't always exactly like to say the Rosary, and sometimes I think that when I'm grown up and don't have to mind you anymore, I

[24]Matt. 6:34.

won't say it," you can laugh. You can laugh and tell her with confidence that she needn't concern herself now about whether she will say it when she's grown. If she will say it now, one day at a time, asking for the grace to love it and say it well, our Lady will fill in what is lacking. If we work hard to help children meditate on its mysteries, and give them the sense of its real power, then we are teaching our children not only how to say, how to pray, the Rosary, but, best of all, how to use it.

Chapter 7

*Nurture a devotion
to Mary and
the other saints*

When a child is very little, his mother is very perfect. She's "the best mother in the whole world, and the most beautiful, and the one who cooks the best, sings the best songs, and makes the best surprises." Everything she does is the very best, and her virtues surpass all others. And then, in a little while, he discovers she has weaknesses like everybody else. She can be cross without very good reason, and lose her temper. She can judge unfairly and punish too severely. She can do lots of things that even a child can see are far from perfect, and this is very sad, because mothers *should be perfect*.

How good our Lord was, then, to give us our Lady. She is many profound and mysterious things, and she ministers to mankind in many ways, but in the lives of children — who see things in such simple terms — she fills the space between what mothers really are and what their children want them to be.

If anyone should ask me what is the most difficult thing I can think of to write about, I would say immediately — Mary. And having tried many times and failed miserably, there's no reason to think another try will be better. There is just one saving grace. To write about children and our Lady, one does not need to know all the Mariology; one just needs to know about Mary. It's Mary that children need because they need so much to have a mother who is perfect.

An example will explain what I mean. The other day, Peter was quite naughty, and finally a spanking was called for. I was quite calm (really) and very sure that he deserved it. When it was all over, and things seemed pretty much all right again, he knocked me right off my feet by asking: "Mother, if our Lady was here in our house really, would she give me a spanking?"

Oh, dear.

No, our Lady wouldn't give him a spanking. Our Lady wouldn't need to give spankings because our Lady is perfect. And Peter would be different if his mother were perfect. And there you have it all in a nutshell: only a perfect mother could form a perfect child, and the only perfect Mother is our Lady.

It's when they say things like that to you that you see all the things that Mary's perfection means to a child. He isn't concerned with her splendors, about which he has not yet any occasion to know. He finds in her all the lovely things he finds in his own mother, and she adds to these things all the things that are lacking in his mother. She never loses her temper, is never too busy, is never too tired. She always listens patiently and always judges fairly. She knows how you are in your secret inside, where you always want to be good, and she never wearies of waiting for it to show on your outside, where all you seem to do is be bad. She's the most beautiful, the most kind, the most loving. She's the most generous, and forever forgiving. It's the truth: she's a *heavenly* mother.

⌒

Teach your child to live under Mary's watchful care

But first, of course, he must know her. If I had not met children who do not know her, I would be tempted to say that, in a strange way, children seem to come already knowing her. That is not true, of course — but they come all ready to know her. And they learn to know her and love her as easily as they learn to know and love God. Her picture, her name, the familiar way of praying "Dear Blessed Mother," the sound of the Hail Mary, the sight of the Rosary, the family kneeling together to say the Rosary — all these things make it clear to the littlest child that there's somebody real whom everybody loves called Mary. And for little children, it's no difficulty at all to learn to live in her presence.

"But Mother, how can you live in the presence of Mary? Our Lady isn't God. She can't be everywhere the same as God is."

I hadn't expected quite so much perception from someone only ten! But it's good to know how easily we can confuse them, and how clearly we must explain if living in the presence of Mary is to be more than a sentimental pose.

"No, she's not God, and she's not with us the same way God is. She's not present as Jesus is in Holy Communion, nor as the Holy Trinity dwelling in our souls. But our Lord made her our Mother, and wherever a mother's children are, there is her love. *She has us in her eye.* When the sun shines on you, you say you're standing in the sun. In the same way, you live in Mary's gaze, and it follows you everywhere. But, then, what else would you expect? Mothers always watch their children."

But the little children need no such explanations. Their faith is so sturdy that they simply accept her presence and the simplest domestic happenings help them to practice it — like hearing their mother say, "Please, Blessed Mother, help me find my hat. I can't go to church without my hat. You children, please say a Hail Mary and ask our Lady to help us find my hat."

This is so commonplace in Catholic households that it seems ridiculous to put it in here. But is the commonness of it not the proof of how practical Mary is in her mothering? Don't children scatter in all directions saying Hail Marys and searching for my hat? Inevitably she finds it, or the gloves, or saves the roast, or whatever it happens to be. And if on occasion she reminds me instead that I left it in the car, none but the rarest of fools expects her to shatter the natural order by the flying entrance of hats. Not that she couldn't. God can make hats fly as easily as birds and if Mary wanted it, He would.

But her concern over her children goes deeper than just saving them the vexations they suffer in their absence of mind. Her work in our lives is to make in us a likeness to her Son, and when we remember the hidden years He lived under her care and the ordinariness of them, we can expect that her work with us will be as hidden and the means by which she forms us as ordinary. For the most part, there will be no miracles — except that staggering miracle at the end of it all, when we find that she has led us to Christ.

But she can't do this if we don't let her, and to let her means asking her to come into our daily lives and teach us how to do everything we must do. She taught the Child who was Christ; who is better able to teach us how to be Christlike? She served the Child who was Christ; who is better able to teach us how to serve Christ? That's how we're like Mary: we're all called to serve Christ, and Mary can teach us best of all, because that was her vocation.

≈

Mary can teach your child many virtues

It begins with the most ordinary things, because we serve Christ with our ordinary things. Now, this is an example of how she taught one child patience with sewing. Monica was learning to sew, and like all little girls with grand ideas about elaborate wardrobes, before ever the scissors cut the cloth, her enthusiasm was two jumps ahead of her fingers. Anyone with half an eye could see that she was headed for trouble.

"Darned old basting — why do I have to baste? Darned old machine — always goes crooked!"

"Well, you will have to baste if you want the skirt to be any good. It isn't the darned old basting that's the trouble, or the darned old machine; it's the darned old impatience. But our Lady can help you with that. She was very patient. She had a loom, and on it she wove a garment for her grown Son, without a single seam. It must have taken her a long time, and she must have been very patient. First, ask her to help you be patient, and then take one stitch at a time, every stitch with love. She will help you, and it will be a lovelier skirt because she helped you make it."

It went along with stops and starts and much biting of the tongue. And finally it was done.

"The long hem was hard to do, and I almost got mad again. The thread broke and I had to rethread a hundred million times. But I did ask her. And I tried to be patient like she was. And she did help me get it done. I know, because if she hadn't, I'd never have gotten it done."

Someone is sure to say, "Don't tell me once is enough, and a child has learned patience!" And they're so right. Next time we'll probably start all over again with "Darned old basting!" But if we do, we'll start all over again with Mary, and things may go on like that for quite a while. But I know (because I've seen it happen before) that one day it will start with: "Now, I'm not going to groan about the basting because our Lady has gotten me used to it." And I, for one, shan't be the least bit surprised.

No one can claim to know exactly how she works in the minds and hearts and wills of children, but even the children will tell you that she does. Monica says, "It's the times you forget to ask her that you don't like doing things. And sometimes even when you do, you don't exactly like it, but she helps you get it done and afterward you're glad. Only you need to be reminded."

So if we would have our children be formed by Mary, we must be forever reminding: "Please, will you watch the baby while Mother gets the supper? Ask our Lady to help. She was so gentle with her Baby. and she'll help you with ours."

"Please, will you gather some kindling? It won't take a minute, and our Lady will help you. You can tell her you'll do it for her — the way her Boy did."

Our Lady can teach children courage; they love to discover she was brave. She knew the prophecies about the Messiah, and she knew that they meant terrible suffering. If the details of the suffering were still hidden, the horror was not. Hadn't she heard over and over, in the Psalms, "I am a worm, not a man; the scorn of men, despised by the people"?[25]

And here was Gabriel asking her to be God's Mother, make all this horror come true by bearing the Son of God. It took courage as well as love for Mary to say yes.

We told our children about Mary's courage when they had to have booster shots for measles. They had twenty-four hours to pray very hard and ask her to help them be brave. Being afraid was the worst part, not the short minute it would really hurt. It wouldn't hurt today and tomorrow, or riding to town in the car, or sitting in the waiting room, or even standing around in the doctor's office. Our Lady could manage both the fears and the pains if they would only ask her. So we had intense prayer for twenty-four hours, and staggering success at the doctor's. No fuss, no muss, no noise — except maybe a couple of short yelps for

[25]Cf. Ps. 21:7 (RSV = Ps. 22:6).

about thirty seconds. And more than anyone else, the doctor was impressed.

"My goodness," she said, patting the last boy. "You're very brave."

"All on account of our Lady."

I do not recommend this on the strength of one test run. It works every time, if they really pray. The latest success reported was from a friend down the road whose little girl, scheduled for a tonsillectomy, was terrified of the thought of the hospital. Her mother, describing it afterward, said, "It was amazing; you never saw such *calm*."

This is not just a form of religious child psychology. It's the means to a grace needed at a particular moment. It may be put in a very simple way, but it's still the teaching of the Church on Mary, the Mediatrix of all grace. When children have faith and ask for grace, it will always come through Mary. Even when we're clumsy with grace, and have to struggle to cooperate with it, when it's mothers trying to keep their tempers, or children trying to behave, turning again and again to Mary is the only way to progress.

"What I don't get, though, is why it's so easy to be bad, and so awful hard to be good." And Jamie sighs, as St. Paul must have sighed when he wrote in a letter about the good he would do, and did not, and the evil he would not do, and did.[26]

"But that's not hard to understand when you remember the Devil, and how he's always pushing and shoving. He's smart. He knows our weaknesses. But you can play a trick on him if you remember to call on Mary. Remember in the story of Adam and Eve, when God promised to make Mary the Devil's enemy? He said she would lie in wait for him and one day crush him under her

[26]Rom. 7:15.

heel.[27] He hates her because he knows he can't touch her, and when you call to her, 'Mary, help me!' he has a regular fit."

We mustn't let them get the idea that because we describe her as gentle and loving, Mary is not a tower of strength. To the Devil she's as terrible as an army in battle array. What does it matter how, in their enthusiasm, they imagine her battle technique?

"She'll do this," and Jamie crushes a serpent with a horrible squish.

"And she'll do this," and John pierces a shrieking Devil with the razor edge of a lance. Boys need to love her with virility, and if there's violence in the way they act out Mary vanquishing the Devil, it's nothing compared with the way it will be with the real thing. That's going to be spectacular.

⬲

Train your child to imitate Mary's purity

Imitating Mary's purity is sometimes hard for children to understand unless we explain it to them in terms of her faithfulness to her vocation. She was very different from us, conceived without Original Sin and with never the desire to sin in the littlest way. We can't be like that. We're born marked by Original Sin; even when it's washed away in Baptism, there's a scar left and a weakness. We carry it until we die and are always in danger of sin. But we can ask Mary to help us love purity. It's easier to be pure when you love purity than when "pure" is something you're supposed to be. And this is the only really helpful way to answer an older child's discovery: "But our Lady was never tempted to be impure."

And for parents, it's important to remember that Mary's purity had no ignorance about it. She was fourteen or fifteen, but she

[27]Cf. Gen. 3:15.

knew about babies, how they're conceived and born. When Gabriel waited for her to say yes, she would bear God's Baby, first she asked him, "How shall this be, since I know not man?"[28] A wholesome knowledge of sex suited to a child's age and curiosity and need is not an obstacle to purity, but rather safeguards it.

We can teach our littlest children to pray to Mary about purity in their earliest prayers, and we can teach our older children, when they're old enough to understand, that one day it may become more difficult to be pure and that they should pray, "Please, Blessed Mother, help me to *love* purity."

And then, for girls, there are all the special Mary virtues that have to do with being ladylike. I often wonder if the word *ladylike* had its beginning in the imitation of our Lady. If it did, it has long since lost this meaning. Now it means proper and well mannered and a lot of things nice girls do, not for the sake of pleasing God — which is why our Lady did them — but usually to impress the company.

It's bound to strike today's youngsters (although few of them come right out and say it) as a little preposterous that they imitate Mary in their dress. Or their hairdos, or, for that matter, almost anything else they do. The reason is that, as soon as you suggest it, they have a mental picture of all the Marys on the holy cards, or the statues, or perhaps even the Mary at Nazareth, dressed far differently from them, in a society far different from theirs. To expect them to act or dress like that is asking the impossible.

But Mary-likeness has little to do with externals first. It will affect the externals after children have formed an understanding of her interior disposition. If they understand something of her humility and are encouraged to pray that she will form them in the

[28]Cf. Luke 1:34.

same humility, then they can learn to reason out Mary-likeness in terms of dress and actions.

Mary was the most sublime creature God ever made, and — what's more — she knew it. She said, "My soul magnifies the Lord," which would sound to us like startling presumption if she hadn't explained "because He has regarded the lowliness of His handmaid . . . because He who is mighty has done great things for me, and holy is His name."[29]

⤴

Mary is a model of modesty

It was because she knew that God had formed all the beauty of her that it did not upset her holiness; and she can teach our daughters this same humility about their pretty faces and their trim figures. To ask young girls to be Mary-like in their use of them, to dress modestly and bear themselves in a manner that will stir up trouble in no one; to ask young boys to put a watch not only over their actions, but over their thoughts about themselves and others — these things are incredibly difficult in a world where the measure for attractiveness is sex appeal.

But we can help our children while they're still very young to learn how to think about themselves (a person is forever thinking about himself — in either the right or the wrong way) by showing them Mary's graciousness with her own splendors. Whether we're correcting our younger daughters about sitting with legs astraddle or spending too much time in front of mirrors, or our older ones about the demerits of peekaboo blouses or strapless evening dresses, the point is never made by saying, "Our Lady would not do that." As a matter of fact, the point is never made at any one time,

[29] Luke 1:46, 48-49.

but, rather, over a long period with many reminders and much prayer.

One of the easiest and most natural ways to discuss this question is when the family is leisurely saying the Rosary together and it's someone's turn to explain the Visitation (which was the occasion of Mary's *Magnificat*), before saying that decade. Another opportunity follows upon jubilant reports of compliments: "She said my dress was sweet, and I look pretty!"

With our little boys, we've had opportunities when, looking through a copy of *Life* or home from watching the neighbors' television, one or the other has said, "There was a lady in the picture who was almost all bare!" Then a mother or father, without seeming to preach, can pick up the thread and develop it nicely and end it quite casually with something like, "Let's remember to ask our Lady tonight to help us remember always that God made our bodies to give honor and glory to Him — not to make us vain or tempt us to sin."

Mary is our Mother

Very little children love being left with our Lady, and many times when I have had to run up to the mailbox or down to the barn and have forgotten to do it, they will run after me, shouting, "You didn't leave us with our Lady." To be honest, they do not always please her when they are left with her, but they almost always try — and that's better than not trying. They'll never learn to please her if they're not reminded to try.

Although I expect some people will think I'm making this up, Mary gives children lots of ideas about things to do. "Why don't you kneel down and ask our Lady? She'll put a good idea in your head about what to do." And she'll keep them company. "I can't go see your mud pies right now, Stephen. I'm mixing dough. Ask our Lady. She loves to see mud pies. Her Boy made the best mud pies in the whole world."

And if you want them to think of her often as "my Mother," try this sometime:

"Your mother is the most beautiful, the most wise, the most wonderful mother in the whole world." Our children looked so startled. They *suspect* that I'm wise (some still look for the eyes in the back of my head), and most of the time, I hope, think I'm wonderful, but Christopher and Philip are the only two innocent enough to still think that I'm beautiful. Then it dawned on somebody. "She means our Lady!"

They think she's wonderful for a lot of reasons, but one of the biggest is because of the bicycles. For three years, our oldest children sighed for bicycles, praying quite regularly. One night, when we were deciding what to think about before going to sleep, I suggested visiting her at her house and asking about the bicycles.

"But I always ask her, and she never sends one."

"She will when the time is right. You have to keep on asking."

The next day, without any warning, a friend drove up with a bicycle. Jamie nearly fainted. And expecting that if our Lady did answer all the prayers, it would be entirely miraculous (like winning a thousand dollars in a contest), he was impressed to see how reasonably and economically she had done it. She had found an old one.

"But I asked for a bike," Monica said, "and she didn't send one to me."

Jamie said, "You have to be patient. She will, when the time is right."

The time was right the following week. The same friend who brought the first bike had a sister with an old second bike; so you can imagine how it is around here when someone gets started telling about our Lady and the bicycles.

≈

Familiarize your child with the saints

Living with the saints is like living with Mary, except that the saints are brothers and sisters. Nowadays saint biographies are written so that their subjects are both believable and interesting; and if families are going to "collect" things, the first thing ought to be a good collection of books about the saints.

Since the saints, unlike Mary, were not born perfect, sometimes the easiest way to come to grips with a fault is to find a saint who had it too. Peter is fond of saying that people who get mad ought to pray to St. Peter, because he got so mad once, he cut a guy's ear off. And children who are piggish about being first ought to know about James and John, the two brother Apostles who wanted the best seats in Heaven. Our Lord was pretty cross about that. He said that people who want to be first all the time and have the best of everything would do better to act as servants to the rest. Anyone who says, "Me first" at our dinner table gets, really fast: "The first shall be last, and the last shall be first,"[30] and Me First gets served last.

Children should be on especially intimate terms with their patron saints. Once a little boy we know named Michael was at odds with the world in a bad way, and his mother, who probably has more patience than any woman I shall ever know, was at her wits' end. She simply couldn't reach him. Then we thought about St. Michael the Archangel. So we drew a great big life-size St. Michael on the back of a strip of wallpaper, with a flaming sword and

---

[30]Cf. Matt. 19:30.

armor, great wings, and radiance all around his head, and on it we wrote: "I am Michael the Archangel, patron saint of Michael, whom I love and watch over always." His mother took it home and put it on the wall in his room, and late that night she called up.

"I wish you could have been here. He looked at it and said, 'Oh, Mother — I love it! Best of all my things!' And tonight he prayed to him for the first time." It's not just that *my* saint means so much to a child, but that *my child* means so much to *his* saint.

The best thing about the saints is that they're heroes. There are no heroic feats in all children's literature or movies or TV or radio that the saints haven't done better. There are all kinds, and there are saints for all types of children.

There are saints who were very bad (at first), such as Paul and Mary Magdalene and Augustine, and there are saints who were very good, such as Thérèse and Blessed Imelda. There are saints who lived "normal" lives, such as Mother Cabrini and Mother Seton and Monica, and there are saints who would stand your hair on end, such as Lawrence the Roasted and the Apostles, most of whom were stoned, stabbed, flayed, or crucified. There are loads of saints who had delightful experiences with animals, such as Martin and Anthony and, of course, Francis of Assisi, and there are saints who had delightful experiences with people, such as Bridgit and Martin of Tours and Philomena (well, after they found her remains anyway). And we have just discovered, of all things, a saint who was the oldest sister in a family with six younger brothers: St. Odilia. Monica is sure this augurs very interesting things for her.

Then there are all the Old Testament saints and their stories — to be found right in your household Bible. There's more to Daniel than the lion's den, and more to David than Goliath, and a quantity of really exciting material in Esther and Tobit.

Nurture a devotion to Mary and the other saints

There are saints with all kinds of afflictions — and still full of joy, such as Margaret of Costello, who was blind and humpbacked, Herman the Cripple, Jeanne de Valois, who was ugly, and Isaac Jogues, who lost some of his fingers. And there were saints who were very poor, such as Benedict Joseph Labre, and saints who were rich, such as Elizabeth, Queen of Hungary. There were kings and queens and noblemen, shepherds and shepherdesses, warriors and warrioresses, cobblers and popes, farmers and priests, nuns and mothers and fathers and boys and girls, smart ones and "dumb" ones, painters, cooks, bakers, lawyers, writers, swineherds, lepers, poets, doctors, nurses, slaves, and beggars. They walked and ran and rode and flew (Joseph of Cupertino flew like mad) and even sat (Simon Stylites) — all for the love of God. Some knew tricks, such as John Bosco, and played jokes, such as Philip Neri, and laughed a lot; if you think the saints are dull and stuffy, you just don't know about saints. We know a great many stories, and we have a great many books; yet (this is the truth) whenever our children ask for a story, they always say, "Mother, tell a saint story."

The fact about the saints that's so important for us is that they were people born with Original Sin — the same as we are. They had the same weaknesses and temptations, and they were saints because they overcame them with the same graces God gives to us.

Jamie will moan, "Oh, golly, I'll never be a saint."

"You won't if you don't try. Ask your saints to show you how it's done. They will because they know."

The making of a saint is the work of grace, and Christ's grace comes through His Mother. That's why our children need Mary, because Mary is the mother of saints.

Chapter 8

*Develop in your
child a love for purity*

"When do you start teaching children about sex?"

"What is the right time, and how much and how far should it go?"

"And who should teach it?"

"Maybe teaching it in school is a good thing, when so many parents seem unable to approach the subject at home."

"But maybe it isn't a good thing, because you can't tell what the attitude of the teacher is going to be."

"What about questions? Should they all be answered, or should we put them off and change the subject and wait until there's a better time?"

These are questions that come up in everyday conversations between mothers everywhere, and more and more these past few years, when the whole subject of sex seems to preoccupy society as it never did before. The answers — at least the *right* answers — are probably just about the same as they have always been; except that now, in the midst of the confusion that follows a wholesale rebellion against the moral law, the obsession with sex has assumed fantastic proportions, and attitudes toward it fluctuate between complete license and fearful puritanism.

Because sex is so little understood as part of the nature of man, coming from the hand of God and created in His image and likeness, people either refuse to acknowledge that God has anything to do with it, or else are puzzled that, having created man a complex enough creature as he is, God should have chosen to include something so confounding, even unsavory (to some), as sex. This is too bad, because nothing God has done is less than perfect. And the creation of two sexes and their endowment with the power of procreation is as perfect as all the other things He has done.

With that truth in mind, it is not so difficult to approach the problem of sex education for children. We ought to leave the word *sex* out, and when we speak of education for children, assume that sex is to be included.

When? That is the burning question. And the answer is just as simple and as reasonable as all the other answers: when they begin to learn about themselves as a whole being with an intimate relationship to God. When they begin to walk and talk and discover themselves — that is when. And if you stop to consider when all these things begin to happen, you discover with a bit of a shock that the proper age for starting the sex education of children is a very early one.

⁓

Approach sex education in terms of God's plan

Now, the idea of starting with the subject with the very young is not particularly new. Ever since the advent of child psychologists, parents of young children have been leaping at texts treating sex and all its attendant problems like hounds after the hare. I do not wish to appear to be debunking all the genuinely good work of genuinely good psychologists. But there's an immense amount of blame to be heaped upon the bad psychologists, for even the science of psychology must be ordered to God's plan, and the havoc wrought by those who do not admit any sort of ordering of life, any relating of life to God and His will for man, to holiness and sin, is terrible to ponder. Their assistance in the matter of opening doors and unveiling mysteries and airing the facts of life is no help at all when it results in nothing more than the public contemplation of a lot of exciting pornographic facts.

For example, the attitude that it's quite normal for children to become interested in their bodies, and that parents should not be too perturbed about it, makes sense. But to proceed to the problems that arise from this early interest, and assure parents that their root lies in insecurity, or rejection, or fear of a thousand and one different things, and that their cure lies in security, or love, or confidence coupled with a complete array of biological data and nothing else — that is no answer at all.

People, even when they're children, want to know themselves. And you can't know yourself until you know yourself in relation to God. So when a very small child begins to ask his mother questions about his body and its functions, it isn't enough simply to explain the functions. It may satisfy the child momentarily, but he's still cheated; for even with such intimate processes explained, there's an opportunity to give honor and glory to God, and no child's education is good or complete unless the one ties in with the other.

Teach your child to respect his body
Usually the first questions of a young child have to do with his eliminative system, and they're not hard to answer. God designed his body marvelously well, and He planned ways for it to function so that it would remain strong and healthy. Once discovered, however, this interesting body is a matter of constantly recurring curiosity, and sooner or later — in the course of quite innocent explorations of it — he will discover that some explorations are

capable of producing very pleasant sensations. Like the untrained animal he is (although an animal with a human soul), he's apt to be quite taken with the whole business, and indulgent, too. This, mind you, at the age of two or three or four.

If there are mothers who do not realize it, this is very common and has been the way with children — good children — since children began to appear on this earth. It isn't at all remarkable. In fact, it's the kind of thing one should expect. Children speak a language restricted almost entirely to the senses when they're very small; what's pleasant to them is good. If no one has explained that a thing is not good, how are they to know? And if a mother stumbles onto her small child in the act of indulging in what she considers forbidden pleasure, her last reaction should be shock. She isn't thrown for a loss when she discovers that, left to his own devices, he would eat three meals a day of candy, ice cream, and cake.

Just as with his greediness for sweets, when she explains that they do not sustain life alone and must be kept in the category of privileges, not necessities, so with his early, innocent physical self-indulgences. It merely needs explaining. With very small children, of course, the answer is no more complicated than seeing that they are securely pantied and given enough other distractions. If the problem arises during the course of training in daily elimination, a very neat solution is a big apron with a big pocket, and a cup or spoon or whatever tucked in the pocket to amuse him. A very little child has practically no power of concentration and is easily coaxed to new pursuits. When it shows up with, say, the three- and four-year-olds, the time has come to start explaining — not just sex, but sex and *purity*.

The whole success of a mother's maiden voyage on the sea of sex instruction for her child lies in being calm and serene, pleasant and never outwardly disturbed. As soon as she shows her alarm, a little one will suspect there's more to this thing than meets the eye, and, along with increased interest, he will note that it makes Mother mad and isn't a thing to be *caught at* again. Because small children will not lie until they have been given a cause to lie — until they have the sense of having done something wrong that calls for a punishment — they are astonishingly candid. Inevitably the small child who is questioned calmly about what he is, in this instance, doing, will answer just as calmly and with complete frankness.

Well, his mother may say, of course she understands that it's all very pleasant, but this is one of the pleasant things we must not do. God designed our bodies with great care and every part of them has a special function. All He asks of us is that we do not abuse their function. To do as God wishes us to do with our bodies is to be pure. *Purity* is a new word he must learn now, and remember, and it means to do with our bodies only those things God wishes us to do.

Sometimes, she may go on, it isn't easy to be pure. In fact, it can be very hard. But the harder we try, the more we please God and the more grace He will send to help us to be pure. There is a kind of secret about being pure: whenever he's tempted to indulge in this pleasure that God forbids, he can fold his hands together tightly, like this, and quick as a wink say inside himself, "Please, Blessed Mother, help me to be pure." She will, because she's so pure herself, and she loves purity so much. She knows all about little children and how hard things can go for them. She will send all the grace he needs, as soon as he needs it, if only he will ask her. She will watch over him, with God, and she will be pleased when he's successful (although, of course, just as sad when he isn't). But he must never stop trying, and most of all — now that he knows what it's all about — he must never stop praying for the grace to be pure.

Sometimes this is all that's needed to sidetrack a near-habit, but sometimes, too, it isn't accomplished so easily. Mothers must be careful always to be patient, always watchful without appearing to be watchful, and always ready to repeat the same counsel over and over again. The little struggle with concupiscence, and that is what it is — as innocent and simple as it is — can be kept a secret between the two of them and the Blessed Mother, and as long as she never gives her child the feeling that he angers her with his lack of success, he will never fail to confide in her when she questions him about it. It isn't good to question too often, but it's such an important thing that it cannot be completely ignored the way one mother does: "When I'm stuck, and don't know what to do about a thing, I don't do anything." In small children, it's certainly not serious sin; it's questionable whether any guilt at all could be attached to it. It could, however, lead to serious sin in adolescence, and at that late date, it's a bitter struggle trying to beat it.

Rather than be discouraged by the immediate lack of success, it's best to keep hugging to oneself the knowledge that Mary, Mediatrix of all grace, will never abandon a child who needs her help, and the two, mother and child, together with the Mother of God, can with prayer accomplish wonders.

Thumb-sucking is a minor consideration, but it's still one of the great unsolved mysteries. A thousand theories have been advanced and as many recommendations. The last time I was naive enough to ask a pediatrician what to do about a thumb-sucker, he sighed and said: "This year, it's in." Some children find comfort in sucking their thumbs; others seem not to need it. Those who suck their thumbs long enough can ruin their bite, which is why dentists are death on thumb-sucking. The remedy seems to be different for each child, with no rule that applies to all. There's only one conclusion unanimously agreed upon: Don't be too determined that a child break his thumb-sucking habit all at once. Occasionally a child who is a dyed-in-the-wool thumb-sucker will finally abandon the habit if he's hounded consistently; but he may substitute something far more disturbing, indulging in other sensory pleasures that trespass purity.

So much for a problem that has bothered mothers, and guardians of children in orphans' homes and state institutions, shelters and nursery schools. It's good to know that the discovery of these problems does not indicate that a child is a monster. For the Christian parent, it can be a matter of rejoicing to realize that out of even such a trying (although innocent) situation in the earliest years of his life, a child can be set on the path to an understanding of purity and the use of grace to fight the good fight. This will be the bedrock of all his education in the serious business of sex. It must go hand in hand with the knowledge of God.

⌒

Be frank, but prudent in explaining
about where babies come from

The next encounter with sex information usually has to do with babies — a subject that's introduced at a far earlier age than it formerly was, but one that cannot be ignored. In families where babies are welcomed as regularly as God sends them, the whole procedure is so normal and natural that children rarely think to isolate the business of Mother giving birth to a new baby and consider it with a curious clinical eye.

Usually, in such cases, the first rumor that all is not so simple as it seems comes from the outside. It was that way with our children. They were informed by a neighboring five-year-old that a new baby was on the way. And having told her that they already knew it (they had been told God was sending us another baby), she announced that she hadn't to be told, she could tell! As this puzzled them, she explained straightway, and they came tearing home, their eyes bugging right out of their beads. N. said that babies were inside their mommies before they were born — was that true? Yes, it was true.

Well! It enchanted the smaller ones for all of fifteen minutes, and then they forgot all about it. The six-year-old, however, apparently mulled it over all day. It was that evening, when she was looking out the window at a herd of expectant cows (having seen a cow deliver a newborn the summer before, and the cat having kittens innumerable times) that she said to me, "They all look like they're going to have babies, too, don't they?"

"Yes, they do."

"Is it the same with mommies as it is with cows?"

And there we were, facing up to a subject I had thought to postpone until she was at least a few years older. It was certainly no place to leave the fate of our blessed fifth baby.

"No, dear, not the same. God makes animals strong and hardy, and they have their babies wherever is best — sometimes in barns, or in the pasture, sometimes, as with kitty, in the kitchen woodbox. But with mothers, it's different. They have their babies in their rooms, or in hospitals, and they have family or friends or doctors and nurses to help them."

"But how do they come? The same way animal babies come?"

You grope for the right words, and you pray that the Blessed Mother will put them in your mouth.

"God has made a place in mothers through which, when it's time, babies come into the world."

Without any more beating around the bush, she asked, "Where?"

Either you lie or you don't. This is probably the most crucial moment in your entire relationship with a child you love with all your soul. You want her to grow up to be pure and holy and pleasing in the sight of God, secure in all the knowledge she will need to govern her own actions, secure in her confidence in you. You want, more than anything next to her knowledge of God's love for her, to know that she will come to you every time she steps into a new phase of her ever-increasing experience with sex information — and ask you first, and accept what you will tell her as the right and the good answer. This is a beginning. The whole future of your most intimate relation with her depends on being honest, and reverent, and calm.

So, you tell her where. You explain that everything God does is pure and good and holy, and that if He had thought there were a finer way to have babies come into the world, He would have done it that way. This is His way; and now that she knows, she can understand even better that one's body is meant for holy things, has very holy functions, and it's important to walk carefully in this body of ours, dedicated with every step to giving honor and glory to God. Now, remembering that the Holy Trinity lives in our souls when we're in the state of grace, the whole thing contrives to surround the body with an aura of reverence and respect. How wonderful: God creates a new soul and then uses a mother's body to bring it into the world.

Sometimes they will ask, "How does the baby get there?" And at such an early age as this, it's never necessary to tell them more than that God plants a seed within the mother, beneath her heart, and from it grows the baby. It's wise, if you're not sure how deep their curiosity really goes, to ask a child very casually to rephrase a question another way. One of my children startled me by asking, "Mother, can't ladies who aren't married have babies?"

"Why do you ask, dear?"

"Oh, I don't know. I was just thinking that all the ladies I know who aren't married don't have any children."

"Well, children have to have fathers."

"Oh, of course. And if you aren't married, there's no daddy, is there?"

It would have been very easy to offer far more information than she needed or wanted, if she hadn't explained her question so simply.

⁓

Help your child to deal with impurity in friends

These are the two most serious, and difficult, steps in initiating a child to sex instruction and purity. Remember, however, that while you're making earnest, prayerful efforts to teach your child what he must know about sex from God's point of view, a host of children they rub elbows with every day at play and at school are picking it up from the grapevine. And they pose no small problem. We have a standard answer to give to children who introduce the subject in conversation or play: "I can talk about that all I want with my mother, and it isn't very nice to talk to anyone else about it." So far, thank God, they've consistently used it.

This does not mean, however, that watchfulness about playmates and off-limits playing can be abandoned. It's a fearful thing, this suspicion that among their acquaintances there may be some who are not quite so wholesome as they look, and it has to be handled very carefully. The best time to check on the attitudes and interests of playmates is during the long, confidential chats mothers and children have from time to time about things in general. Children will rattle on endlessly over bread and butter and peanut butter after school, and it's during these gushings forth of school gossip that you can trace the personalities of their playmates. What is Mary Jane like? Nice? Well — yes, but . . . But what? Well, sometimes she isn't so nice. No? How is that? Well — sometimes she says kind of bold things. . . .

As carefully as you'd unravel a thread, you slowly unravel the thread of Mary Jane's "bold things," what she talks about, what she likes to play, and so on, all the while being as casual as possible. Finally, if there's something to be told, it will be told, and you can throw yourself into the business of shoring up your child's moral values — but still very casually.

"That's too bad, isn't it? That Mary Jane doesn't understand that saying such bold things, and suggesting such games, are very offensive to God. Poor Mary Jane — she doesn't know about her soul and how much the Holy Trinity wants to live there and shine in it as bright as the sun. Do you tell her it isn't nice to talk that way? That's good. Next time you must remember to tell her, as gently as you can, that she's hurting our Lord very much when she acts like that. He wants her to love Him, and be very pure so He can live in her. You remind her that unless she remembers that purity is thinking sweet, clean thoughts, and respecting her body very much, she won't be able to please Him. Tonight, when you say your prayers, ask the Blessed Mother to help you to be pure, and to help Mary Jane to be pure, too."

All this will help, slowly and surely, to develop that instinct for things pure with which the soul is so marvelously endowed, so that a child can sense what is unwholesome in a situation that has not even been identified as unwholesome.

I remember one summer day, when some of the neighborhood children came up to play "show" under a big maple on the edge of our pasture, rigging up a stage with two sawhorses and a large plank. Because they are children who go frequently to the movies, "show" consisted of doing imitations of what they saw at the movies. Looking out the window from time to time, I was suddenly startled to see a visiting twelve-year-old do an amazingly accurate imitation of a burlesque dancer — complete to the last detail. My own daughter, then seven, was watching, fascinated. When it was finally her turn, she climbed up and, in the most pathetically clumsy way, tried her best to imitate the imitation. I could have wept. Inwardly I raged. It's like a knife in one's heart to see a child who's pure of heart tricked into doing a caricature of all that is hideous and ugly, flamboyant and blatantly impure.

After they had all gone home, she came in the house. "What were you playing?"

"Oh, we were playing show."

"Oh? And what did N. do in the show?"

"A kind of dance, I guess. She said they do it in the movies. I was trying to do it, too." She thought for a few minutes. "You know what? I don't think it was a very nice kind of dance."

"Why?"

"I don't know. It just didn't *feel* nice."

"Well, I'll tell you something. I just happened to be looking out the window, and I saw you all playing show. And you are quite right — it wasn't a nice kind of dance. I'm glad you could tell. It doesn't look, or feel, like the kind of dance to make a pure and holy body do, does it? Dancing isn't bad. It can be very beautiful. It can tell exciting, beautiful stories, if it's done well. Even stories about God. Although it doesn't have to all the time. But what dancing must say is that the body that's dancing is good, and knows its dignity, and knows that all its movements and energy and rhythm are gifts from God. When you dance, thank God that He gave you a fine, supple body that can do all kinds of good things, even dance."

Develop in your child a love for purity

⁓

Discourage vulgarity in speech

Vulgarity is another perplexing problem that falls into the category of things modest and pure, for the young and the old alike. Man is naturally vulgar. Supernaturally he may overcome it, but Original Sin seems to have left a broad stripe of vulgarity right down the middle of his back, and from time to time it will assert itself in the broadest kind of humor. With small children, it's what is commonly known, among mothers, as bathroom humor.

Just the other day, a mother was here, discussing her two fine little boys, and at one point, she rolled her eyes and said, "We're going through a stage now that's about as trying as anything so far: bathroom giggles. It drives me wild!"

Even the nicest children will indulge in it from time to time, repudiating all the wholesome training and thinking they've been given.

The best general approach to it is a dry one: "Well, it doesn't take much to amuse you, does it?" And then go on to remind them that, but for the daily bodily functions, one would soon depart this life via one of a number of painful complications — and isn't God good to manage our health so sensibly?

One way to hurdle a child's titillation over bathroom terms is to adopt the completely unprovocative anatomical terms used in the hospital. I had not given this too much thought until we had to ship our three middle boys to the hospital for a mass tonsillectomy. The day after the operations, when I called to see them, one of the nurses said to me: "So you're the mother of the three little boys? Well, I must say, the way they ask about going to the bathroom has all the nurses dumbfounded. So professional! You should hear what most of them say — it's awful! Why in the world do mothers allow children to use such unpleasant words?"

How to Raise Good Catholic Children

With all the use of proper terms and constant reminding about keeping the body and its functions in the proper place, small children — usually in the attempt to get attention or strike back at some older brother — will now and then fling the most unsavory words about with riotous abandon. There are apparently two attitudes to take. Either ignore it (recommended by most of the books on child care, with the advice that being ignored will cure it, because it will fail to get the desired attention) or take firm steps to suppress it. We have tried both in our family and have concluded that ignoring it is no cure at all.

A child knows instinctively what annoys his mother, what is bold and forbidden. Even when she possesses such remarkable self-control as to be able to let the naughty words pass unnoticed, he knows that, down deep inside, he has succeeded in getting the attention he desired. So — and here we go out on a limb — we use an old and time-honored cure: a good lick on a bar of soap. It doesn't do children any harm, and if it's accompanied by a few words to the effect that since they have used their tongue to offend God and their fellows, therefore the naughty tongue must have the punishment, it will soon discourage bandying about with unacceptable words.

Then there are the inevitable shrieks of laughter over baby as he chugs off after having stepped out of his diaper. There's no doubt about it; there is something delightfully funny about babies and their smooth, round bottoms. But little boys are apt to be carried away and start applying themselves too heartily to the whole subject in general, and that's where a little anatomical information comes in handy. It puts an entirely different aspect on the large muscles of the lower posterior torso to be told they are called the *gluteus maximus,* and were designed by God to cover the sharp corners of the pelvis. Now, the pelvis, uncushioned, would hardly support baby — or anyone else for that matter — comfortably for more than five minutes at a time; and if you want to see what it would be like without the gluteus, bang your elbow hard on the table: you'll see. Even in the prosaic occupation that is the act of sitting down, God's infinite wisdom, and mercy, are evident.

⁀

Emphasize God's wisdom in designing the body

As for other anatomical interests, in large families where older children have to help younger children in and out of the tub, and so forth, it's only normal and natural that in the process they become quite used to the way they're put together. Where there's only one child, or two of the same sex, the simplest way to dispense with the anatomical mysteries is to permit them to help other mothers bathe young babies, ask their normal quota of questions, and get the right answers. Enough of this, and they will cease to be curious or even very much interested. Always, however, this is most successful with young children. Get them over this bump while they're still small. Little children have no sense of modesty during their earliest years at least, and it's the most reasonable way in the world for everyone to learn about the differences between boys and girls. Of course, when a child is old enough to bathe and dress himself, he expects to be left alone to do so; that's only right and proper.

The final item that must be accounted for within the home — or it will be elsewhere (and at what a cost to the whole edifice of a child's purity!) — is the feminine bosom. Today's entertainment and fashion industries have successfully limited the definition of feminine charm to one qualification alone, a physical measurement — a far cry from what God intended. Again, life in the family where children are fed at their mother's breast offers the most natural, most beautiful, most wholesome explanation — without any words at all. It's the fine hand of God showing once more: infinite wisdom in the matter of teaching about sex and life and reproduction. That seeing his mother nurse her babies does form a child's whole vision became quite clear to us when one of our little boys, after seeing a visiting child play dress-up and add to her other paraphernalia a reasonable facsimile of a seductive bosom, commented: "You know, I didn't think that was very nice, going around pretending to be a *mother* all day."

Little girls are not little for very long, and in no time at all choosing their own clothes poses another problem in modesty and in purity. A child who has grown up secure in the knowledge of the divinely ordained purpose of the body will have a yardstick against which to measure the seemliness of her dress when she's a young woman. Someday she will be fully grown, young and fresh and clean and promising, and out of the wide embroidery of her fancies and dreaming, perhaps she will discover that the way to God for her will be through marriage. What she brings to her marriage, and what a young man brings to his, in the way of virtue and holiness, will be the fruit of all that has been sown many years before in a Christian home, the fruit of wise, patient, intelligent, and reverent understanding of the human body, coupled with its great destiny as the instrument of divine sowing.

This is why sex education in the Christian home is important and good and holy, and why there's no setting so perfect as a Christian home for imparting it.

Chapter 9

*Help your child to
participate in the Mass*

⁊

If the Mass is to be understood at all, it must first be understood in terms of sacrifice — not an easy subject for children. This chapter does not claim that they will grasp its entire significance with the first telling, but with repetition they will learn and, learning, love it, and their parents will both learn and love the more.

Sacrifice is a word that appears in the history of man since the very beginning. Man has always offered sacrifice to God. There are two reasons for sacrifice: one, to give adoration and praise to God, the Lord and Maker of all things; two, to show sorrow for sins, the offenses of men against the all-holy God. And because it contains these two elements, there are two important parts to a sacrifice: the offering itself, and the destroying (or consuming) of the offering.

⁊

Explain the meaning of sacrifice

Now, in the beginning, man did not count his riches in money, or houses, or cars, but in the flocks that fed him if he was a herdsman, or the food his gardens produced if he was a farmer. These were his treasures. When he thought to choose something to offer as a sacrifice to God to show Him how he loved Him, he chose the most precious things he owned: the finest lambs or kids born to his flocks, or the most perfect fruits that grew in his fields. The things he would like to keep for himself were the things he offered to God. It was as close as he could come to offering himself; in short, these things were a *sign* of himself.

That was the first part of sacrifice. The second part had to be a sign of his sorrow for sin. Now, to sin against God is a terrible thing. Once a sin is done, it cannot be undone. And God could, in all justice, demand the life of a man as payment for his sins. It would be quite fair. But He is merciful as well as just and is willing to accept a truly sorrowful heart. So instead of demanding the life of the man who had sinned, He mercifully accepted the *sign* of this, the life of the animal that man offered in sacrifice. For this reason, it was necessary that whatever was offered in sacrifice be consumed or destroyed in order that man could never take it back. A sacrifice acceptable to God had to be entirely surrendered.

This could be explained to children with a very elementary example. Suppose a little boy has offended his mother in the worst way. After his rebellion is done, he's filled with remorse and feels he must somehow show her that he's sorry and that he loves her. A gift would show her that he loves her. So he decides to buy her a gift. But how will he show, also, that he's sorry? He thinks for a long time, and then he decides that if he spends his *whole allowance* — money that his mother knows he has been saving to spend on himself — then surely she'll understand that he's sorry. Spending all he has to buy her gift will be a sign of his love *and* his sorrow — as perfect a sacrifice as a little boy could make.

The first mention of sacrifice comes in Genesis, in the story of Cain and Abel. It's a terrible story, and it tells not only of sacrifice, but of good and evil sacrifice. Cain and Abel were brothers, the sons of Adam. Just as God said, they had inherited their father's Original Sin and through it a weakness for sin. Cain was a

husbandman, or farmer, and Abel a shepherd; so when they decided to offer sacrifice to God, Cain chose the fruits he had grown
in his fields and Abel the firstling of his flocks. Now, Abel loved
God and was truly sorry for his sins. For this reason, after he placed
his sacrifice on the altar, God sent a sign from Heaven (perhaps
fire), and the animals were consumed. It showed that God accepted them. But when Cain put his offerings on the altar, nothing happened. And he became very angry. Then God spoke to him
in words like this (and all this has greater force if it's read aloud
from Scripture): "Why are you so angry, and why do you have such
a scowl on your face? If you do right with your sacrifice, will it not
be received? But if you do wrong, won't your sinfulness continue?"

And God made it very clear to Cain that He saw no true love
or sorrow for sin in Cain's heart; his sacrifice was not acceptable.
This made Cain very angry indeed, and in a fit of jealousy, he invited Abel to walk with him in the fields, and killed him. Which
goes to show that God was quite right: a man who is not sorry for
his sins will go on to commit even worse sins. Cain himself came
to a dreadful end, but that's another story. What this story tells is
that God considers every sacrifice very important, and it's an evil
thing to offer it without the right intention.

Now, when the family of Adam had multiplied to such a vast
number of people that they were performing their acts of worship
in large groups, priests were appointed to offer sacrifice for the
people. This was their special service, to act as intermediary between the people and God, offering their sacrifices for them, praying that they would be acceptable to God. Generation after
generation of priests and people continued to praise God and try
to atone for their sins against Him with sacrifice.

But, of course, no lamb, or hundreds of lambs, or kids or fruits
or any *thing* could really pay God back for even one mortal sin.

God is perfect. How could men, who are imperfect, make it up to Him once they had offended Him? They couldn't.

It's like the case of a boy who has stolen a dollar from his master. When it's discovered, and he must pay it back, he has lost it. All he has of his own money is a penny, and all he can say is, "I will pay you back, but with a penny." But a penny does not equal a dollar, and it never will, and the boy, no matter how sorry he is, will never be able to pay his master back. It can't be done — unless someone with a dollar comes along and offers to pay the boy's debt for him. And that's what happened between mankind and God.

↷

Only Christ could atone for our sins

God accepted all the sacrifices as signs of man's sorrow for sin, and still the debt wasn't paid. But God loves man. He wants man with Him forever in Heaven. That's the only reason He made man. So, hardly had the story of the Jews gotten under way than God began to hint that someday He would send someone who would be able to pay the debt of man's sin. He would offer a *perfect* sacrifice, this someone, wholly acceptable to God. He would offer it as the priests did, for the people. And he would pay in full not only for all the sins that had been committed, but for all the sins that would ever be committed until the end of time.

But who could do all this, except God Himself? And that is the answer. God will repay God; it's the only way it can be done. So God the Father promised to come Himself in the person of God the Son, to be born a man and die as a victim for the sins of all men in a sacrifice on a Cross. We're getting closer and closer to the Mass.

When Jesus was born in Bethlehem, He was born to die. All men die, of course, but God has work for them to do before they die. But the most important of all the work our Lord had to do was to die on the Cross. We shall skip all the other years of His life and go to the part that begins His Sacrifice. At the Last Supper there was the first sign of anything that would appear later in the Mass.

Long before, when Abraham, the father of all the Jews, had gone out to rescue his nephew Lot from four warring kings, he returned and was welcomed by the priest-king of Salem, Melchisedech, who took bread and wine and offered a sacrifice of thanksgiving and praise to God. This is why Melchisedech is mentioned with Abel and Abraham in the Canon of the Mass, where bread and wine are changed into the Body and Blood of Christ and offered as a sacrifice to God. Jesus, who is the divine Priest as well as King, was following the example of the priest-king Melchisedech when He used bread and wine at the Last Supper.

After Jesus had taken the bread, giving thanks, He broke it and gave a piece to each of the Apostles, saying, "This is my Body, which is being given for you: do this in remembrance of me." Then He took wine, gave thanks, blessed it, and said, "All of you drink of this, for this is my Blood of the new covenant, which is being shed for many unto the forgiveness of sins." And for the first time in all the world, men received Holy Communion.

But something was missing. Jesus had not yet died. He had not yet become the sacrificed Victim. He had to fulfill the form of the old sacrifice where the victim was slain to satisfy God for man's sin. So He left the supper room to start the terrible journey of His agony and Passion, and it was when He did this that He offered Himself, as priest offering sacrifice for all the people. It was at the end of His agony, the moment before He died, that He cried out to God the Father, "It is consummated."[31] Then the slaying of the

[31] John 19:30.

perfect Victim was complete. God was paid, for all eternity, for the sins of men.

If He had not done this, we would never have had the Mass, for the Mass is the offering, by Jesus and the priest and the people — all one in the Mystical Body of Christ, the Church — of the perfect Victim (already slain) as a gift of praise and a reparation for sin. That's why it is called "the Sacrifice of the Mass."

Encourage your child to
participate as best he can during Mass

There's no hard-and-fast rule about the minimum age at which to start taking children to Mass. I remember going to Mass when I was very little in a town along the Mexican border where the mothers brought their babies with them, set them in the aisle, and Mass was heard over a chorus of howls, chirps, and yammers. No one seemed to mind the noise, nor the puddles in the aisle afterward. If you want to start your small fry when he's six months old, there's plenty of precedent.

North of the border? Unaccustomed as we are to babies in the aisle, I personally believe that the temperament of a child is the determining factor. A tranquil baby can attend from infancy, disturb no one, and absorb much that will contribute to his growing affection for the Mass. A volatile child can be a scourge, not only to his parents and those around him, but especially to the priest who, for all he loves little children, is duty bound to get the Gospel and the sermon across to his parishioners. This is the child who is better off waiting it out a while at home.

There's one reason for not taking children to Mass that's no reason at all, and that's the high-sounding dodge that it doesn't make sense to take them until they can understand what's going

Help your child to participate in the Mass

on. How are they to learn if they don't go? Most children should be going by four, and all, it seems to me, by five.

When to start taking them isn't the important issue. The great mistake is the assumption that anywhere from three to five to even ten years will have to be spent in quiet, unenlightened attention. Even before they can read, children can be given a sense of the Mass and a rough knowledge of its form, and can participate in it as intelligently as many adults — more so, in some cases.

As a prayer ending in sacrifice, the Mass contains merely an elaboration of the four principles involved in a child's daily prayer: contrition, petition, offering, and thanksgiving. None of these ideas is over his head. If he has had any spiritual training at all, they ought to be quite familiar ideas. Helping him attend Mass intelligently is a matter of applying these familiar relationships to God and pointing out that the priest and the rest of the people are doing the same. From that point of view, the Mass is no longer a mystery. It's a form of prayer, the kind that gives God the highest praise it's possible to give. In its simplest terms, it says, "I'm sorry," and "Please, will You . . ." and "I offer You," and "I thank You."

All this explaining, of course, should be done at home. At best, however, home study cannot substitute for being there; so it's inevitable that there be some whispering between parent and child at Mass. For this reason, it's best to get nicely settled in the front pew. The view is unimpeded, distractions are minimal, and the rest of the people are least apt to be disturbed.

For little ones who are really too small, a Mass book (and not the kind with pictures showing the priest doing what looks like the same thing on every page) and a nodding acquaintance with statues, pictures on the windows, and the symbols in the decoration will help keep them occupied. Since satisfactory Mass books are sometimes hard to come by, if you can't find one that suits, it's best to make one yourself with the children's help. A small album or notebook with holy pictures that symbolize what's going on is fun to make and will teach them at the same time. The more fun a thing is, the more it will teach.

Then there are the usual instructions about behavior during Mass. My own technique inclines to firmness. I'm about as thick-skinned as any mother around and can take plenty of distraction; but carrying on at Mass has nothing to do — at least not in the first place — with distraction. Mass is a solemn and holy occasion, and I think it's extremely important that children learn right from the start that they're to face the altar at all times, keep their feet still, and pay attention. I was briefing Peter, at three, about "no talking out loud," and failed to point out the one outstanding exception.

He reminded me, loudly, from the front seat, "Father Burke is talking."

Although the Mass is the most formal kind of worship, it must be kept as informal as possible for a child, with constant reminding that Jesus who is in the Tabernacle is the same Jesus who is with him all day long. The chattier the relationship with God, the better; so let their greeting to Him when they arrive at church be reverently (although not audibly) chatty. You even have to tell them what to say in the beginning. Something like, "Dear Blessed Jesus, I am so glad to be here, and I love You so much. Please help me to offer the Mass nicely."

⇾

Show your child how to participate
attentively in the prayers and readings

Then the Mass begins. The *Confiteor* comes first because one wants to have all this confessing done before getting on to the more sacred parts. It's said in the spirit of the daily examination of conscience and act of contrition, the only difference being that, at Mass, we confess sinfulness not only to God, but to the Blessed Mother and all the saints, and ask them please, will they pray for us too? The priest and the altar boys and all the others in the Church are begging the same pardon. A child needn't know the *Confiteor* to be part of it. You can say, "This is the part where we all ask God to forgive us our sins. You ask God and the Blessed Mother and all the saints to pray for you so that you'll never be naughty again."

Children who say the litanies now and then at family prayers will recognize the translation of the *Kyrie eleison:* "Lord have mercy on us." Because the tune of the chanted *Kyrie* is easy to learn, it's nice to sing it at home. Perhaps it will be children's first introduction to singing liturgical music. It's a beautiful prayer, crying out for mercy. We should use it more often.

The *Gloria* is next. Children love knowing about the *Gloria.* All Christmas carols say, in some form, *"Gloria in excelsis Deo."* Although the entire prayer at Mass is a little too much for them, they will be very happy with their heads full of pictures of what the words are saying.

The readings will mean little, or much, depending on how familiar a child is with Scriptures read at home. If there's no time for anything but baths, shampoos, and polishing shoes on Saturday night, someone should tag along with the Sunday readings and Gospel and read them aloud.

The only people who think reading the readings and Gospel to small children is going too far are those who have not tried it. Granted, some of them are over their heads, but not so many as you would think; and if you translate the words into their language as you go along, they'll love it. A good example is St. Paul's text,

"Brethren, put ye on, as the elect of God, holy and beloved, the cloak of mercy, benignity, humility. . . ."[32]

"See? St. Paul says that you must put on kindness, like a coat, and wear it all day, and let people see that you're kind just as they can see the real coat you wear. When you're kind, people know it. They'll love you for it, and they'll say to themselves: 'She would do nothing to hurt me, because she's kind.' "

The same technique applies to the Gospel. Preparing the Sunday Gospel with children is the best way to develop their interest in the whole Gospel. Some of our most successful sessions with the New Testament have grown from such Mass preparations. Indeed, the children thought they ended far too soon. Adding the daily Gospel to night prayers during the penitential seasons, Advent and Lent, is an ideal way to follow the meditation of the Church. The order of their arrangement is not accidental: they were chosen especially to lead our minds toward a more intelligent and joyous celebration of the great feasts that climax these seasons.

We had one such Mass preparation (ordinarily they must be fairly brief; there are a lot of children to put to bed in our family) which lasted two hours, with first the missal and then the New Testament open on the end of the ironing board while I ironed and the children sat on the floor in their pajamas. They were the ones who asked for more.

At Mass, there's a short pause between the readings and the Gospel, for the prayer before the Gospel. This would hardly be noticed if it didn't include something *to do*, but making the three crosses on the forehead, the lips, and the heart is not only very appealing; it also teaches children a lesson they learn easily: "Please

[32]Col. 3:12-17.

help me to love Your word with my mind, keep it on my lips, and hug it to my heart."

Then they're ready for the Gospel. If it has been read the night before, Father will be heard through with attention to see if he really does read the same text, and the sermon is listened to with far better attention if children have been promised a discussion of it after Mass.

After the sermon, the Creed. Then comes the Prayer of the Faithful. This prayer is a collection of all the intentions and favors we ask, from the Holy Father down to the smallest member of the Mystical Body. In it we ask God for blessings for the Church, for the Pope, for the people; we ask for grace and peace and prosperity, and we ask for all the things we so dearly need (or think we need) in the temporal order.

Here a little lad may apply himself passionately to the serious (and quite legitimate) business of asking for the bike, the puppy, the wallet (we're all asking for wallets at the moment, except Mommy and Daddy — they're asking for something to *put in* the wallet), quite encouraged to know that the prayers of the Universal Church beg, too, that his intentions be granted according to the will of God.

Teach children what the Prayer of the Faithful means, and then, when you help them with Mass preparation the Saturday night before, watch their eyes shine when they think about what they will ask in the Prayer of the Faithful.

⥲

Encourage your child
to contribute to the collection

With the Offertory comes the confusion of the Sunday collection, and as a consequence its meaning is often missed. Since, of all the parts of the Mass so far, this is the one I most want my children to watch, it must be carefully reviewed at home. A reminder before Mass helps: "Now remember, have your envelope ready so you won't have to fish around, and see if you can't follow the Offertory."

In the early Church, all the catechumens (those preparing to be baptized but still not members of the Church) left after the Creed, and only the faithful remained for the part of the Mass called "the Mass of the faithful." At the Offertory, the people brought their own gifts of bread and wine and presented them to the priest, who, in turn, presented them — unconsecrated — to God.

Now the collection substitutes for the offering of gifts by the faithful, and the Offertory collection is meant to buy the things needed for the Mass.

For this reason, it's expected that children who receive allowances will provide at least part of what goes into the weekly collection. If someone ever makes a survey of reasons for adult nonsupport of the Church, I wouldn't be surprised to find that the explanation lies in this handing out of collection money to children, year after year after year. Every baptized child is a member of the Church and has an obligation to support it, but at the age of seventeen, he's rarely inspired with the nobility of his role as supporter of pastor and parish if he has never been made to face it before.

Generosity can be made compelling for small children if it's explained that the money put into the collection is used to buy the hosts and the wine that will be consecrated and become the Body and Blood of Christ, to buy the candles, the sweet incense, and all the other beautiful things that delight the eye and the ear and the nose at Mass.

Help your child to participate in the Mass

*Help your child to visualize the
hidden grandeur of the Holy Sacrifice*

At the Offertory, the priest offers the unconsecrated bread and wine to God, asking Him to accept it for our sins. Here is the sign of ourselves, which we explained in our talks about sacrifice. We might have lived ages ago and had at best only a lamb to offer as a sign of ourselves, knowing that it would never be enough to pay for our sins, but here is a sign that soon will be changed into a Victim who *can* pay for our sins.

"Watch, dear, and when you see the priest lift the paten with the bread and lift the chalice with the wine, pretend you are lifting them with him. Pretend you are there, being lifted up with them. That is what it means — that you offer yourself. Soon he will change the bread and wine into the Body and Blood of Jesus, and He will be the perfect Victim offered to God for us." Children love to do this.

The priest washing his hands at the *Lavabo* is something they always see. Over and over the Church uses water as a sign of purity and purification — for instance, in Baptism and in the holy-water font as we enter the Church. Telling our children about the *Lavabo* in the Mass, that it's a sign of the inner purity of those who offer this sacrifice, we can remind them also of other things: "Why don't you try to remember, every time you wash your hands, how pure you must keep your soul in order to please God." It is only one of the many ways mothers can use homely, domestic things to teach their children a spiritual vision, but it will be the occasion of repeated small meditations, and the multiplication of small meditations can be the beginning of contemplation.

The Preface is a thank-you in which we ask God to let us join the angels to sing, "Holy, holy, holy." Every time I've explained the *Sanctus* as the song the angels sing forever before God in Heaven, some small child has asked: "But is that what we're going to do in Heaven? Nothing but sing, 'Holy, holy, holy' all the time?"

And there's a wonderful answer to this in the story of St. Perpetua and St. Felicity. In a vision describing the saints' arrival in Heaven, they, too, heard the angels singing, "Holy, holy, holy" without end. But after they had greeted God the Father and kissed Him, and He had passed His hand over their faces, the elders standing beside the throne of God said to the saints: "Go and play." O blessed relief. The angels sing, but the children play!

If you suggest to them to imagine how the sanctuary is filled with millions of angels, waiting to bow low before the Body of Christ, it helps make the *Sanctus* very exciting for them. Now and then, when I have to go to a late Mass alone, a little boy creeps into the pew beside me to follow the Mass, and I've explained parts of the Mass to him. One morning, at the *Sanctus*, he whispered, "Is this where the angels come in?" So you see, it does make an impression, and they do remember.

The Consecration is the changing of the bread and wine into the Body and Blood of Christ. After the consecration of each species, he elevates it so that the faithful may make an act of adoration.

The traditional prayer at the Elevation is "My Lord and my God," the words of St. Thomas when he saw Christ's wounds after the Resurrection.[33] If the children know the story of St. Thomas and his doubts, they like to use his words. Be sure to tell them there's an indulgence of seven years attached to saying this prayer devoutly, and encourage them to use it as a gift to the souls in

---

[33] John 20:28.

Purgatory. If they're too little to understand this prayer, they can say simply, "I love You," at each Elevation, whispered, of course (but an accidentally louder-than-whispered "I love You" is a deeply moving thing).

Here, at last, is the perfect Victim. Here we ask God to accept our offering as He accepted the offerings of Abel, Abraham, and Melchisedech, and now we see why an understanding of sacrifice, identifying it with the sacrifice of Abel, is absolutely essential if a child is to understand anything about the Mass. I admit it's complicated, that it takes a long time for them to learn. But it's not impossible to learn.

The mementos in the Canon of the Mass will keep the children very busy, and they like to be reminded, "This is where we pray for the Holy Father, Bishop Weldon [always give the bishop's name], and all the Catholics in the world" and, "This is where we ask God to remember us — Daddy and Mother, you children, all our relatives and friends and everyone here."

Next comes the memento for the dead, where the children can be reminded to pray for the dear departed relatives and friends and all the souls in Purgatory.

Next — and even if they catch nothing else, they should be helped to catch this — the Our Father. Even the very little ones can say the Our Father.

If they can hear it, they love the *Agnus Dei*, because it is a prayer to Christ as the Lamb of God; entirely logical when they understand about the old sacrifice of the lambs.

It is at Communion that the priest, and after him the people, consume the Victim, the last part of a sacrifice necessary to make it complete. But Communion is also a banquet, a feast of love. I don't know why we never talked about this as a banquet, unless it was because we didn't want to confuse the children with too many concepts at one time. But Monica stumbled on it all by herself at nine.

"Mother, why don't we receive our Lord in both bread and wine?" So I explained about His Body and Blood being present in each species, that it wasn't essential to receive both, and receiving Him as we do is simplest when there are so many people going to Communion, so many Masses each Sunday.

"You know, if we did, it would be like a party, wouldn't it? Like God giving a party." Wonderful are the ways of the Holy Spirit in the mind of a child. It is God's party, the eucharistic banquet, and the food that's served is the bread of heavenly life. The One who comes to us is Love, and when we consume this Victim at the unbloody sacrifice, we join Him in a feast of love.

One or two things to add for the older children: first, the meaning of "Lord, I am not worthy to receive You . . ." which is said before Communion. The story of the centurion who spoke these words to Christ, "Lord, I am not worthy"[34] will help them learn and remember always.

You can suggest to a child what he might say for thanksgiving after Communion (realizing that when the time comes, it's something he must do alone), something like: "Dear Blessed Jesus, thank You for coming to me in Holy Communion. I love You. Please teach me to love You more." Repeated each time children receive the Eucharist, this moment of prayer perhaps more than any other will open the door to real spiritual growth. Christ wants to teach us to love, but we must want to be taught.

And there's no better time for fathers and mothers to pray, "Please, teach my children to love You. Please, make my children want You."

[34]Matt. 8:5-13.

They must also be taught to remember the intentions of all those they love — indeed, of all the world — and to ask for help with some particular weakness.

The Sign of the Cross at the end of Mass is like a seal. After offering our Victim to God, knowing that His sacrifice pays for our sins, we trace on our own bodies the Cross that is His sign. Although I try to make our children bless themselves reverently always, I want this one at the end of Mass to be especially proud. "Make it big, dear; make it beautiful. It's His sign, and you belong to Him."

Then comes, we hope, the demonstration of proper manners: we wait until Father is off the altar and out of the sanctuary before stepping out of the pew. Then a good, deep genuflection because God is in this place. No bobbing, please.

"Tell Him, 'Thank You, Blessed Jesus, for letting me come to Mass. Thank You for coming to me in Holy Communion. I love You. Please help me to love You more.' And think for a minute of the thousands of people in the world who can no longer go to Mass, whose priests have been murdered or put in prison. They long for Mass and Communion. Ask our Lord to restore them, and to free His priests and nuns who are imprisoned."

Teaching a child the Mass takes a long time. One or two steps at a time is fast enough. But little by little, he'll learn.

We can give a child all other knowledge, an appetite for all other devotions, a familiarity with every other aspect of the Faith; still, if he does not have reverence and awe and finally impassioned love for the Mass, he's spiritually only half-alive. It's probably one of the most intricate of all the lessons to teach, but it's the one he will thank us for the most, all the days of his life.

Chapter 10

≈

Teach your child that
death is the gateway
to eternal life

Death is not the happiest subject there is. But it ought to be. If it isn't, it's because we're still too much attached to the world, and not attached enough to God.

Joan Windham (who writes very fine saint stories for children) describes St. William (the French St. William) and his attitude toward death in a way that makes death sound as delightful as it ought to sound, and it's quite the cheeriest kind of introduction to death for a child. It goes something like this:

After living a very busy, holy, apostolic life, St. William decided he wanted to go off to the missions. So he packed his bags, settled his affairs, and went to bed one night with plans to leave in the morning. In the middle of the night, his angel awakened him and said, "Get up, William. We're going someplace."

"But I can't," said St. William. "I'm off to the missions in the morning."

"Oh, we're going someplace better than the missions," said his angel. "We're going to do something you want to do more than anything else in the world."

"You mean going to see God?" cried St. William. "Oh, *fine!* Of course I'd rather do that than anything else, even going to the missions. What you mean is it's my time to die. Well, that's great!" And off they went to see God.

It's almost impossible for most adults to feel that way about death. The world doesn't think death is the best thing of all — even death and going to see God. The idea has been universally accepted that death is a calamity to be staved off at all costs and that none but the mentally deranged look forward to it.

Children, however, don't view things the way adults do; if they've been told that Heaven is the most wonderful place of all, that God is there, and life is but a kind of test with Heaven the reward, then they're quite excited about going there and death holds no terrors for them. In fact, they're so fascinated by the idea sometimes that, like a small four-year-old who invented a song about it, they're even shockingly cheerful.

Grown-ups think of death first of all as synonymous with one or all of these: pain, suffering, cold, stiff, coffin, grave, corruption, and, nowadays, the mystery story. In fact, the rage for murder mysteries probably has its roots in the fact that death has a morbid fascination for most people, as long as it's someone else who is dead. To think of themselves as one day dead is just morbid, without any fascination.

Until impressed with their elders' creepy notions, children think of death as synonymous with a place where you have fun all the time, never have to go to bed, can have anything you want, and are with Jesus and Mary and the angels and the saints. But because death is a combination of both sets of ideas (barring the mystery-story trimmings except in a few rare cases), a little theological know-how does not come amiss. It's good to brush up a bit before the small fries start asking their questions.

"Can you have bicycles in Heaven?"

In Heaven the soul's desires are wholly satisfied. One wants nothing because one has everything — in God. This is all that the soul desires, yet at the same time, it possesses Him to the very brim

Teach your child that death is the gateway

of its capacity, so that its desire is immediately fulfilled. Now, this is all very confusing for a child. It's possible, however, to arrange an answer that will be theologically correct, and at the same time satisfy his momentary conviction that Heaven must include bicycles or else it will not be heavenly.

It's quite truthful to answer, "In Heaven, dear, you may have anything you want."

"Birthday cake and ice cream, too?"

"If you wanted birthday cake and ice cream in Heaven, then ice cream and cake you could have."

Isn't it so? *If you want* . . . You see, he will *not* want ice cream and cake. He will want only God, and since he will possess God fully, he will want nothing. It's a slightly foxy answer, but it's the truth. Heaven, for a child, must be seen as the essence of all that's good and desirable. As he puts the years behind him, it will be many things in turn, from a place where one has ice cream and cake all the time, and bicycles and tents and sailboats and an infinite number of party dresses and slippers, to (gradually) a place not necessarily so heavenly because of its furniture but because it's where one is eternally loved and admired and satisfied. It's all quite normal, and pleasing to God, who understands best of all how a small child's mind works.

It's certainly a wholesome attitude. To translate Heaven into an unending choir session with nothing but "Holy, holy, holy" all the time (see St. Perpetua and St. Felicity in chapter 9) is to make it sound hopelessly dull and to turn their hearts from desiring Heaven to desiring wherever it is one can have an infinitude of bicycles, tents, and party dresses. The world promises these things if they will set their sights right, but the price is pretty high, and they don't satisfy for very long. This describing Heaven accurately may seem one of the accessories to the spiritual training of a child, yet it's one of the most important points of all. We're basing the whole undertaking on the assumption that they will *want* to go to Heaven. We had better be careful to make it sound like a good place to go.

"Mother, don't you wish we'd all die soon?"

⌁

Calm your child's fears about death

It's discovering that we can't shove off on the next bus, even though Heaven is such a great place to be, that introduces complications. Why can't we all die the same day and go up to be with God? When will we die? Will it hurt? How will it happen? And the door is wide open for all the grisly answers to rush in and destroy the child's ease with death as a nice idea, a happy eventuality.

"I don't want you to die and go off without me."

"Who will drive the car if Daddy dies?"

"I don't want dirt in my mouth."

"It will be dark in the ground. I don't want to go in the ground."

We won't all die together unless God wants or permits it to be that way, because we're not here on earth just to please ourselves and do as we wish. We're here to do special work God has planned for us, and it's reasonable to think that Mother's work will be done before Monica's, and Daddy's before Jamie's. When the work is done, God calls us to eternity; even if the time has been wasted and the work left undone, we're called to eternity all the same. That makes for sober thinking.

As for who will drive the car, "take care of me," or whatever insecurity is suggested by a possible death, God will take care of all these things, just as Jesus promised so many times in the Gospel that He would. The Polish folktale mentioned in chapter 5 is perfect for putting thoughts of insecurity to rest.

About "dirt in my mouth," which occurred to Peter after watching a baby goat's burial one day, and how it is "dark in the ground" — well, we aren't going to be here to worry about those things. "The *you* part, the part that's sitting here now and thinking, putting the thoughts into words, that part isn't even there anymore when your body is put into the ground. The *you* part will be off somewhere else, quite busy, and if you give any thought at all to your body, it will be just to look down momentarily and say, 'Oh, so that's where they put my body. Well, well.' "

"But what does happen to your body?"

Well, barring the kind of coffins that guarantee preservation until the Second Coming, one will probably end up a sifted pile of dust and maybe a few bones (maybe in spite of the guaranteed coffins; I have often wondered how they can be so sure). That's what God said we were when He sent Adam and Eve out of Paradise; it's right there in the Old Testament.[35] Nice to know it happens to everybody. Country children will explain earnestly, "You turn into a kind of fertilizer."

Well, don't you? It's silly to pretend you don't when you *do*. They mean no disrespect. They observe that the birds and small animals whose funerals they have conducted will disintegrate in time, and they will happen on the old bones of a cow now and then (last year the skull of a cow in our woods, with moss and ground pine growing out of it — all quite beautiful), and it seems good and right and as it should be.

The great excitement is discovering that God will put it all back together one day and that it will be whole and sound and full of beauty. That, for instance, removes the shock of realizing how many members of our society today are amputees. The mental

[35]Gen. 3:19.

picture of a lovely new leg winging its way back to join its body on the Last Day leaves everyone quite content.

⁀

Give honest answers to questions
about suicide and murder

There are other aspects of death even more distressing than corruption, and they can hardly be missed by any child old enough to read the headlines — suicide, for one. Suicide is a serious sin because God has a special time for us to die, and until that day we're supposed to keep working away at the things He wants done.

But suppose someone does kill himself. If it's such a serious sin, does he go to Hell? How to answer that one and not be guilty of consigning souls to Hell on our own initiative? If suicide, by definition, is to be treated as the greatest of all sins of despair, because it's a sin against hope, a sin against God's mercy, how do you explain it to a child so that you leave the judging to God, yet not take the mortal out of mortal sin? The answer is fairly obvious to an adult, but not so to a child. God alone can judge whether the person who killed himself really meant to break the divine law, really understood what he was doing. It isn't necessary that we know. It's only necessary that we hope. We hope for the soul self-dispatched into eternity and pray for it with special charity.

There's all the difference in the world between sentimentality for the dead and Christian hope. Sentimentality is first cousin to a kind of blindness in which adults murmur to other adults that still other adults have "gone to Heaven" as soon as they die. It's far wiser to remember the possibility of Purgatory and pray like mad.

No Catholic child who has studied as far as Purgatory in the catechism, or had it explained at home (and it can be explained reasonably to a four- or five-year-old), is going to be offended at the possibility that some soul near and dear to him does not get to Heaven immediately. It's unnecessary to make an exception because a beloved grandmother, for example, has died, and the parents think that the child needs the security of thinking she's in Heaven. The Church gives her children security when she provides the sacrament for the dying, the great reparative value of the Mass, and prayers for the dead. To allow children to believe fuzzy half-truths when they are little, then try to substitute the blunt reality of Purgatory later is risking their never taking seriously the necessity of reparation for sin.

Too many times such sentimentality results in families' not warning their loved ones of impending death while there's time to prepare for it, not calling a priest and availing them of the last great mercy before they must meet God face-to-face. "We didn't want to frighten him. . . ." And a soul is allowed to slip out of life unprepared. Children must learn the necessity of the soul's impeccability before it meets God forever in Heaven.

So, in the matter of suicide, it isn't prudent to let sentimentality take the sting out of the sin, not even in the minds of children. Out of Christian hope and charity, we can pray for the souls of those who have killed themselves, begging God to purify them speedily if they should be in Purgatory. All of this will come up if ever a child asks about suicide. Several years ago, a suicide took place not far from where we live, and the subject had to be wrung dry before the children would let it rest.

Murder is an ugly word, but it's right there on the front page of the paper. As soon as a child learns to read, he asks about it. Most of all, children are scandalized to think God would let it happen, especially to innocent people. It's hard even for grown-ups to understand, but hardest of all when they forget that this life isn't everything and eternity is. It's man's bad will, not God's, that instigates such things as murder; never tampering with the gift of free will, God will not interfere with murder. Obviously it isn't good to let children dwell on it, but once it has caught their attention, their questions must be answered, or they will never forget it.

About the best way to take the worry out of murder for them is to compare it with martyrdom. The martyrs' deaths were murders. Our Lord's death was a murder. The difference between martyrdom and murder is that one who is killed for the love of God, defending His truth and His law, is a martyr. No one wants to die a violent death, but the saints who were martyrs were willing to die violently, after the example set for them by Jesus. From our point of view (lacking the graces given to the martyrs), of course it would be much nicer to die the kind of death that isn't so messy. If not, however, it will not matter too much how one dies, as long as he's in the state of grace. If he has tried to serve God perfectly with all his strength, then maybe he's a saint and so much the better.

⌒

Take the worry out of death

As for how badly it might hurt: we know that God will never desert us, that He will never permit us to go through anything without sufficient grace to bear it. We don't know what kind of death we will die, but we can always pray for the grace to die bravely. If we remember how much it hurt our Lord to die for us, then we need not fear that He will forget to help us if dying, for us, should hurt. We should always pray for the grace of a happy death, but happy in this instance means that we will receive the Last Sacraments — not that death will be especially painless.

"But death is sad, and people cry."

It *is* sad to lose someone who is a part of your life, whom you have loved and depended on, and whom you are going to miss.

That's why even people who believe all these things about the blessedness of a happy death cry when they lose their beloveds. They *miss* them. But God helps them to be happy again. He helps them to look forward to the time when they will be together again in Heaven. To forget this is to accuse God of being mean when He finally takes someone you love, when all the time we know He must take them, sometime. It's to forget how really lavish He is with the joys He originally planned for us when He made us, the joys He so gallantly died to buy back for us.

Die? Of course we're going to die. When? Maybe tomorrow. Maybe even today. Who knows? The thing isn't to waste time worrying about when, but to spend time as though we might be dying today, *would* be dying today.

"Oh, I don't want my child worrying about dying today."

Why not? And why *worrying?* If he knows God and His love, and loves Him back, if he knows about Heaven and is free from the gloomy nonsense with which other people belabor the subject, where is the harm in his considering that he might die today? No harm, and much good. Much good for all of us, because then we would stop postponing the good we mean to do, the ways we mean to reform. The real Christian is very cheerful about death. It's the doorway to Heaven, and all of life is a hurrying up to it. It's the doorway to Purgatory and Hell, too, but as long as we're going to receive enough grace to be saints, the thing to do is try. Let's not dampen the high spirits of the young. Just as they think it's going to be easy to be saints (and, really, in their secret hearts they do think so), so they're sure they will go to Heaven. They just *have to.*

Chapter 11

*Train your child in his
vocation as a student*

When a child goes to school, he takes his soul with him. What he learns will have an effect on whether he saves his soul and how he fulfills the purpose for which God made him.

"Well, yes," someone will say, "if he goes to a parochial school. But you cannot say that what he learns in the public school has much to do with his soul."

But it does.

You can't learn anything that doesn't affect your soul. It may be that learning in public schools is rarely related to the soul, but it's an error to think that it has no relation to truth. So simple a thing as the sum of two and two is a truth. People who do not believe in God will admit that two and two make four. It's simply a truth. And it's a truth God knew before man did. In fact, man could not know if God had not given him a mind to know it. He could not even know with his mind if God did not give him the grace to understand it.

St. Paul says, "Not that we are sufficient to think anything of ourselves, as of ourselves, but our sufficiency is from God."[36] Thus, going to school involves God every hour and minute and second, and everything a child learns that is truth, he learns with the help

[36] 2 Cor. 3:5.

179

of the Spirit of Truth. That is why going to school has a particular relation to the Holy Spirit.

⌒

Teach your child the Faith at home

The reason Catholics have parochial schools is to teach what is called formal education — all the things that seem to be remote from God — in relation to their Source, and in relation to the whole purpose of man on this earth. This content is fitted into the pattern of sacramental life by which a child will save his soul and know his obligation to help save the souls of others. He's taught all the lessons a public-school child is taught, plus the truths of the Church that are necessary for salvation, and he's taught these last as commands imposed by divine authority.

So parents who can send their children to parochial schools are blessed in a special way. But there's a danger some will thrust on the parochial school more than it proposes to do. Teaching sisters and brothers are not the equivalent of parents, and no parochial school can substitute for a home or the example and teaching of parents. Together, the home and the parochial school can work into a whole piece the two phases of life that do the most to make the man. Without cooperation from the home, what is taught in the parochial school may very well, for some children, remain forever on the level of something "Sister says."

For instance, "Sister says you're supposed to be a saint."

"Yes? Well, all I hope is that Sister knows you're supposed to earn a living."

And it becomes quite clear to a child that being a saint has nothing to do with earning your living. Sister may say, until she's blue in the face, that it does have a connection, that how you earn your living may very well be the difference between saving your soul or losing it, but attitudes at home indicate that it's far more important to earn money; and pretty soon sanctity is relegated to the birds. Or at least to the nuns.

"What I like about the parochial schools is that children get such a good foundation in their religion. You can't really teach it at home." And sometimes parents retire permanently from the field, reluctant to encroach in any way on Sister's province, secure in the knowledge that, under Sister, the children will get the full treatment.

Sister may be a genius, but she cannot give the full treatment. She cannot follow a child home and take over the part of a child's education learned between three in the afternoon one day and nine in the morning the next.

You can't really teach it at home? *But that is what the home teaches* — if it's fulfilling all its purpose. There are no two sets of truths for anyone, and what is taught in the parochial school is supposed to continue the teaching already started in the home, not to isolate a child from reality between six and eighteen. Parents have as heavy an obligation to teach and apply the truth about God to their parochial schoolchildren as to teach and apply it to preschoolers. There is no time when the nuns "take over." There's only this great blessing: there are nuns to help.

❧

Children in public schools can be mindful of the Faith even at school

There are, however, parents who cannot send their children to parochial schools, and they need not despair that sending them to public school is abandoning them to the tides of faithlessness — not unless they intend to relinquish their role as teachers of the Faith. It will involve more work for these, a constant application of Christ's teaching to school life as well as the awareness that godless teachers can do great harm; but there's a special joy reserved for those who will turn to it with all their energies. There's the joy of discovery. Even for parents well grounded in the Faith, learning to see it in a fresh and simple light, to apply it for children, can be the beginning of falling in love with God.

The danger for public-school parents lies in disinterest in their obligation to teach. Having no parochial school, they may shrug and say, "No parochial school — what can you do?" and let it go at that. There will be catechism once a week, Christian doctrine classes weekly for the high-schoolers, and the burden of making the children attend. There will be the nuisance of fitting catechism lessons in with homework. But for many, that is the whole of it. What more can parents do?

Parents can teach it all, if they want to. There is no shortage of doctrine to teach or grace to help with the teaching. There are the Gospels to read and apply, discussion groups to attend, pastors and nuns and libraries and literature within reach of a phone call or a postage stamp. There is the Mass, the sacraments, the prayers of the universal Church offered for all her members, the love of God, and the help of the Holy Spirit. There are the tremendous graces peculiar to the vocation of parenthood, given especially to help with this most important duty of all. We're not in this thing alone. God is in it more than we are. All that is necessary is to understand that it must be taught, and to pray for the grace to do it.

We send our first-graders off to school in the fall, scrubbed, dressed, and shod outwardly, and inwardly resplendent with the virtues of faith, hope, and charity infused in their souls at the moment of Baptism. Our knowledge of this, and the end for which God created our children, can be the focus through which we see the relationship of formal learning to the whole of a child's life.

Train your child in his vocation as a student

We need not stir up in very small children declarations of great faith. They possess faith. When they reach the age of reason, we must help them make a habit of acts of faith, for belief in God is the only way to make sense of the world. And when they go off to school for the first time, it's as easy as pie for them to understand that now they're going to use the mind God gave them to learn things they must know in order to do the work God has laid out for them.

This sounds like such a simple thing that it shouldn't need to be put down in a book. But so many times we know these things ourselves and don't think to point them out to our children. A five-year-old, learning this, understands why it makes such good sense to pray to the Holy Spirit every morning as he goes out the door to catch the bus.

"Please, Holy Spirit, help me in school today."

Even children attending public schools can say a prayer to the Holy Spirit before their reading, recitations, work sheets, and test papers. Thus, in many small ways, faith becomes the vessel in which school life is contained.

≈

Remind your child that learning is his vocation

The virtue of hope helps us to know that God wants us eternally happy with Him in Heaven and will help us get there. What has this to do with school?

All the things God gives us, or permits to happen to us, are the means by which we work out our salvation. Going to school is part of it. When we teach our children that Heaven, not just a diploma, is the end of going to school, with the help of hope they can keep their gaze fixed on the end and work harder in school because it's a means. Whether they learn easily or with difficulty, hope says: Do not be discouraged. The ease or difficulty is part of the way to Heaven.

One of our children had great difficulty learning to read. By the end of the year, it was recommended that he repeat the second grade. He didn't seem to be unintelligent, and was able to keep pace with the other children in other things, but his reading was only a little short of hopeless. We tried to prepare him gradually so that he wouldn't be too hurt to discover he wouldn't pass, but in the end, it was a terrible shock, and he despaired of ever holding his head up in public again. His only comfort was little enough, for him, but it was leaning very hard on hope. Somehow, if we all prayed hard enough, surely God would help him to accept it and send him the grace to learn, and whatever it cost him in embarrassment he could use to help him get to Heaven.

We tugged mightily at hope all summer, and before school began again, part of the answer came. We discovered with the help of a child guidance clinic that he had a remedial problem. He was left-handed and right-eyed and had been trying to read from right to left. The rest of the answer came the first day of school. Armed with hope, he marched off to school and there in front of all his friends, went once more back into second grade. I think no one could reckon the cost of this to a small boy. When he got home that night, he was beaming when he said, "Gee, nobody even cared."

Then we could show him the beauty of the virtue of hope. He had prayed so hard just to hope that the disgrace of repeating wouldn't destroy him, and now what looked like an unbearable cross had worked so much good. It had revealed his remedial problem, and we knew how to help him. Better than that, he had learned a little bit about trusting that God knows what He's doing when He lets hard things happen to us. He uses the everyday kind of things to draw miniatures of what the way to Heaven will be like. Hard work, obstacles, and always spells of walking blindly and making yourself pray for hope, because with hope you won't despair, and with hope you can always wait just a little longer until God works things out the way He wants.

Even the child who is retarded, who will be a poor student always, and will be passed from grade to grade merely to keep pace socially with his fellows, must not be permitted to despair. Hope says that both he and his parents may find serenity even in his failures, because he was not created just to get good grades in school. This isn't a sentimental substitute for scholastic brilliance. It's the essence of hope.

And hope, on the other hand, keeps the self-sufficiency of a good student in check, reminding him that this is not his final end, but only a means; that he must beware of pride, which easily substitutes a successful scholastic career for eternal happiness as the end of going to school.

St. Paul says that charity is greater than either faith or hope, and without charity we have nothing. Charity is the fire that warms faith and sustains hope, because charity is love. It has the most obvious relation to school life.

Charity is patient, is kind; charity envieth not, dealeth not perversely; is not puffed up; is not ambitious, seeketh not her own, is not provoked to anger; thinketh no evil; rejoiceth not in iniquity, but rejoiceth with the truth; beareth all things, believeth all things, hopeth all things, endureth all things.[37]

Charity is the virtue by which we're able to love God above all things, and our neighbor as ourself. And from the first moment of

[37] 1 Cor. 13:4-7.

starting to school, we are riding, sitting, walking, learning, talking, eating, and playing with new neighbors.

Whether or not we may talk faith, hope, and charity in complicated terms to our first-graders doesn't matter. We can talk faith, hope, and charity in their own terms. What is important is that we understand them and use them as our rule for seeing the years of going to school in relation to the purpose of life. Without this understanding, we'll be fooled into thinking that the purpose of education is merely to accumulate knowledge. There's a difference between an educated man and a knowledgeable man. The first knows why he's here and uses knowledge to discover his relation to God. The second does not know why he's here and uses knowledge as the end itself.

We have an obligation to teach our children a right respect for education and to rejoice that they live in a land where it's available to everyone. Going to school is so commonplace in America that not many people remember to rejoice about it. It's a privilege that's so much taken for granted that, for some, it isn't even a privilege, but a burden, and they drop out of school as soon as the law allows.

Homework can be an opportunity to practice and explore what has already been learned; yet often parents and children alike consider it only an odious burden heaped on helpless victims by teachers who have (they are sure) forgotten what it means to be young. On the other side of the world, Korean children are sitting on crates by the bank of a river, gleefully happy because once more they can go to school. African children walk ten miles barefoot to get to mission schools where they can learn to write their names, read the communications of other men, add, subtract, multiply, analyze the soil of their farmlands, master the principle of self-government, and learn about God.

Train your child in his vocation as a student

Our own attitudes will color the way our children look at school. It can be a dismal prison, an automatic babysitter, or the opportunity to discover the gifts that are in us and the ways to use them, depending on which of these attitudes a child absorbs from his parents. Granted, there is lack of space and teachers. There are antiquated buildings. There is confusion in many quarters as to whether the end should be purely scholastic, "practical," or merely social adjustment. In spite of all these, we still have schools. If there are improvements to be desired, it's our burden to work for them. If there are dangers to beware of, it's our burden to beware of them. But it's a blessing to have schools. And if we teach our children that the knowledge they accumulate in school will help them discover God-given vocations, we must also teach them to be grateful that they may go to school.

⌒

Instill in your child a love of learning

The plaint of educators everywhere is that children seem to lack eagerness and enthusiasm about learning. This zest is the hallmark of the beginner, but somewhere between first grade and high school, it dries up. Parents can do much to help a child sustain his eagerness by participating with him in the things he learns. This is not to imply that all parents don't; yet often our contribution amounts to no more than a constant admonition. "You buckle down and get to work. Learn while you have the chance. You'll be sorry later you didn't take advantage of school."

A routine assignment for a geography class, for instance, can become exciting when we discover its contact with our own daily life. One child was supposed to collect pictures of five agricultural products grown in Mississippi, but the pantry cupboard produced the products themselves, so her display consisted of little plastic bags filled with cornmeal, oatmeal, whole-wheat cereal, a string of peanuts in their shells, and a wad of cotton.

A child who needs practice in addition learns how necessary it is to daily life when he adds up the checkout slip accompanying the grocery order. Fractions seem to have some reason for being when they are the means of tripling a cake recipe; a youngster who hates fractions but loves to cook will discover that they aren't quite so inscrutable or detestable as she thought.

Applying phonetics to reading new words is fun when a child is handed a letter from Grandma or Aunt Martha and told that he may read it to the family.

We don't have to be professional teachers to interest our children in what they learn in school. Our role is to stimulate their interest by tying knowledge in with family and civic life. Encouraging self-control in the matter of radio and TV programs, those thieves of time and enemies of concentration, is easier if we plan constructive projects to correlate with homework. It's surprising how easily children can be weaned from too much TV if they're given something more interesting to do instead.

⌒

Support and respect your child's teacher

Then there are the lessons in obedience, silence, respect, responsibility, and honesty to be learned in relation to school. If we have taught our children that obedience to parents is important because they are the visible representatives of God in the family, they can understand why it's important to be obedient to the teacher in the classroom. Obedience is not something the teacher is challenged to wrest from a child. Obedience is *due*. A Catholic child is taught to confess disobedience. I asked an eight-year-old why he obeyed his teacher.

"Because it's wrong not to."

"Why?"

"Because you aren't home, and she's like your mother and father are at home, only in school. God wants you to be obedient to the teacher."

Certainly, "we all have our rights." But we also all have our obligations. If we teach that obedience is expected by God, then the personality of the teacher has nothing to do with it, and even the child who is not obedient knows, in his conscience, that he's *wrong,* not clever. The childhood of Christ is the example of obedience we may instill in our children; and if obedience is difficult, we can pray with them, asking Him to give them the grace to learn it.

Because their teacher is given her authority from God, we must help children to respect her, even when they may not like her too much. If she is *Sister,* they must understand that, in her vocation, she is a Bride of Christ who has left father, mother, sisters, brothers, and all the world to serve Him. She is not and does not care to be considered a "regular guy." She's a dedicated woman, quite human (why people are surprised that the religious are human is beyond me), who loves, teaches, corrects, and endures for a supernatural reason. She did not take the habit because she's a saint, but because she wants to be one; if her weaknesses show now and then, so do ours (probably more so). We must pray for her and with her, as we know she prays for us.

If the teacher is a layperson, the same respect is due. Lay teachers are people with private lives like ours, who suffer the same worries and pains and bear the same obligations as the rest of the world. Theirs, too, is a dedicated vocation. We need not go into the economics of teachers' salaries with our children, but it's easier to see that teachers are dedicated when we ponder the salaries they might be making if they were doing something else. If now and then we meet a teacher who is not, to our way of thinking, understanding and patient, by our own understanding we can help her be the best sort of person she may be.

≈

Work with the teacher
to help your child improve

Religion plays an important part in the lives of many teachers; and even when we don't meet in the same specific faith, we do on the broad plain of belief in God. I have never met a teacher who was amused to learn that our children prayed for her. Nor have I ever met one who, working with me on some child's problem, did not respond warmly when I asked her to remember the child in her prayers.

Since conflicts between teacher and pupil are not uncommon, a conference with the teacher is the best way to determine the real cause of the trouble. No parent ought to judge after hearing only the tearful one-sided report of an aggrieved child. Often, the parents can explain puzzling behavior by revealing some secret fear, embarrassment, or disability in the child about which the teacher knows nothing. If it's a remedial problem, the teacher can tell the parents how best to help at home, and more important, what measures to avoid. Overanxious parents trying to help a slow reader at home often contribute more to his difficulty and tension by adding the fear of failing before his parents to the already terrible fear of failing before his class.

Conferences with the teacher can explore far more than the child's scholastic progress. The teacher is also an observer, and she can help the parents discover areas of social behavior where a child needs help. Frequently, however, she will not mention these unless asked, because to oversensitive parents, it may sound only like tattling.

For instance, a boy who is taller and heavier than his class-mates is likely to be rougher, not deliberately, but because of his size. Parents seeing him at home in the company of larger or smaller brothers and sisters have no way of knowing the compara-tive size of his classmates. A teacher can cue the parents to remind him of his obligation to be considerate and protective of children smaller than he.

A child addicted to tattling on the school grounds can be a scourge to the teacher and slowly develop a warped idea of how to solve difficulties met in play. Once they realize this, parents can help by giving him spiritual motives to help control peevishness, by promoting lightheartedness and coaxing him to laugh off fan-cied abuse.

A teacher can also spot physical irregularities the parent may not notice, such as squinting, slouching, difficulty in hearing, and inevitably she will discover special aptitudes that parents will want to encourage, such as abilities in art or music, leadership, or service. And conferences concerning the child who has real diffi-culty learning can help both parents and teacher to work together with patience and love to eliminate all semblance of disgrace from his failures, stressing praise for effort, and assuring him that their opinion of him rests on his value as a person, not on his I.Q.

Above all, we must inspire our children to love their teacher. She, too, is another Christ of whom He said, "What you do to these . . . you do to me."[38] She is a dearly beloved of God, re-deemed by Christ on the Cross; and we must be as eager to pro-mote love of a teacher as love of all human beings. No matter what

[38]Cf. Matt. 25:40.

happens, we must not criticize a teacher to a child. If we have critical opinions, they're not the affair of our child, but one to be settled between the teacher and us. Criticism of teachers to children is the collapse of all classroom discipline.

⁀

Help your child
develop character in school

Responsibility is a manifold duty. Not only must a child try to see his schoolmates as other Christs, with the obligation to love them, but he must also see that he has a responsibility to give good example to the individuals as well as the group. By his obedience, he will help the entire group to be obedient. By his silence, he will help the group to be silent. By his courtesy and cooperation, the group profits. He must defend the weaker ones when they need defending, and give praise freely for the talents and good work of the others.

This is, indeed, a "hard saying." But the beauty of early childhood is that the virtues *are admired.* It's only after bad habits have glazed over the first willingness to be good that children begin to scorn goody-goodies. Often such scorn is the clearest indication that a child envies the virtues of the good, the accepted ones. This is very evident in adult society. No one has a corner on goodness. We can help our children by giving them, in the beginning, really stiff ideals to live up to, but ideals that are warm with the example of Christ, the beauty of His personality.

Responsibility also means that we must take care of school property and make restitution as far as we are able for any damage we've caused.

"Mother, will you please write a note to the librarian and explain about the library book?"

But Mother did not let the baby get the library book; someone else did. So Mother would not write a note. The only course was to pray for the grace to admit full responsibility to the librarian and ask what could be done to make up for it. It ended up with allowance money spent to replace the ruined book, and much respect for library books ever since! Insignificant as these experiences seem to be, once the fear of facing up to responsibility has been conquered, honesty is never quite that difficult again. These are very small things perhaps, but they are the making of integrity.

Silence in the classroom can be directly related to the silence of Christ in the Holy Eucharist. Silence is really terribly hard, but the efforts to be silent for His sake, to join Him in the poignant silence of the Tabernacle, will be repaid — who knows with what riches of grace? And perhaps in the struggle there will be the first intimation to a child of the sweetness of silence, which one day he must learn to love if God is to speak to him.

Honesty in school means many things. It means not cheating, neither telling answers nor asking questions when you're not supposed to. It means telling the truth always, to the teacher as well as to your fellows. It means never taking anything that doesn't belong to you, and knowing that things one "finds" are to be given to the teacher to dispose of. And it means doing all these things in order not to *sin*, not just because this is the nice way to be. Our Lord bade his Apostles have such a love for truth that they should not swear by anything on earth or in Heaven, but merely speak the truth with a simple yes or no.

"God is there with you in school, too, dear. Even if you could fool the teacher, you couldn't fool Him. When you pray to the Holy Spirit for help in your work, remember that He's the Spirit of Truth. You can't expect His help if you're not going to be loyal to truth."

How to Raise Good Catholic Children

Again, if we can remember to teach our children to pray for the grace to be honest, the Spirit of Truth will strengthen them before each trial. Answering an invitation to be dishonest with, "No, it's a sin," helps them grow stronger in their conviction of sin and is one of the obligations of correction St. Paul pointed out to his newly made Christians.

But there are obligations in charity that forbid our publicizing the dishonesty of others. Children will sit in judgment constantly over the actions of classmates and bring many a long tale home about who swipes rulers and pencils and does mischief and then blames it on "me." There are delicate problems involved, and the greatest service we can do is to help our children look with charity upon the weaknesses of their friends. If someone has a yen for stealing pencils, it's best not to leave any pencils around for him to steal. Our own carelessness may be a temptation for him. If someone has selected us as his pet "scapegoat," we can ask our Lord for the grace to bear what abuse he dishes out, and only when it's beyond endurance, tell the teacher.

Tattling isn't the only thing to do with difficulties on the playground or in the classroom. But unless we show our children how to handle them, how to concern themselves for the souls of their tormentors, it's the only thing they know how to do. Our Lord's words about good doing to our enemies are just as effective in the schoolyard as they are anywhere else, and most of the disagreeable characters in this world respond to kindness and love. Many a child will become intrigued by the idea of trying to be nicer than ever to persons who are mean to them — just to see if it "works." It almost always does.

Reading the Gospels and letters of the New Testament at home, with an eye to discover solutions to social problems at school, can become an exciting chase, and in the bargain we are

Train your child in his vocation as a student

teaching our children to look to the right source for their guidance all through life.

For instance, in his letter to the Romans, St. Paul poses a real challenge: "Now, we that are stronger ought to bear the infirmities of the weak, and not to please ourselves. Let every one of you please his neighbor unto good, to edification, for Christ did not please Himself."[39]

Just these few lines pose a whole new attack on "stinky old So-and-so." "Stinky" usually turns out to be a pretty good guy after all, after he has had a chance to see that you really want to be his friend.

"Know what? He's not so bad. I didn't used to like him, but I do now."

᠉

Encourage your child
to witness to his Faith

School is the first experience away from home when a child will have to give reasons "for the faith that is in you."[40] Why doesn't he have meat sandwiches on Fridays during Lent? Why doesn't he have desserts in his lunchbox during Advent and Lent? Why does he go to Church on certain weekdays during the year? He begins to take part in the lay apostolate in a real way when he answers these small things that set him apart a bit from the others. There are people who do not know why they eat fish on Friday. But a child can understand easily enough that it's a self-denial in memory of Christ's sacrifice for our sins on the first Good Friday. Learning it, he will comment, "That's not much to do, is it?"

[39] Rom. 15:1-3.
[40] Cf. 1 Pet. 3:15.

How to Raise Good Catholic Children

Self-denial during Advent is a form of purification, a preparation for meeting the Infant Jesus on Christmas with a clean heart and a clean mind. During Lent it's a penance, an attempt to atone for the sins that made it necessary for Christ to die on the Cross, so that we can greet Him at the Resurrection purged of evil and ready to start anew.

He goes to Mass on the feast of the Ascension to rejoice that Christ has gone to Heaven before us, to prepare a place for us. He goes on All Saints' Day to rejoice that men and women, born in Original Sin like us, can rise to the heights of sanctity with the help of God, and to celebrate with special love the joy of his own patron saints, begging their intercession for him before the throne of God. He goes to Mass on the feast of the Immaculate Conception to greet the spotless Virgin who bore the Son of God within her body and gave Him to the world on Christmas Day.

The graces of these feasts and all the feasts of the liturgical year can be applied to school life as well as home, and the child develops in his awareness that the mysteries of the Faith apply to the whole world, not just his house, his yard, and his family.

Two little boys whose families celebrated the Epiphany at home produced fat pieces of Epiphany cake in their lunchboxes the next day at school.

"Epiphany cake, Epiphany cake, hurrah, hurrah for Epiphany cake!" they yipped.

"What's Epiphany?"

And when they explained, someone said, "Gee, I wish we had Epiphany."

But *everyone* has Epiphany. Christ was manifested to all men on Epiphany, not just to a few. One teacher became so much interested in an account of St. Valentine that she asked a mother to write it out, whereupon it was read in the elementary classrooms of a public school. That was something new indeed — that valentines could speak of love as coming from God. When another mother encouraged her children to make Nativity puppets, they gave a show in the classroom — at the teacher's request.

None of these things was calculated. They were the spilling over from the lives of children whose parents have tried to teach them that religion embraces all of life — home and school (in this case, public school). The children simply took their joy to school with them.

The Faith governs all of life, not just a fraction of it. If we forget that the hearts and minds and souls of men were created to be the dwelling place of the Holy Spirit, we leave our children to find their way, outside their homes and especially in school, as though they were blind. Light has always been symbolic of learning, and Christ is the Light of the World. The love He shares with His Father is the Spirit of Truth. Our children will be educated only when they see knowledge in relation to Truth, use it in the service of Love, and know that the end of it is eternal life.

Chapter 12

Celebrate Baptism

The best way to teach children about Baptism is with babies, either an infant brother or sister, or an infant neighbor. Then they learn about Baptism in terms of *someone*, not just something.

A newborn baby is not in the state of grace; he's marked by Original Sin, which he inherited from his first parents. To a child who understands what the state of grace is, this is a terrible shock.

"But Mother, that's not fair. It isn't his fault they committed Original Sin." So God looks mean, or the Church looks mean, and an older sister will make a private reservation that they may *say* he isn't free of sin, but he *must* be.

It doesn't help to answer, "Well, he is. You'll have to believe it because it's true." Too many answers like this can add up to future apostasy, all because truths that could be explained (if we would bother to explain them) were not explained. Many of the mysteries cannot be explained, but it isn't hard to explain Original Sin.

Explain the reason for Baptism

Suppose God had given Adam a stack of money. "Now you are rich," He would have said. "Take good care of the money. Don't lose it, because one day you will have a big family, and they will need it. It will buy them food and clothes, keep a roof over their head, and all these things will keep them happy and well. If you lose the money, your children will have a very hard time. They will be cold and hungry and naked, and have no home, all because of a wasted inheritance you might have left them."

Now, suppose Adam paid no attention to God and wasted his money instead. He would have had none to pass on to his children. Even if it wasn't their fault, the inheritance would be gone. Nothing could bring it back. So they would suffer because of their father's wastefulness.

God didn't give Adam money. He did give him sanctifying grace. That was the wealth Adam could have passed on to his children. But he lost it, and what he did not have, he could not pass on. Because he disobeyed God by committing Original Sin, the only thing he could pass on to his children was his sin. That's why even the dearest new baby is born with his soul stained by sin.

Only two people were *conceived* without Original Sin, and we must teach our children about this. One was Christ, the Son of God, who was like men in every way except sin, and the other was His Mother. Logically, God could never had permitted His Son to be born of a mother stained by sin, and Sacred Scripture proves it: if Mary had inherited Original Sin, the angel Gabriel could never honestly have addressed her as "Full of grace."[41]

A third person was *born* free of Original Sin, although his soul was stained by it at his conception: St. John the Baptist. He was sanctified in his mother Elizabeth's womb at the moment of her meeting with Mary, at the Visitation: "For behold, the moment the sound of thy greeting came to my ears, the babe in my womb leapt for joy."[42]

---

[41]Luke 1:28.
[42]Cf. Luke 1:44.

This is why our Lady's birthday and St. John's birthday are the only two birthday parties for saints in the entire liturgical calendar. The other feasts of the saints celebrate events in their lives, or their deaths — the day they were born to eternal life in Heaven.

So, in terms of the Mystical Body, a lovely new unbaptized baby doesn't belong. Even though he's born into our family, and we're Catholics, he isn't a member of the Church. If he died with Original Sin on his soul, he wouldn't go to Hell. He wouldn't suffer in Purgatory. But he wouldn't see God, because no soul stained by sin can enter into the presence of God. He would be as happy as he was capable of being, without ever seeing God.

⌇

How Christ instituted Baptism

Far too many people fail to realize that this is made very clear in the Gospels. If we are to teach our children convincingly about Baptism, we will have to use the Gospels as our source. The Church teaches what Christ taught about Baptism, and He made it so clear that it isn't possible to misunderstand His words.

Rites like Baptism, ceremonies that include washing in different ways to symbolize purification, have been part of almost every religion ever since the beginning. At the time of our Lord, St. John the Baptist was baptizing crowds of people who came to hear him preach repentance for sin and the coming of the Messiah. This baptism was not a sacrament. It was a symbolic ritual, which signified that those who asked for baptism had repented of their sins and resolved to live a holier life. John baptized them by submerging them completely in the water, then raising them up again. Disappearing under the water was a sign of their death to sin, a symbol of descending into the grave. Rising out of it was a sign of their desire to live a new life.

Now, St. John had not seen his Cousin since He was a little boy, so he had no way of knowing Him. But the Holy Spirit revealed to him that Christ would come one day, and that there would be a sign for John by which Christ would be known. So one day, when a crowd of people came to be baptized by John in the river Jordan, Jesus came with them. Although St. John said later that he didn't recognize Christ, still he must have wondered, and he asked Him: "I ought to be baptized by Thee, and comest Thou to me?"

Our Lord told him to baptize Him just the same, because there was a reason. So John baptized Jesus, and the heavens opened, and he saw a dove descending and heard the voice of God the Father saying, "This is my beloved Son, in whom I am well pleased."[43]

Certainly Christ had no need of baptism, but by submitting to the rite, He sanctified the waters of Baptism and gave an example to those who would follow Him. Even at this time, however, He did not affirm the absolute necessity of Baptism.

One night not long after, a sincere Pharisee named Nicodemus went secretly to Jesus to question Him about His role as a worker of miracles. And to Nicodemus, Jesus said, "Unless a man be born again, he cannot see the kingdom of God." Now, surely Nicodemus knew that Christ did not mean literally "born again." But to find out what He did mean, he asked, "How can a man be born when he is old? Can he enter a second time into his mother's womb?" And then Jesus described the necessity of Baptism.

"Unless a man be born of water and the Holy Spirit, he cannot enter the kingdom of God."[44] We should memorize this and teach it to our children. It's one of the doctrines about which Catholics are most often questioned.

[43] Matt. 3:13-17.
[44] Cf. John 3:3-5.

Between that time and the post-Resurrection period, both Jesus and His disciples baptized, but not until after the Resurrection did He *command* His Apostles to baptize. With this, it is clear that Baptism is to be a sacrament.

"Go, therefore, and make disciples of all nations, baptizing them in the name of the Father, and of the Son, and of the Holy Spirit, teaching them to observe all that I have commanded of you."[45]

We should know and love these words.

"But suppose someone were dying and wanted to be baptized, and there was no water?"

Water is always necessary, even if it's not clean. The water used by the priest for Baptism is especially blessed, but in case of an emergency, where a layperson must baptize, if there's no plain water, liquids composed of water with some flavoring added could be used. Tea, coffee, carbonated beverages, even beer, may be used in an emergency. Milk, vinegar, wine, or any other liquids may not be used. Unless a child should ask about these exceptions, it would be more confusing than helpful to mention them, but it's always good to know the facts.

There are two other kinds of Baptism, baptism of blood and baptism of desire, and they show God's infinite mercy. Baptism of blood is received by those unbaptized who die as martyrs for the love of God or for some Christian virtue. Baptism of desire is received by those unbaptized who, sorry for their sins, die desiring either Baptism or the complete will of God, so far as they are able to know it. This answers the question of children who worry about pagans who die without any knowledge of Baptism (although only God knows who receives these kinds of Baptism). Even a pagan, if he believes sincerely in one he thinks is God, tries to do his will

[45]Cf. Matt. 28:19-20.

perfectly, and is sorry for his sins, probably dies with baptism of desire. Such a pagan, put to death for the one he believed was God, would probably receive baptism of blood.

God's demand for Baptism is just, and we must help our children understand this. Sentimental substitutes for it are no good. We should be satisfied that His mercy provides for those faithful souls who are unable to receive Christian teaching about it in time.

❦

Answer questions about babies
who die before being baptized

In families where the children know that a new child is expected, and then are told that the baby will not live to be born, the children may ask whether he's able to be baptized; then it's good to know that the Church insists that a fetus be conditionally baptized. Doctors and nurses are instructed how to baptize conditionally the stillborn, even if the fetus is unrecognizable, and husbands and wives should also know about conditional Baptism if a miscarriage takes place at home. The procedure is the same for any emergency Baptism: pouring water on while saying, "I baptize you in the name of the Father, and of the Son, and of the Holy Spirit."

We have near us a state hospital for the mentally impaired, and our children have asked about baptizing the babies who go to live there. Babies born mentally impaired may always be baptized, up to the age of reason, and should be, and it makes a child very happy to be told such a baptized child is a temple of God. Such a child is always in the state of grace because he's incapable of committing deliberate sin. An adult who is mentally diseased may be baptized if, in a lucid moment, he shows a desire for it or if, in danger of death, he has ever shown a desire for it before losing reason.

These points are included to provide answers to questions that may and probably will be asked. Just as children will ask about suicide and murder and we must answer in a way that gives them confidence in God's mercy, so we must answer their questions about the necessity of Baptism in the same way.

✎

Explain the symbolism of the baptismal rite

Learning about Baptism can really be fun when it's a feature of the preparation for a real Baptism, or the celebration of a baptismal feast. Celebrating the birthday of St. John the Baptist on June 24 is a good time for learning about Baptism. A group of children sitting around the kitchen table while their mother mixes a feast-day cake will listen far more attentively to her talk about Baptism than the same group sitting around the dining-room table, catechisms in hand — especially if there's a bowl to lick afterward.

We ought to invite more people to attend our babies' Baptisms — that is, the *sacrament part* (which no one seems to want to attend) instead of the party (which can't always accommodate all the people who think they should attend). And we ought all to celebrate our baptismal feasts with as much enthusiasm as we celebrate our birthdays. After all, this is *the* day, for the Christian: the day he's born again in Christ. Moreover, learning about Baptism in connection with all these occasions means learning *more* than the catechism teaches.

It's a lovely custom for the family to provide their own baptismal garment and candle for a baby's Baptism. White garments can be bought ready-made and embroidered with liturgical symbols, or can be made and embroidered at home. Sometimes they're like a bib or sacque or, as in our family, a piece of fine linen cloth can be used for each child. This is embroidered with the symbols of each sacrament as the child receives them, and parts of it are appliquéd to a First Communion dress, a Confirmation dress, and a wedding dress; or it can be made into a pocket handkerchief to carry at a boy's First Communion, Confirmation, wedding, or even as an amice at Ordination.

The candle used at a Baptism (two are used, but one is handed to the sponsors) must fit the candlesticks in the baptistry; hence, it's usually more convenient to have a blessed candle of ordinary size, decorated either before or after with appropriate symbols and lettered with the child's name and the date. For baptismal feasts at home, there are large liturgical candles available at religious-supply stores. These can be taken to the church before Candlemas (February 2), when Father will be glad to bless them with the rest of the candles.

Decorating a baptismal candle isn't difficult, even for people who can't draw a straight line. Liturgical symbols are all over the place, in missals, prayer books, on the walls of churches, on altars and vestments, on religious greeting cards. If none is found to describe a child's patron saint, it's quite all right to invent them. First, a thin coat of white shellac goes over each spot where a design will be painted. Use a cheap paintbrush (shellac is death to good paintbrushes), and remove the shellac from the brush with rubbing alcohol.

Next, the designs are drawn or traced on paper with a soft lead pencil, then reversed and transferred to the candle by rubbing. Be sure to plan the spacing of the designs to leave enough room near the bottom of the candle for the child's name, date of birth, and date of Baptism. Oil paint with a little turpentine for thinning and a small pointed brush are best for the designs. After the paint is dry, another coat of shellac over them will be protection against handling.

The first three symbols at the top of our candles (reading down) are for the Holy Trinity, to remind the children that their souls become the dwelling of the Trinity after Baptism. There are many symbols for each Person, but we have chosen those easiest for the children to remember. A hand describes God the Father as Creator. The crown of thorns, three nails, and five drops of blood describe God the Son as Redeemer. A dove describes God the Holy Spirit. Very little children must have it clearly explained that *the Holy Spirit is not a dove*. A dove has been seen at times as a sign of the Holy Spirit, but the Holy Spirit is really the love of the Father for the Son, and the love of the Son for the Father.

Next comes a shell with water, because water is the most important outward sign of the sacrament of Baptism. Then we use a cloud with wind, to remind them of the priest breathing three times gently on the face of the child at Baptism, bidding the evil spirit to depart in the name of the Holy Trinity.[46] Next, a salt cellar with grains of salt. This is the symbol children love best, because it's so interesting to see a baby taste the salt at his Baptism, and because it's symbolic of things they know in daily life. At home we use salt to bring out the flavor of our food and to preserve such things as cucumbers (pickles), cabbage (sauerkraut), and fish (codfish cakes). In Baptism, a little blessed salt is put on the baby's tongue as a pledge that it may have a taste for heavenly wisdom, and that it may be preserved from the corruption of sin. It reminds us of the words of our Lord: "You are the salt of the earth. But if the salt lose its savor, wherewith shall it be salted? It is good for nothing anymore but to be cast out, and to be trodden on by men."[47]

[46] Although some of the details explained here and in the following pages aren't generally included in today's baptismal rite, they're nonetheless edifying to ponder. — ED.

[47] Matt. 5:13.

Then we add a little oil lamp, a symbol of the holy chrism with which a child is anointed after the pouring on of water. This is a sign that he's now a member of Christ's Mystical Body and has some share in the work of Christ's Priesthood. In this sense, he's a lay priest. He may offer the Mass with the priest and Christ, as an act of adoration to the Father. A man and a woman administer the sacrament of Matrimony to one another, with the priest present as witness. In this, they act as lay priests.

Next, there's the white garment. This is a symbol of the gift of sanctifying grace that infuses the soul at Baptism. In the early Church, the candidates for Baptism wore white garments, but more recently the priest has used a fine white napkin, laying it across the child's head. Last of all on the candle is the child's name and birth date, and then — lettered in red — the date of his Baptism.

⬎

Celebrate your child's Baptism each year

An English translation of the Rite of Baptism for Infants is needed if a child is to renew his baptismal vows at a baptismal feast. These leaflets cost very little and are available in religious-supply stores or from a number of publishers. A brief rehearsal the day before helps the child to understand what each part means and what's expected of him. On the evening of the feast, before the meal is served, the family stands around the table, and the father reads the questions asked of the sponsors when the child was too little to reply for himself, then gives the responses, which the child repeats after him. The father does not imitate any of the things the priest did, but merely explains them, and for little children, it's best to keep the explanation short and interesting rather than risk boredom with too many hard words or long prayers.

It starts with "N., what do you ask of the Church of God?"

"Faith."

"What does faith bestow upon you?"

"Life everlasting."

Then the father explains how the priest breathed upon the face of the child, signed him with the Cross upon the forehead and breast, laid his hand upon the head, and said a lovely prayer asking God to keep the child from sin and help him grow in perfection day by day. Then he explains about the salt and the prayers of exorcism.

Next comes the Apostles' Creed, followed by the Our Father. Once too small to speak for himself, now the child can do it alone. It's very moving to hear it.

Then the father explains how once more the priest commanded the Devil to depart and then, using the words of our Lord when he cured a man deaf and dumb, he touched the child's ears saying, "*Ephpheta*, that is, be opened," and touching his nostrils he said: "Unto the odor of sweetness. But thou, Devil, begone, for the judgment of God is at hand."

Then come the "Do you renounce?" questions that children love to answer.

"N., do you renounce Satan?"

"I do renounce him."

"And all his works?"

"I do renounce them."

"And all his pomps?"

"I do renounce them."

"But what does *pomps* mean?" someone will ask. *Pomp* is defined as "a show of magnificence, display, brilliant splendor." It's easier to explain to grown-ups than to children. It could apply to the way the Devil uses worldly displays to make us forget the holy meaning of the great Christian feasts, such as Christmas and

Easter. It could apply to the way the splendor of impure movies or TV shows can blind us to the fact that they might arouse temptations in us and be occasions of sin.

Then the father explains how the child was anointed with the oil of catechumen on the breast and between the shoulders, and the priest changed his purple stole for a white one, to signify the joy of the Church receiving a prospective new member.

Next the "Do you believe?" questions, and then the priest asked the sponsors, for the child:

"N., do you wish to be baptized?"

And the sponsors answered for him, "I do."

Then came the wonderful moment. Pouring water over his head, the priest said the words of Baptism, and the Holy Trinity came to make their home in the soul.

The bestowing of the three gifts came last of all. First, the anointing on the crown of the head with the sacred oil of priesthood to signify membership in Christ. Second, the presentation of the white garment to signify the gift of sanctifying grace. Third, here the father hands the lighted baptismal candle to the child, saying as the priest did, "Receive this burning light and safeguard your baptism by a blameless life; keep God's commandments so that when our Lord comes to the marriage feast, you may be worthy to greet Him with all the saints in the heavenly court, and live forever and ever."

With, "Go in peace, and may the Lord be with you," everyone kisses the child. It's a very proud moment, and seeing him there with his lighted candle, a symbol of the living Christ, whose life he shares, everyone feels the same — so glad to be baptized.

Chapter 13

Teach your child to make good confessions

It's wonderful the way kitchens lend themselves to the teaching of catechism. And it's wonderful how much fun catechism can be for children when mothers make it kitchen catechism. Consider, for example, the task of preparing a child for his first Confession.

A long time ago, a friend of ours wrote a book whose purpose was to make catechism come to life. Among other things, he invented what he called a "catechemical method" for teaching children about their souls and the state of grace. Lacking the chemicals he used, we adapted his method to the kitchen and, with leftover tea and coffee, got the same effect. Some Saturday morning when the communicant-to-be is helping wipe the dishes, lift a glass of water to the window and, with the sun shining through it, point out, "See how the sun shines through clear water? It's that way with God and the soul in the state of grace. He can enter it, His grace fills it with light, and it's beautiful. Have you ever thought how the soul is different when venial sin is present? It's something like this," and you hold a glass of tea to the light.

"See? The sun still shines through, but not so clearly as through water. God can remain in the soul even when there's venial sin there, and He does, because He knows we're weak and He chooses to remain to strengthen us as much as possible. But the soul isn't so beautiful as it was when free of all sin. And God isn't so happy there as when the soul is free of sin and He can fill it with Himself and His grace."

You go on. "Mortal sin is different. It's the worst offense of all and, in the presence of mortal sin, God cannot, will not remain. With mortal sin in the soul, God is not there, nor any grace, nor any light — only ugly darkness, like this," and you hold up a glass of black coffee to the light. A little girl whose understanding of mortal sin has been limited to a perfectly memorized definition will suck in her breath and whisper, "Oh, I see."

"What to do then, if the soul's beauty is changed by venial sin? Or worse still, if it's ugly with mortal sin? Why, go to Confession, of course, as fast as you can. You tell your sins to the priest with real sorrow, meaning never to commit them again, promise to say your penance, and through His priest, God forgives the sin, and grace once more enters the soul. It's something like this," and a glass of tea, followed by a glass of coffee, is held under the faucet. The water turned on full force pours into the glass, displacing all the color. Water is an eloquent symbol of grace. The Church uses it often. St. Teresa of Avila liked it best of all for teaching souls about grace.

Children love learning like this, and it helps them remember something about the sacrament of Penance that we are all inclined to forget: its sacramental grace. We get accustomed to going to Confession in order to go to Communion, and we forget that, in receiving absolution, we receive a separate sacrament. We forget to take advantage of its special grace. After Confession, the soul is filled not only with grace, but also with an overpowering cheerfulness — one of the effects of grace. We *feel* as though we shall never want to sin again. It's one of those times when an emotion can be made to serve us well; so we must teach our children how to use it.

Teach your child to make good confessions

Because children, when making their first Confession (and for some time after), usually ask their parents' help in defining their sins, parents become, in effect, their childhood spiritual directors. Not that the priest isn't capable, but there's a limit to his time and he isn't often able to know each child well enough to do more than direct in a general way. Using the same method as a spiritual director, a mother or father (one or the other consistently, if possible) may point out the importance of using this sacramental grace and suggest that the recital of penance be followed by special pleas for help with one outstanding fault. It's best to work at one fault at a time and get somewhere than try the whole field and grow discouraged getting nowhere. Our Lord is there in the newly washed soul, waiting to help. Years can be wasted by regular penitents because they have not been reminded to *ask for help*.

≈

Help your child to examine his conscience

Even children who examine their consciences daily usually need help preparing for Confession. The important thing for parents to keep in mind is to avoid assuming an accusatory air. If there has been endless bickering with brothers, it's a big mistake to say, "What! You mean you can't remember all those fights with your brother?"

Even when he honestly can't remember, it isn't up to us to hit him over the head with it half an hour before Confession. It's our job to help him to remember and to be sorry he fought with his brother. "Well, you did get pretty rough with your brother, remember? Fighting offends God. Don't you think you'd better confess that?"

Then, as everyone knows, children should be taught to mention the number of times they've committed some sin. "How many times did you fight with your brother?" "Gee, I don't know. About a hundred times, I guess." Our pastor is satisfied to have them say "several times" and cautions mothers not to grow too emphatic with children about how serious a sin it is. Sometimes (most times, I would say), there's no deliberation at all, merely an explosion; it might better be called an imperfection than a sin. There is, however, no need to whitewash quarreling entirely. Penance is the sacrament that helps eliminate the imperfections; so it's good to keep track of these.

As for the times he was saucy or disobedient to his mother, this is Mother's big chance — if she wants to take it. But she had better not. If she's going to send a little boy off to Confession to confess sins against his mother, where does God come in? Certainly he should obey his mother, because God expects him to obey his mother. His mother can help him be sorry for disobedience if she's gentle when reminding him of this.

"Remember the time Mother asked you to leave her pen alone, and you didn't, and you broke it? That would come under disobedience, wouldn't it? I know you didn't mean to, and I know you're sorry. God knows, too. He always forgives sins the minute you're really sorry, if you mean to go as soon as you can to tell them in Confession."

There are others besides parents whom children must obey: teachers, their school-bus driver, policemen, and more. At the proper time, each one of these is a "duly constituted authority," and helping children remember disobedience to them as a matter of Confession helps them develop a more reverent respect for authority.

As for missing prayers, I suspect that children who miss saying their prayers rarely do so on purpose. At the last mission in our parish, the missionary made a point of saying that to miss morning prayers is not a sin (deliberately neglecting prayers is another matter). I rebel against afflicting children with scruples because now and then they forget their morning prayers in the hectic rush to the bus. For this reason, we have our children say their prayers on the way to the bus. It takes about five minutes to get there; there's plenty of time for the Morning Offering, said together and aloud; and because they say it this way, they help to remind one another. Another mother has her boys kneel at their chairs and say the Morning Offering while she dishes up the oatmeal. I would hold myself more to blame than my children if they consistently forgot their prayers, and the best way to prevent this is to train them to pray aloud and together.

Naughtiness at prayers is easy to observe; we need only remind them to confess, "I didn't pay attention at prayers." Distractions are harder: "Mother, I mean to pay attention when I say my prayers, but I keep thinking of other things."

How you can be sure a child isn't wasting time with distractions, I don't know. You can't look into his mind. You can say, if you suspect he's distracted, "Try to think about what you're saying. If your mind goes wandering to other things, try hard to make it turn back." And we can remind him that praying without attention will probably get no results. It helps to have a picture for meditation, or a family shrine to pray in front of. When it's time to go to Confession, the best we can do is say, "If you purposely thought of other things at prayers, you had better mention that."

Missing Mass is one of the things very few children are themselves to blame for. They must understand that to miss Mass deliberately is a mortal sin. But they must also understand that to miss Mass because their father was sick and couldn't drive them, or the ice made the roads impassable, or the car had a flat tire — whatever valid reason it was — is not a mortal sin. Even when there's a valid excuse, however, it's good to recall it during preparation for Confession so that they won't make the mistake of treating the Mass obligation lightly.

Being late for Mass is something else again, and here sometimes children are to blame. It should be clearly explained to everyone in the family that oversleeping on Sunday morning, tearing out of the house, and barely arriving at Mass in time for the Offertory, is very bad business. The deadline for being late for Mass is the Offertory. Later than that, you've missed Mass. This makes sense when you recall that the purpose of the Mass is to offer Christ in sacrifice to God the Father. If you aren't there to help with the Offertory, you might as well not be there at all. Racing down in time for the Offertory, however, is hardly the way to assist at Mass and should be frowned on severely.

A child who will not get his clothes ready the night before (if it's expected of him and he's reminded), and will not get out of bed when he's called, and will not cooperate after being reminded that he must can very well be to blame for the whole family's missing Mass. If this is the case, he should be reminded when preparing for Confession to say, "It was my fault the family was late for [or missed] Mass."

Telling lies is clearly a sin, with a possible exception. Children who spin tales do not fall into the category of liars. Most parents can tell the difference, and the time to make it clear is when the tales are spun: "Oh, go on. You're inventing a story. It's a pretty good story, but really only a story, isn't it?" And you laugh. He will laugh, too, and everyone will understand that it was all fun in the first place. But lies are serious; so remembering them with Mother before Confession is important. If it's hard for a child to tell the truth, perhaps this should be the fault Mother will suggest he pray about after Confession is over.

Teach your child to make good confessions

Eating meat on days of abstinence is hardly ever the fault of the child, and if his mother is to blame, it's matter for her Confession, not his. He need not even be reminded. It's good to recall this obligation when preparing for Confession, however, so that he will never forget. "Let's see, you didn't eat any meat on the days of abstinence [we should teach them the difference between fast and abstinence]; so you don't have to remember that."

Almost all children think rebellious thoughts about their mothers and fathers after punishment; so it's good to help them be sorry for this — but not until resentment is gone and the world looks good again.

"You know, when people get mad at their mothers — especially after punishments — they usually think pretty mean thoughts of them. Now, I'm not saying you did, but it's possible. So if you did, stop now, and remember and be sorry. You know you were naughty, and you know you had to be punished. God expects mothers and fathers to punish when punishment is called for. Tell our Lord tonight that you really didn't mean it, and remember it next time you go to Confession."

This really works. Not long ago, an embarrassed youngster came to me and said, "I have something I want to tell you, but I'm afraid." We got cozy, and I said he must not be afraid, and finally he screwed up his courage and said, "When you made me go without dessert tonight because I was acting so bad at the table, I went upstairs and said in my mind, 'Mommy is a stinker. I hate Mommy.'" He was quite relieved to hear me say that I already knew it. It had been written all over his face. I knew he didn't mean it, and I wasn't mad; but next time, he might try not to say it again. Because he never *really* means it.

Stealing is always listed among the sins children might commit, but I've honestly had no experience with it. Stealing involves

How to Raise Good Catholic Children

not only the confession, but also restitution; hence, I would think it wise (if the act were repeated) for a mother or father to consult with the child's confessor. Not for the sake of telling on him, but because, if the confessor is alerted, he can single this sin out in Confession and give it his special, gentle attention.

Great care should certainly be exercised in devising some means whereby the child can make restitution that would not expose his theft publicly. Usually a conference between parent and victim will develop some way for him to return what he has stolen, or the value of it, as gracefully and contritely as possible. I've never heard of a teacher (and apparently much childhood stealing takes place in the classroom) who was not eager to help the culprit, keep his secret, and encourage his determination never to do it again.

One thing should be understood very clearly about confessing bad words and naughty thoughts: *the priest is not interested in hearing the words*, only in having the child confess saying them. *Vulgar* is a good word for describing bad words; would that no one had dreamed up the word *dirty*. Vulgar words usually have to do with bodily functions, and these should never be thought of as dirty. If "bathroom humor" is a problem serious enough to confess, a child nearly dies when he thinks he must confess it. How to tell Father about *that!* We help greatly by not appearing to be shocked (if your mother is shocked, think how Father will feel — he's a priest!), and calmly suggesting that he phrase it "immodest thoughts" or "laughing and talking about immodest things."

Children must have help phrasing such sins for Confession so that they can make it clear to their confessor and not be frightened into some serious omission. I remember a woman's telling about trying to confess a little sin of immodesty when she was a small child. It involved using a word that had no meaning except to the snickering neighborhood children. She had no help preparing her

Teach your child to make good confessions

confession. When she finally got there, worked up her courage, and spilled it out, the priest said, a little impatiently, "What? What's *that?*" All courage failing, she hastily covered up her confusion, and for years she was tormented by the specter of a bad Confession. Children *can* develop terrible scruples and grow to hate Confession rather than love it. Parents can prevent this if they will take the pains to help their children prepare for Confession with sympathy and understanding.

⌐

Train your child to distinguish
between perfect and imperfect contrition
Technically speaking, one may receive Holy Communion as long as his soul is not in the state of mortal sin. Frequent and well-prepared Confession, however, is important if there is to be real spiritual progress. The ideal is once a week; twice a month is fine. But there are families living in rural areas without easy access to Confession, and for these it would be presumptuous for me to prescribe. As often as possible is the best rule, and when parents are really interested in their own and their children's progress, they don't have to be told that.

While they are little — and so confident of Heaven one day, so sure of God's love — is the time to teach them the difference between imperfect and perfect contrition. A perfect act of contrition is true sorrow for sins because we've offended God, who loves us and deserves our perfect obedience. An imperfect act of contrition is sorrow because we're afraid of the pains of Hell. It's a healthy thing to be afraid of the pains of Hell, but when we teach our children to tell God they're sorry for their sins, we can emphasize this difference and urge them to be sorry most of all because they have offended His goodness.

How to Raise Good Catholic Children

"But Mother, sometimes when I say an act of contrition, the Devil puts a thought in my mind that says, 'You're not really sorry. You don't really mean it.' "

How true, how true. And it isn't just children he torments this way. St. Teresa had some mighty sharp things to say about the way the Devil can stir up an imagination. This is the time to understand the value of an act of faith.

"Of course he'll say it, dear. He'll say it to you lots of times all your life. He wants to upset you so you suspect you aren't sorry. Our Lord doesn't insist that you be all droopy and weepy with sorrow. Maybe someday He will give you the grace to weep for your sins. Until then, He's content when you say to Him firmly, 'I'm truly sorry!' Tell the Devil to get along, push his tempting thought out of your mind, and apply yourself to a firm, careful act of contrition. That's all that's necessary."

One night I heard the children at their prayers, and before their act of contrition, this same child said, "Let's all say: 'Dear Blessed Jesus, I mean everything I say.' " He doesn't ask for more.

Encourage your child to pray for his confessor

Last of all, confessors and their human weaknesses. It must call for heroic patience to stay cooped up in a box for hours, listening to the deadly repetition of one sin after another, and retain a disposition that's all sweetness and light. Should a priest finally break down after a long day of "hearing the kids," and give someone's pride and joy a short, sharp answer, please — let's give Father a break. It's an occasion that could, if parents encouraged it, inspire compassion and a few Hail Marys for the priest who's hot and tired, weary of hearing how many people have wounded our Lord once again.

Teach your child to make good confessions

"Perhaps Jesus is testing you. He has forgiven your sins; now He waits to see if you will forgive Father for being a little cross with you. He didn't mean it. He's just tired. You say three Hail Marys for him, and next time he'll be able to stand that stuffy confessional even longer without losing his patience."

It's important that children be taught to pray for their priests always. We cannot live in Christ or die in Him without them — and especially after Confession. If it weren't for that man in that box . . .

"Thank You, Blessed Jesus, for forgiving my sins in Confession. And thank You for Father, who heard my Confession."

Chapter 14

*Instill in your child a
love for the Eucharist*

Receiving Holy Communion for the first, or the hundred and first, time is like nothing else in the world. It's a wonder we can take it so calmly. Of course, if we could grasp what happens, we would die on the spot. Saints have. Blessed Imelda died after receiving Communion from the hands of our Lord, but for the rest of us, there's little chance of that. The rest of us have trouble remaining recollected long enough to say, "Thank You" with simple graciousness. We salute baseball stars and Hollywood beauties with wild enthusiasm, and we take Communion so calmly. We greet new cures for our physical ills with bounding optimism, and we consider whether to communicate daily without even a quickened pulse. We act as though the important thing is how long men will live, not how many will get to Heaven.

Young children can have faith in
Christ's Real Presence in the Eucharist
Unless we carefully reassemble our values, helping a child to prepare for First Holy Communion is apt to be the sum of catechism lessons learned, trips to rehearse the procession, shopping tours, dress fittings, and last-minute reminders to get film for the camera. All these things are normal and good and in the right

scheme of things, humanly speaking — but they're not the heart of the matter.

Perhaps it's necessary to justify the early reception of First Communion. "After all, do you honestly think they understand what it's all about at *seven?*"

The objection that a child should wait until he can understand what he's doing when he receives Holy Communion is no objection at all. He understands as well at seven as at seventy. The Holy Eucharist is a mystery as profound and unfathomable as the Trinity. One does not *understand* how Christ can assume the form of bread and wine. One *believes*. A child must believe, and if it helps to substitute the word *understand*, then he must understand that the bread looks like bread but is not bread; it's the Body of Christ. The wine looks like wine but is not wine; it's the Blood of Christ. To ask him to understand the mystery of it is asking of him something that even his elders do not understand.

"But how can you be sure they're really reverent enough?"

Before we protest too loudly on this score, we should weigh a child's supposed incapacity for reverence (as compared with the more perceptible adult) against his purity of heart and mind and soul. Enough said. The relationship in Communion is a two-way thing. There is not just the child receiving Christ. There is Christ also, wanting to come to the child. "They are my delight."[48] "Suffer them to come unto me."[49] First Communion at seven is not an imprudence. It's not a piously sentimental occasion. It's world-shaking.

Reading the lives of the child saints is apt to leave the parents of the average child properly depressed. St. Thérèse never refused

[48]Cf. Prov. 8:31.
[49]Cf. Matt. 19:14.

God anything after she was three. Blessed Imelda desired Christ in the Eucharist with such longing He brought it to her Himself, in secret. St. Tarcisius died at the hands of pagan soldiers rather than surrender the Eucharist he was carrying to the early Christians.

We look at our own children, who seem to be taking it all so calmly, and wonder how to stir up in them any of the awareness of these blessed ones. Unless God wills it, we never will. For some mysterious reason, it was His will that these small saints enjoy a conscious intimacy with Him in the Eucharist that sends our souls reeling. But although our own children may not receive the same privileges of grace, they have this in common with the child saints: Christ comes to them as wholly as He did to the saints. What the child saints experienced by divinely cultivated intuition, we must substitute for as best we can with teaching, with illumination, and with the feeding of their faith. And all the while there will be sufficient grace.

How to prepare a child to receive Christ in Holy Communion? There are a thousand ways for as many children. If there are frustrations that go with teaching catechism class, the most poignant of all must be having to teach children about First Communion en masse. This is a subject that demands long, intimate interludes, with time to ponder and weigh and imagine. Here's one of the times when a mother and a father will stop short and suddenly see what a tremendous thing it is to be a parent. A soul, whose creation waited upon them, is about to receive the Body of the Son of God, who has waited for this since all eternity.

"Just think, dear, since before the beginning of the world, God was thinking about you, and His Son was wanting to come to you in Holy Communion. He always knew what day it would be, what hour, what minute. He won't divide Himself into twenty bits of Jesus, so that the twenty in the First Communion class may receive a piece of Him. There's no such thing as a *piece* of Him. He will come to you as though there were no one there but you. Where the Holy Eucharist is, in each host, or even each piece of a Host, Jesus is wholly there. He's the same God who made the heavens and the earth and all things, and who is surrounded by the angels and the saints in Heaven. He's the same Jesus who was born in Bethlehem, and the same Jesus who died on the Cross."

"But Mother — why bread and wine?"

If we've talked to them about the meaning of sacrifice, about the reason for the Mass, this isn't hard to explain.

"Remember when we talked about the Mass, and I showed you the name Melchisedech in the missal? He was the priest-king of Salem, and Salem means "Peace." When Jesus offered bread and wine at the Last Supper, He was imitating this unique priest in the Old Testament who offered a sacrifice of bread and wine to thank God for Abram's victory. (Abraham was first called Abram; God changed his name.) Jesus is the divine High Priest, because He's God, and He offered Himself in sacrifice for our sins. And Jesus is the King of Peace. Remember when Pilate asked Him, 'Art thou a king?' Jesus said, 'Thou hast said it.'[50] And after the Resurrection, which proved He was God, when He first appeared to the Apostles, His greeting was 'Peace be to you.'[51] It wasn't an accident that Jesus offered the same things Melchisedech offered. He wanted to remind us that He's also Priest and King of Peace.

"And isn't it good that it *is* bread and wine, which are easy to get and easy to prepare on the altar? Suppose it were a lamb, or fruit? That would make it very complicated for priests to offer the divine Sacrifice.

[50]Cf. John 18:37.
[51]Luke 24:36.

"There's another thing about the bread and wine. Think of them first as wheat and grapes. Before they can be made into bread and wine, they must be wholly crushed. They suffer a kind of passion all their own in order to become bread and wine, the substances used in the Mass. Our Lord was wholly crushed on the Cross, so He could be the perfect sacrifice for our sins." Children love to know the meaning of the liturgical symbols on the altar and around the church. Understanding about the wheat and wine makes for a momentary meditation every time they see these symbols.

Furthermore, bread is called the staff of life. When men are poor and have nothing else to eat, they can exist on bread. Our Lord is the staff of our spiritual life. The Holy Eucharist is a divine bread with which we feed our souls.

"Give us this day our daily bread" doesn't mean just the bread on our tables; it asks God the Father also to let us receive His divine Son daily, if possible, in Holy Communion.

~

Emphasize the importance of the
soul's beauty over exterior beauty

There are temporal concerns as well as spiritual when it's time for First Communion. First is the effect of the costume, especially for the girls. White dress, white shoes, white socks, white *veil* — how to bear all this glamor and not succumb? Once a little girl confessed to me, after five minutes of dreamily surveying her veil in the mirror: "Mother, I think it's very pretty, and I think I look pretty in it. But I think maybe Jesus doesn't want me to think I look pretty. Maybe it's wrong, and that makes me feel kind of funny."

That sums up very well, I think, the struggle between pride and humility. And it's a real problem for girls, always. On First

How to Raise Good Catholic Children

Communion Day, you want to look as pretty as possible to please God. I don't think the solution to pride and vanity lies in telling comely little girls they're ugly. It isn't going to develop the right kind of humility (you couldn't properly call it humility), and it's apt to set up defensive attitudes that could cause really serious trouble. Part of perfect humility is to be able to admit possessing the talents and gifts God has given you, and take no personal credit for them. You must learn to wear them like garments God has bestowed, happily, gratefully, honestly. They're not essentials, but extras, attached to which are certain obligations of stewardship. Along with learning how to live with them, you must learn also to beware of the Devil, who loves to tamper with them.

"If you think you look nice in your veil, it would be wrong to pretend you don't. Jesus would prefer you to be honest. You can't fool Him anyway, and if He has given you a nice face and a pretty veil, you must thank Him. But the beauty of your soul is far more important, and that's what the Devil would like you to forget. He's forever trying to stir up trouble with the good gifts God has given you, so when he tempts you to think only of your face, turn your thoughts around to your soul, and remember that the prettiest face in the world is as nothing if the soul is not beautiful.

"All this lovely white is not meant to tempt you to be vain about how you look. It's a symbol of the purity and beauty of your soul. If you were to forget this, and forget that it is for Jesus that you dress nicely, then it would be better if you were dressed in rags."

I had an experience that leaves little girls — big ones, too — pondering beauty in a new light, and it's a nice story to tell around First Communion time. A long time ago, I became acquainted with a little nun at a retreat house, a lay sister whose work was making the beds, sweeping the floors, and setting the table. Each

Instill in your child a love for the Eucharist

year on retreat, I would see her, and we would nod and smile at each other, and usually at the end of the retreat, we had a few minutes to chat. Finally I asked her name.

"My name? Sister Felicitas. That means 'happiness.'"

"What a beautiful name, Sister, and especially good for you."

"Oh? Why?"

"Why, because you look so happy. Yours is a very happy face."

"Is it? I wouldn't know."

"What do you mean, you wouldn't know?"

She was embarrassed. Something had slipped out that she had not meant should slip out. "I haven't seen my face in fifteen years."

"Fifteen years! But, Sister, what about the mirrors in the bedrooms?"

"Oh? I just close my eyes tight when I walk past them."

She had no way of knowing that she was a radiant beauty: apple-cheeked, skin so smooth, and a freshness in her face that would turn most women green with envy. Her age was a mystery. Only her walk, her frame, and some of her ways hinted she was no longer young. All this without mirrors, without creams, without cosmetics. Beauty for her equaled convent soap and water and total preoccupation with God. If ever there was a walking sermon on the adage that beauty is from within, it was Sister Felicitas.

We are all dust, and children must know it, too. A pretty face, someday, is a pinch of dust. First Communion Day is an appropriate time to contrast the two kinds of beauty, physical and spiritual, and a good time to remember that our obligation is to raise young women who will be holy, not necessarily beautiful.

Why some children giggle and squirm even at their First Communion is hard to say, unless they haven't had enough preparation beforehand. Sisters do a magnificent job, but they still can't take each child aside and spend as much time as they would like with

235

him, explaining, helping with meditations. This is the parents' work. Reverent behavior even when all eyes are on him — even when someone next to him is taken with a fit of self-consciousness and has no outlet for it but giggles — will probably depend on how far a child has been helped to penetrate the beauty and mystery of this day. It would help, too, if most of the comments from loving family and friends — both before and after — had to do with what has happened rather than how pretty we all look.

~

Teach your child to make an act
of thanksgiving after Communion

We've said something about acts of thanksgiving after Communion in the chapter on the Mass. Unless a child is constantly reminded, even given the words to say until he's able to phrase his own thanksgivings, he can easily forget to make any thanksgiving. It takes time and patience to form the habit, to learn how to fight through the distractions and pay perfect attention to God. It isn't necessary that a child *feel* the grandeur of his union with Christ in the Eucharist. In all probability, he will feel more like looking around to see who else is receiving. But if he can learn to apply his will to making a thanksgiving, close his eyes or cover his face so that distractions are shut out, his thanksgiving has as great a value as if he were dissolved in sweetness. It's the action of the will that gives the value to prayer; it's too bad to wait until you're twenty or more, and have "discovered" prayer for the first time, to learn this. How much nicer to learn it at seven — and why not?

For emphasis, we repeat the three most important things for children to say in their thanksgiving: "Thank You for coming to me in Holy Communion. I love You. Please help me to love You more," phrased however each child would phrase them. Then we can remind him to remember Father, from whose hands he has received the Body of Christ, his family and friends, special intentions, the souls in Purgatory, and everyone in the world. The child who, at this age, wants to go on talking to Jesus is probably unusual (although they should all be encouraged to do this). The child who lifts his head to watch what's going on has at least said the necessary things before distractions set in. Grace will work on even the least of these things, like yeast in a dough, because they're pure now, and very innocent. We must not let them waste their innocence.

In our family, there's always a family feast following First Communion. Here, with the table beautiful in white linen and the best silver, with Granny's Delft china, with a lovely ceramic statue of our Lady and her Son as the centerpiece, the First Communion child is the honored guest. His gifts are at his plate, and a little bouquet of flowers, his baptismal candle is lighted, and after saying grace, before sitting down, the honored guest receives a kiss from everyone in the family. Every year the feasts of First Communions are kept, if not on the exact feast day, then on the parish First Communion day.

One more member of the family receiving Communion is a thrill all its own. At the breakfast afterward, if the preparation has been thorough and the emphasis where it belongs, a First Communicant will put what it all means in his own words. "Daddy has Jesus in him, and Mother has Jesus in her, and Granny has Jesus in her . . . and Jesus is in me!"

Jesus Christ, the Son of God, in *me* — is it not world-shaking?

Chapter 15

⁀

*Help your child to grow
spiritually in Confirmation*

As a Baptism or a baptismal feast is the best occasion for beginning instruction about Baptism, so Pentecost is the best time to begin instruction about Confirmation.

For a long time, we've made the mistake of thinking that little children aren't interested in Confirmation. They ought to be. They're interested in all other phases of growing up. "When I'm big, I'm going to be a policeman," they'll say. And the next day it's a fireman, then a truck driver, then a priest, and one of ours has decided to be a bishop. They're going to be brave and strong, do good things, help all the poor and the suffering, buy their mothers the most beautiful presents in the world, and help their daddies with their work. And no matter what else they're going to be, secretly they're sure (for all the outward reservations) that they'll be saints.

If you're going to be a saint, you need all the help you can get. Take the Apostles. They knew for certain they were destined for great things. Peter knew he was head of the Church. All of them together had been told by our Lord, "Go forth and teach all nations." Even so, after He ascended into Heaven, they stood on the hillside, lonely and afraid. And an angel came and said to them, "Men of Galilee, why do you stand looking up to Heaven?"[52]

---

[52] Acts 1:11.

⁐

The Holy Spirit helps your
child to mature in the Faith

It was a small uncertain group of people who went back to the Upper Room in Jerusalem. They were really afraid. Christ had made many enemies, and now He was gone. His enemies were *their* enemies. If they were to go out and try to convert people, they would certainly need help. But our Lord had promised them help. He was very tender with them at His discourse at the Last Supper, calling them "little children," and telling them that although He would leave them, "I will not leave you orphans."[53]

"I will ask the Father, and He will give you another Advocate to dwell with you forever . . . the Spirit of truth."[54] This Advocate was to be the Holy Spirit, who would comfort and strengthen them. When we remember that the Holy Spirit is God's love, so real that it's spoken of as another Person, we can understand why the Apostles looked forward to His coming with such longing.

But this is confusing. We have taught our children that with Baptism they become the dwelling place of the Holy Trinity. Theologians hold that when the Holy Spirit enters the soul at Baptism, the soul receives His virtues of faith, hope, and charity, and His gifts of wisdom, understanding, counsel, fortitude, knowledge, piety, and fear of the Lord. Then why do we need another sacrament to bring the Holy Spirit?

It isn't too hard to explain. There's a parallel between being born into the life of the flesh as an infant and growing up to be a man; and being born into divine life with Baptism, and growing up through Confirmation.

[53] John 13:33; 14:18.
[54] Cf. John 14:16, 17.

Help your child to grow spiritually in Confirmation

The little boy who says, "When I grow up, I'm going to be a policeman," knows he's not grown up yet. He's busy now learning about himself, how to feed himself, dress himself, tie his shoes, read his books, and write his name. One day, he says, he will be grown up and be a policeman, and then he will help other people. He will help children cross the street when school is out. He will help people shopping on Saturdays to get their cars about safely. He will walk the street at night and guard the homes of the community.

The difference between the baptized child and the confirmed child is somewhat the same. When he's baptized, he's born into the Mystical Body. According to our Lord, he's "born again of water and the Holy Spirit." And in the years following Baptism, he learns to know and love God, learns what sin is, and learns how to pray that he will save his soul. He learns about Christ in the Eucharist and receives Him often to help sanctify his soul. His world is still very small, even his spiritual world. It's all in terms of "me." From time to time, he reaches out and puts his arms around the world, gives it his help with prayer and sacrifice, with daily work and play offered to God. Essentially, however, he's learning the place of himself in relation to God.

⮎

*Show your child the difference
the Holy Spirit can make in his life*
Confirmation marks a child's spiritual growing up. With Confirmation, he's launched on the social aspect of his spiritual life, with which goes an even greater obligation to pursue his own sanctification. But self-sanctification is now dependent upon his relationship with all men. With Confirmation, he's equipped, by the strengthening in him of the gifts of the Holy Spirit, to look at

the world with new eyes, to desire its conquest for Christ with new love. He sees more clearly (if he's helped to see by his parents and teachers) what it means to be a member of the Mystical Body. Like a cell in his own body, he's a cell in the Body of Christ. Each cell is important, a part of a whole. Without it, the whole would be less whole. If one cell is sick (in sin), the whole is less well. Now he begins to see that it's up to him, as well as to the other members of the Body, to work for the total health of the Body; not only that — but to work for the further growth of the Body.

Now the time of merely learning what he must do to save his own soul has come to an end. He must use what he knows, think of it in terms of everyone in the world, and want with all his heart to bring others to the knowledge of Christ. It's exciting, becoming a "soldier of Christ." It's a role filled with unknown challenge, invitations to unknown bravery. The child needs much more strength than ever before to face the challenge, and the strength comes to him through the special anointing at the hands of his bishop in the sacrament of Confirmation.

There's an account in the Acts of the Apostles that tells of St. Peter and St. John, both bishops, confirming, in Samaria:

> On their arrival they prayed for them, that they might receive the Holy Spirit; for as yet He had not come upon any of them, but they had only been baptized in the Name of the Lord Jesus. Then they laid their hands on them, and they received the Holy Spirit.[55]

It's easy to understand what a difference this special coming of the Holy Spirit implies if we picture the Apostles before Pentecost. They had been baptized. They had even been ordained. Peter

[55] Cf. Acts 8:15-17.

was not only a bishop, but the first Pope. But they had not been confirmed. Seeing the difference between their fear and their zeal as a matter of Confirmation can be the beginning of not only a child's interest in Confirmation, but his *desire* for it.

Read from the Acts, it's a very exciting story, which tells of their nine days' prayer, the sound of the great wind, and the tongues of fire as a sign of the Holy Spirit. Suddenly, fear was gone. *Love* was with them. And their knowledge was multiplied miraculously. Not only were they eager to preach the word of Christ, but they knew many new languages in which to preach it.

St. Peter rushed out and there on the streets of Jerusalem preached with such enthusiasm that some thought he was drunk. When he was done, he had made three thousand converts.

Never before had they been so inebriated with their love, so fearless in their desire. They had loved Him before, but not like this. The night of His Passion, they fell asleep in the garden. Later all but one ran away. Peter lied that he did not know Him, even cursed that he should be thought His friend. Only one stood at the foot of the Cross. One of them would not believe that He had risen from the dead until he saw His wounds.

They were not more fearful than the rest of men, but it was a terrible bravery He demanded. They were the bravest men He could find. It was dangerous even to be His friend, and they had walked and lived with Him openly for three years. But what He asked of them in the end was the impossible. It was asking them to walk to certain death. They *wanted* to — but they were so afraid.

We're like that. We want to defend the Faith. We want to explain the doctrine. We want to go out and convert people and bring them to new happiness in Christ. But it takes such courage. We're used to being "tolerant," "not interfering," "respecting the opinions of others." All these things we know are good. Yet with our knowledge of Christ, the riches of grace, the joy of being a member of His Church, the certainty of salvation through perseverance in the Faith, we ought to see that even the opinions we "respect," if they are error, need to be replaced by truth.

If we see our children licking up poisonous fly spray, we're not so respectful of their opinions that we allow them to continue. If we see them eating nothing but their dessert and leaving their meat and vegetables, we take effective measures against this regimen. We want our children to be whole and healthy, wise and holy; so we give them all our love and help and knowledge and understanding. And we're obliged to feel the same way about the souls of our brothers in the world. We cannot want this enough, nor work for it enough, without the strength that comes with Confirmation.

Not all of this can be adapted at once for small children. It's hard for them to understand such things as their role in the Mystical Body of Christ when they're only five years old. But when the Church celebrates with such joy the Feast of Pentecost — which St. Augustine called the Nativity of the Holy Spirit — we can use this day every year, as well as the many days of the Pentecostal season, to prepare their hearts and minds and souls for Confirmation.

All children say, "I can't wait till I grow up." If we understand Confirmation and are on fire with gratitude for it, we can help them experience the same impatience in wanting the sacrament of spiritual growing up. Then, when the time has come to receive it, preparation is more than a sum of well-memorized catechism lessons. It's the climax of years of loving the story of the Apostles and understanding that with this sacrament, they also will be ready to be apostles for Christ.

Help your child to grow spiritually in Confirmation

⤺

Teach your child how to
use the gifts of the Holy Spirit

In what ways must they use this new strength? We can't know
how to use the gifts of the Holy Spirit if we don't understand them.
Somehow we must make this simple enough for children.

♦ *Fear of the Lord.* The first gift is fear of the Lord. There is a
phrase in the Act of Contrition that helps children to understand
this gift. "O my God, I am heartily sorry for having offended Thee,
because I dread the loss of Heaven and the pains of Hell, *but most
of all because I have offended Thee, my God, who art all good and de-
serving of all my love."*

Fear of the Lord is part of love of the Lord, because He is great
and good and created us, not because He needed us, but because
He *wanted* us. There's a difference between being good for the love
of God, and being good because we're afraid of Hell. When we
know we possess such a gift as this, we can pray harder for the grace
to love God more, and to love goodness for the sake of pleasing
Him. As we grow in the use of this gift, we understand that fear
means awe and wonder at His omnipotence, not just terror at the
thought of His judgments.

♦ *Piety.* Piety also has to do with loving God. Often people who
are "pious" are so sour about it that they give children an active
distaste for any and all piety, and children are quick to single them
out and label them as pious frauds. One of the definitions of *piety,*
much more to the point, is "loyal devotion." The gift of piety helps
us to be loyal and devoted to the three Persons of the Blessed Trinity, to the Mother of God, to the saints, to our guardian angel, to
the other angels, to the souls in Purgatory, to our parents, relatives,
and friends, to our enemies (remembering their worth in the eyes

of God), to our Church and country, Pope and President, and so on. We must have a sense of reverence about all the things God made, about the blessings He has given us. The gift of piety has a special bearing on how we obey our parents. St. Francis of Assisi is an example of one who overflowed with the gift of piety, having such love for all God's creatures, even His animals, that he called them his brothers and sisters.

• *Fortitude*. Then there's the gift of fortitude. Children are afraid of many things: pain, embarrassment, being lost, and much more. To tell them they must practice fortitude may only make them secretly afraid that they're cowards. Talk is cheap. Suppose that down deep inside, you're afraid you may lie rather than take a punishment, run away rather than defend your brother, keep silent when your friend is called a derogatory name. What good does it do to have the gift of fortitude if it doesn't change you into a daring-do? But fortitude does not guarantee courage tailor-made. It reminds us that Jesus said, "Without me you can do nothing."[56] Then it explains, "But with me, you can do all things." Fortitude teaches us to ask for the grace to do the things that need doing, little things as well as big. If we use this gift in all the challenges every day, we'll be ready when God asks heroic things of us later on.

• *Knowledge*. The gift of knowledge is easily misunderstood. It might seem to apply to how well a child knows his geography, his arithmetic, his spelling, and his history. No parent would permit a child to think these things don't matter. But it matters more that we do God's will. The gift of knowledge refers to learning the things we must learn in order to do God's will. It helps us to discover how we are to serve Him on this earth. For instance, a boy

[56]John 15:5.

Help your child to grow spiritually in Confirmation

who likes science and studies well will learn much about the physical universe. If he is to be an intelligent scientist, he must know that God is the Creator of the universe and that it's subject to Him. Scientists are morally bound to use their knowledge of the universe to do God's will.

• *Counsel.* The gift of counsel "warns of the deceits of the Devil and the dangers to salvation." One of the neatest deceits of the Devil is to point out that we all "have our rights." Within the law, we may insist on them, which is true. The law defines what is right and wrong. But sticking stubbornly to the letter of the law rarely makes saints of people. Counsel is the gift that helps us to know what course of action is more perfect, and to follow it. For instance, the Church teaches that to receive the sacraments of Penance and Holy Eucharist once a year, between the first Sunday of Lent and Trinity Sunday, satisfies the obligation for the year. But it's certainly the least we can do, and sticking to the letter of this law is not going to help us grow in perfection.

Children respond to the gift of counsel when they take their many small voluntary steps toward perfection. The child who goes without dessert (when it has been portioned out equally among himself and his brothers) because the baby has spilled his and will not be comforted unless he has more, is doing more than is asked of him. He's making an unnecessary self-sacrifice out of love for his baby brother; in this, he responds to the gift of counsel.

• *Understanding.* The gift of understanding helps us to know more clearly the mysteries of the Faith. The mystery of the Eucharist is an example. It's sufficient if a child knows that bread and wine, consecrated, look the same, but are truly the Body and Blood of Christ. But we can help him understand some of its mystery by pointing out how the crushed wheat and grapes that make the bread and wine are symbols of the crushing Passion of Christ, in order that He may become the sacrificial Victim. The symbolism of the water used at Baptism, the sacrament that washes the soul free of sin, is another aid to understanding more clearly this mystery of the Faith.

• *Wisdom.* Lastly, the gift of wisdom. "Fear of the Lord is the beginning of wisdom."[57] This gift is like all the others together, working in us as long as we're in the state of grace. The gift of wisdom accounts for the soul's instinctive hunger for God. It's truly a gift and has nothing to do with schooling or books or diplomas. Even the smallest child, baptized, filled with grace and shining faith, loving God and wanting to be a saint, is a witness of the gift of wisdom. Many of the child saints couldn't read or write, but they had the gift of wisdom. With it, they were illuminated by grace, they understood and believed truths that the most learned sages have sometimes resisted. It should be our greatest comfort as parents, seeing so many differences in our children, to realize that each one possesses this gift and may use it in his own way to give honor and glory to God. Quick children, slow children, alert, clumsy, talented, plodding, whole, deformed — whatever our children are — they all receive from the Holy Spirit the gift of wisdom. There's no one who cannot use it, only those who *will* not.

⮌

Explain the symbolism of the Confirmation rite

The bishop is the usual minister of Confirmation, although, under special circumstances, certain priests may also confirm. We should take particular pains to acquaint our children with their

---

[57]Ps. 110:10 (RSV = Ps. 111:10).

bishop, if not in person, at least with his picture in the newspaper, and to teach them to pray for him every day. Our relationship to our bishop is that of child to father, and the bishop at the head of his diocese, with the people under him, is a miniature of the Mystical Body.

All these things can well be learned before it's time for Confirmation. On the Feast of Pentecost, a lovely family dinner at a table decorated with red ribbons in honor of the Holy Spirit and a cake with tiny sugar doves, a lighted candle to remind us of the tongues of fire, will help the children enjoy the lesson of Pentecost and respond to the graces of the feast.

There's another common occasion for recalling Pentecost and Confirmation: the Third Glorious Mystery of the Rosary. Our Peter is only five, but when it's his turn to lead a decade, he always asks for this one. "My best one," he calls it. He explains that the Apostles were afraid until the coming of the tongues of fire; then they were brave and full of the Holy Spirit, and they went out to do Christ's work.

"What first feast was it, Peter?"

"Pentecost."

"And like what sacrament?"

"Confirmation."

We will not see tongues of fire, nor hear the sound of a great wind, but when the bishop anoints our children with the holy chrism and strikes them lightly on the cheek as a token of persecutions to which they may be exposed for the Faith, we will know that the time of their *real* growing up has begun.

Chapter 16

⁓

Celebrate the liturgical year

Everyone is liturgical. You don't believe it? Then look up the definition of *liturgy* in the dictionary. After some revelations about liturgy and the Christian Church, there comes a definition that calls *liturgy* "a rite or body of rites for public worship." As Americans, we certainly spend plenty of time publicly worshiping at one shrine or another. Some of it is good, some of it is confused, and some of it is silly.

For instance, it's good to conduct traditional patriotic rites on national holidays, recalling the birthdays of great presidents, celebrating our independence, honoring the memory of our war dead. On Lincoln's Birthday, statesmen read the Gettysburg Address, Republicans hold Lincoln Day dinners, and children in school cut out pictures of log cabins. On Washington's Birthday, ceremonies are held at Mount Vernon, schoolchildren cut out hatchets, and mothers bake cherry pies. On the Fourth of July in New England, everyone used to eat salmon and new peas. Now on the Fourth of July, everywhere, people shoot off firecrackers (where they're legal), eat hot dogs, and drink beer at picnics. On Memorial Day we visit cemeteries; on Labor Day we have parades. On Thanksgiving Day we remember our forefathers (or the forefathers of some of us), give thanks for our blessings, and eat turkey and cranberry sauce.

How to Raise Good Catholic Children

There are the popular confusions of religious feasts. There's Christmas in terms of shopping, Santa Claus, trees, and presents. There's Easter in terms of new hats, bunnies, Easter eggs, and candy. On Halloween there's trick-or-treat, and New Year's Eve is the time for too much drinking. In the lowest bracket are the commercial rites in the name of the gods of industry. Queens are thick as flies all over the country, with coronations and attendants and balls and free samples to the people: cotton queens, orange queens, popcorn queens, kiddie queens, snow queens, freckle queens, beauty queens. In the name of patriotism, or a confused form of Christianity, or out-and-out materialism, we celebrate public rites with gusto all through the year.

The Liturgy of the Church has one thing in common with all this: it's year-round. It has a thousand points of difference. The biggest difference of all between celebrating for the sake of celebration and celebrating in the name of Christ is the difference between mere commemorative rites and the rites of divine life. They celebrate the *now* of Christ's life as He lives in His Church today. They're the public worship of Christ, the Head of the Mystical Body, together with His members, addressing God the Father in praise, in expiation, in thanksgiving.

⮜

Advent

Living the Liturgy gives a Christian his focus. Because it is life in terms of grace, the end of each year should find him a little more holy. He lives with Christ in the Church Militant, celebrating the same mysteries with the Church Triumphant. The Liturgy is a bridge between earth and Heaven.

Holy Mother Church is very wise. She knows us better than we know ourselves. For this reason, she designs her year with unerring instinct. She begins rather than ends with Advent and Christmas, for life makes no sense except in the view of eternity — and the key to eternity for us is the Redemption. Advent is a four-week condensation of the four thousand years mankind waited for the Redemption. It's our time to reflect on the meaning of Christ's coming, to long for it, to purify ourselves so that we'll be ready. It's a penitential season, with penance done with joy.

The lighting of the Advent wreath, the family praying together nightly in its presence, the weekly ritual of candle-lighting to remind us of His coming (He who is the Light of the World) — these rites are sermons in themselves. Since on Christmas He will be a birthday Child, He must have birthday presents; and the family chooses mortifications to make beautiful gifts for Him.

The feast of St. Nicholas is December 6, the time for learning about Santa Claus. No rival to Christ, this saint, but one of the elect waiting in Heaven as we do on earth for the glory of His birthday to break over the world. Fun with St. Nicholas, stockings filled with cookies for children who are good, is a reminder of the reason we give and receive gifts. He gave out of his love for Christ and His little ones, out of gratitude to God, who gave Christ to him.

The feast of St. Lucy, on December 13, is the day for a feast of lights, for thinking of the Child who is Light, for planting the Christmas wheat. Sprouted, soft green by Christmas, it reminds us of our daily bread, the bread of life on our altars, the *end* of the story that has its beginning at Christmas. All through the weeks of Advent, the harvest of mortifications increases, counted with little beans in tiny boxes, or with straws in an empty crèche. The children watch self-denial fill the gift box, make a soft bed in the crèche; every day passed means one day closer to His birthday.

Christmas Day the Beloved is here, tiny, helpless, newborn. The crèche is His throne, and we are like shepherds, invited to adore. Gifts are given and received because we are the pampered children of God to whom He gives the gift of His Infant Son. Following Christmas come the days when we greet and honor witnesses to His glory: St. Stephen, St. John the Evangelist, and the Holy Innocents. Then comes New Year's. Now the Church reminds us to look back at the sins of the past, and forward with holy hope to the opportunities of the future, and calls us to the altar to pledge our good intentions at the Mass that celebrates His Circumcision, the day He received His beautiful name.

Epiphany . . . and the children are Magi, crowned and bearing their gifts. They journey to Bethlehem, meeting Herod and his scribes on the way, taking counsel from the angel, going back by another route. Laughter in the hall while Herod grumbles. Then the scene is over, and the family sits before the fire and eats Crown Cake in honor of Christ's manifestation to men.

February is the Feast of the Purification, Candlemas, the day for the blessing of candles, for recalling Mary's obedience to the law, the ransoming of the Christ Child in the temple. Dinner this night is bright with candles; on the cake are two little doves. Afterward the candles are carefully put away for sick calls, for baptismal rites, and for use during family ceremonies and blessings.

⁀

Lent and Easter

During Lent, unlike Advent, penance will be done in sorrow. Ash Wednesday begins with a terrible blow to our pride: "Thou art dust, and unto dust thou shalt return." The lesson of the Ash Wednesday Mass bids us to sanctify a fast, that all must observe the season. The young, the old, the bridegroom and the bride, even the babes at the breast — whether we're big or little, the spirit of Lent is for all because all are in need of Redemption. In the

Gospel, Christ tells us to fast and pray and to lay up our treasures in Heaven. "For where thy treasure is, there is thy heart also."[58]

Once again the family bends to mortification. Purple beans count out each act of death to self, signs of the treasures stored in Heaven. Nightly we say the Stations of the Cross, and follow the mind of the Church with the daily readings and Gospels. All over the house, it's Lent. The Crucifix alone is on the mantel; purple shrouds are dyed and await Passion Sunday, when they cover the statues and pictures. Even the baking speaks of the Cross, with symbols of the Passion cut in the piecrusts, with crosses of seeds marking the bread.

Laetare Sunday is a feast of joy, for the end, we know, will be a triumph. Rose color on the altar, rose vestments on the priest, flowers and feasting at home, and the following Sunday we plunge deep into meditation of His Passion. Now is the time for final perseverance. Unlike Advent, this penitential season takes us deeper and deeper into sorrow.

Palm Sunday, with the raising of Lazarus, He has proved that He's the Divine King. Greeting Him at Mass with hosannas and joy, we're puzzled: why this triumph, when we have forebodings of death? Where is the Cross that was prophesied? The words are hardly spoken when betrayal comes. All through Holy Week the Gospel tells His suffering. We are there. We are to blame.

Holy Thursday is the Paschal Supper, a feast in honor of the Holy Eucharist. The story of Exodus is read at the table to explain the meaning of the Paschal Lamb. Before the end of the meal, we read the Gospel about the Last Supper; after that we wash the children's feet. Holy Thursday is all tenderness and love, with the Master acting as servant. "If, then, I, being your Lord and Master,

[58]Matt. 6:21.

have washed your feet, you also ought to wash one another's feet. For I have given you an example, that as I have done to you, so you do also."[59]

On Good Friday we try to be silent. There are no words of our own that make any sense. We betrayed Him. We abandoned Him. We lied and wept and ran away. And still He can love us this way.

Holy Saturday we wait. Running from morning until night, we wait. In the morning, we set the Easter bread, sweep the hearth, lay the wood for the new fire. Eggs are decorated with the symbols of the Redemption, with the symbols of the children's patron saints. The paschal candle is ready, studded with five tiny cloves like the nails of wax and incense that stud the candle in the church. The purple beans are divided, and, after the children are in bed, wrapped with an Easter gift — a symbol of the treasure stored in Heaven. But first, the story of Easter morning with Mary Magdalene weeping in the garden. And then we understand: He appeared to her first because she was the great sinner. We are with that Mary. We are other Marys. He comes to us as He did to her because He did it for sinners.

Since we live in a parish where there's no Easter vigil, we celebrate a vigil at home. Reading from the missal, we recall the blessing of Easter water. We bless the hearth and read the blessing of the fire. We read the blessing of the paschal candle and light it from the new fire on the hearth. And we're silent for a while, and shiver at the thought of the morning.

Easter morning the children rush downstairs, light the paschal candle, that symbol of Christ with us, and sing a great Alleluia. Off to Mass, bursting with joy like the newly baptized, and home to

[59]John 13:14-15.

the Easter table. Eggs must be hunted; gifts must be unwrapped. This is the day the Lord has made!
"I arose and am still with Thee. Alleluia!"
All through the week it is Alleluia. With grace at meals, after prayers, in all our hearts. The story of Jonah is read. "I give you no sign but the sign of Jonah."[60] The paschal candle burns at family meals. The graces of the season are rich and beautiful, and food and rest and play and joy are sweeter for six weeks of fasting.

Forty days fly by. The stories of His appearances are full of mystery and glory. Seeing bread at table recalls the supper at Emmaus. A family breakfast outdoors on a spring morning recalls the picnic He made on the beach. At Mass, the Elevation recalls Thomas doubting, then adoring: "My Lord and my God." Everything that grows, everything that becomes green is a witness to the triumph of the Resurrection.

Then, at last, comes the Ascension. Human nature, glorified, ascends into Heaven, and we rejoice. But it isn't hard to understand the Apostles and their sadness. "Men of Galilee, why do you stand . . . ?" The paschal candle is out. His visible presence is gone. And for nine days we pray to the Holy Spirit, begging that we may be worthy to take on the responsibilities that come with growing up.

Pentecost Sunday is our birthday. The birthday of the infant Church. And we, with Him, are the Church. No mere historical event, Pentecost, happening one day in time. God exists out of time. The Spirit descends even now. We're in Christ, too. The graces that came to the Apostles come to us. Now we're ready to go forth and teach all nations. Love is with us always; we need never be afraid again.

[60]Cf. Matt. 12:39.

How to Raise Good Catholic Children

⌒

*Incorporate blessings and
sacramentals into your family's life*

Then the long summer, the feasts of the saints. We share life with them in His Body. We are fledglings, learning to fly. They're like mother birds, coaxing, cajoling, promising their help. "I was once little like you. Don't be afraid. Lean on faith — and try."

August . . . and with the feast of the Assumption, we have the blessing of herbs and flowers. All year long we've had blessings: the blessing of throats on St. Blaise's day; the blessing of the land and the sprouting seed on Rogation Days before the Ascension; blessing before childbirth for expectant mothers; blessing after childbirth for those who have brought forth new life; blessing of cars and of houses; blessing of typewriters; blessing of foods at Easter, of Christmas trees at Christmas. Like radiances shining out from the sacraments are these sacramentals and the blessings. We've learned to love the use of blessed candles. We've learned to love the use of holy water. We've learned to give the most beautiful blessing of all, the blessing of our own children.

Fall comes, and the earth grows brown and bare. Wise in her motherhood, the Church reminds us of death. The vigil of All Saints is Halloween, and we celebrate it as a vigil, with a party that grows out of ancient Christian customs, with begging at the door and repaying soul cakes with prayers. The next day is the great day, the feast of All Saints, with a procession to the dinner table in honor of our special saints, stories told of their triumphs, charades acted out, and, best of all, the Litany of the Saints that night. All through November we pray for the dead, the soon-to-be-saints we would hasten on to their glory. Not just one day, or one speech, or two minutes of silence, but thirty days of prayers, Masses, and intentions as we go about our work. With this, the year comes to its end.

≈

Help your child to grow holier
through liturgical celebration

The liturgical year is a cycle unfolding from life to death to glory. Observing it year after year, joining Christ with our love, our wills, and our understanding, we live the union of member to Body, no longer branches of the vine that are dead. We are living, bearing fruit — or at least aspiring to. How can one be any closer to Christ?

Perhaps it sounds easy, this living the liturgical year. Or perhaps it sounds impossible. It's neither. But it's slow. It will come to us, and we will grow in it only as fast as the Spirit allows. It's not just a matter of pasting over our lives with liturgical stickers. Its outward forms — its Advent wreaths and crèches and Christmas bread, its candles and blessings, its penitential purple and ashes and palms, its stories and customs and celebrations — are nothing if interiorly we're not on fire with its spirit. It's the reality of Christ's life, and it cannot be separated from the struggle to grow Christlike.

It's the same old struggle to love, be kind, grow in patience, work well and play well, to please God in everything we do. But it's supported now by the graces loosed every day by the prayer of the Church. That's the big difference. Living liturgically, we're really united to Him, praying the prayer of His Church. Raising children liturgically, we're using all the treasure at our command.

We asked the children, "How do you feel about being Catholics?" They answered, "Oh, being Catholics is fun! You have feasts, and saints, and stories, and things to do — and when you go to Mass and Father holds up our Lord, you say, 'I love You!' "

Chapter 17

*Show your child
the dignity of work*

A great many people seem to think that work is a curse. If they know enough to offer it up, this makes it a prayer, but it makes a better prayer if they know it isn't a curse in the first place.

When God the Father made Adam, He put him in the Garden of Paradise "to dress it and to keep it."[61] It wasn't until after Original Sin that He said, "Cursed is the earth in thy work."[62] Even then He didn't curse *work*. He was referring to the earth, whose harmony had been spoiled.

Where formerly Adam could plant seeds and expect them to grow and bear fruit without ever poking a hoe at them, now he was going to have trouble. Stones that were meant (I suppose) to lie about and give glory to God, were going to sneak down into the soil and break his plow. Plants that had kept to their own, raising their young from seed and lifting their heads in praise, were going to scatter their seed in his wheat and corn and potatoes, and Adam would have to pull them out. His work could once have been pure joy. It was now going to involve a struggle.

There's nothing very new about this. Many a work-weary parent has announced plaintively to his children, "Just wait till you

[61] Gen. 2:15.
[62] Gen. 3:17.

grow up and have to work for a living. Then you'll find out money doesn't grow on trees!"

Money doesn't grow on trees, and people have to work for it, but it's a mistake to think money is the only end of work. Even men who get past the point of needing money continue to need work. They retire at sixty-five, and at sixty-five and a half, they discover that they can't bear to be retired. There's a very good reason.

We are the children of God. Our Father is a creator and worker, and we "take after our Father." He made us the finest of all His visible creation, but a little less than the angels; He gave us the universe and made us lords over it. His work continues in the continuing miracle of life in all things, and we are the custodians on earth of all its life and the abundance of its treasures. With our own work in imitation of our Father, we make things, do things, grow things, create things, always with the things He has given. This is the dignity of work. This is why work is holy. This is why, when we do it as well as we can and with the right intention, work gives great glory to God.

For me to presume to say anything new about work would be wild. But for mothers and fathers raising young, who fluctuate so rapidly between periods of liking and disliking work, it's helpful to return and consider some of the fundamentals with an eye to adapting them for children.

$\approx$

The home is the training ground for life

The home is a world in miniature, a mystical body with the father as the head, the mother as the heart, and the children as the members. As every member in the physical body, each muscle and nerve and cell, contributes to the perfect functioning of the body, so every member of a family is needed for the perfect functioning of the family. The father is its support and protector, the mother is its center of order and fruitfulness, the children share in their own way in the work and the joy of both, and the whole has as its primary end the training of souls whose destiny is Heaven. Out of the family will come responsible — or irresponsible — men and women who will form — or malform — society, and society belongs to Christ. He bought it with His Blood on the Cross.

Our ultimate work in the world is merely an extension of this training in work in the home, and no matter what specific work we do, its end is first of all Heaven. Whether we're mothers or nuns or nurses or workers in the fields; whether we're fathers or priests or truck drivers or policemen directing traffic, when we do our work with the right purpose for its end, we're working with Christ for the salvation of men. And always we begin it at home.

For very little children, work is play. It's an imitation of something grown-ups do, and it's the beginning of learning. Stephen is three and a half and is quite a hand at wiping the dishes — also at dragging dish towels all over the floor. This is very trying, and the pile of dish towels to be thrown in the wash mounts rapidly when Stephen is "helping." But to rebuff him constantly (once in a while, when speed is of the essence, he must be sweetly but firmly removed) is to discourage an instinctive desire to serve, and he must not only be allowed to serve, but *encouraged* to serve.

Christ gave us the example when He washed the feet of His Apostles, doing as a servant would do, then bidding them to follow His example. When a child is discouraged too often in his attempts to serve, the desire can easily wither away until his whole impression of the world is that it's a place where other people serve him, and his role is that of the served. Mothers are quite right when they state that little ones can be more hindrance than help;

yet if home is to be a training ground for life, we're going to have to sacrifice a certain amount of efficiency and begin the training. There are too many victims of overefficient mothers, roaming around knowing how to do nothing, to argue much with this.

～

Motivate your child to help with work

It would be nice if the "work is play" stage lasted longer than it does. Children soon discover, however, that the wary in this world shy away from work, and now begins the real struggle. Little girls who loved trying to make their beds, to run the vacuum or wash the dishes, discover that these are the last things they want to do. Then we can help them by emphasizing that work is prayer. This is the highest motive for work, and the best way to use it; and while it's quite likely that we'll have to remind them daily, it will help considerably, especially if we also remind them to pray for the grace to do their work well. Even so, we must not neglect to fuel this not-so-roaring fire for work with common courtesy and much gratitude.

It's easy for harassed parents (I should know) to take refuge in complaints during these times. "I can't do it all myself. You helped get it messy; now you help clean it up." And if we're convincing enough, or maybe just big enough and loud enough, we can get them to do what we want. But it will be reluctant help, probably accompanied by the private observation that Mother is, indeed, a stinker, and it will hardly make reverent prayer.

Such simple things make a difference! If the emphasis is moved from "You do it," to "I will be so grateful if you will," it's much easier; and no one can resist the glow that comes with being thanked. Sometimes we get the idea that thanks are not necessary when children have done something they were supposed to do. If we

Show your child the dignity of work

always thank them, and add to our thanks a reminder that God is praised by work well done, little by little (but it adds up) they learn to associate work with praise and prayer. Then one day it isn't so necessary to them to be thanked. So many times people contribute their services or their work and ask nothing in return except human appreciation, only to find that even that is not forthcoming. But if we have a right purpose in our work, knowing it can praise, be prayer, be the will of God for us at a particular moment, we can learn not to fret for lack of appreciation.

≈)

Show your child how his work
can help Christ carry the Cross

This whole work affair would be much easier if children were naturally tidy. But they aren't. Life is too full, they're too busy tasting new experiences, to bother being tidy.

They enjoy tidiness, but not the making of it; so it's a lesson learned only through constant repetition. It's good to point out the effect of tidiness on the whole family. For a while, the carefree life is delicious. Away with work — today we're free! But when things reach a state where nothing can be found in its right place and there isn't a chair left to sit on, tempers begin to fly, and peace is out the window. Then it's time to get things in order before we fly at each other's throats. Children are not so easily disturbed by untidiness as are adults, but they respond to it by becoming sloppier, more careless, and eventually more quarrelsome. They can learn that disorder is not only unattractive, but sours the family disposition, and that the spirit does respond when things are put in order.

"I don't believe it," one of the boys said when I told him that cleaning up the chaos in his room would make him feel better. Later he came down and said, "Gee, you were right." Another time he helped to tidy a sick child's room "because she'll feel better if her room is tidy." These little lessons in order as a symbol of peace and well-being will help them in maturity when they must recognize really grave ills in terms of spiritual disorder.

But, of course, the whole idea can be abused when tidiness becomes an end in itself. Mothers of many children are rarely, if ever, able to achieve a very lasting order in their houses while their children are young. Would that their neighbors were not quite so critical of the confusion that must be in a house where a mother knows that love comes first, and then order. Without the love, order is a tyrant that's quite as able to destroy the family disposition as the loving struggle to achieve order can warm it.

Even when adults understand that work is prayer, obedience to duty is beautiful, and all of it service to God, we're still loath to do the things we like the least. These are the moments and hours of work that bear a resemblance to the Cross. There are other crosses, like suffering, betrayal, death, loneliness; but with work, it's the fatigue, the pain, and even in tasks we love (such as caring for the sick, or for babies) there are moments of revulsion. Putting off such tasks can destroy one's whole peace of mind and ruin the beauty of an entire day. Done, the whole spirit sings. Children can be *made* to perform the tasks that are most hateful to them as a matter of obedience, but we can help them make strides in obedience (without even mentioning it) if we show them how to use such work as a cross. Simon of Cyrene, carrying Christ's Cross with Him, is a great challenge to children and helps them to see how doing what is distasteful can really be carrying a cross. Especially during Lent and Advent, these lessons in work and the Cross can be put to good use.

"It feels so good," John has said after finally getting out in the wind and cold to water the goats. "Now doing everything else is like nothing." Nothing but the Cross will justify watering the goats to John.

Our teaching about the really difficult jobs will bear only as much weight as our own example, however, and my reminder about using the hateful work as a cross, doing it first instead of last, is so much prattle if the children see all the time that I am postponing a smelly washing. So honesty with our own weaknesses will help us be patient and understanding if we wish to correct the same weaknesses in our children.

What all this seems to imply, and smugly, too, is that once on the track of work-is-prayer, children will hold the vision forever. Ha! I only wish that were true. The day comes when they say they don't feel that work is prayer at all. It doesn't mean that all the teaching has gone with the wind. It isn't really lost, but as they approach adolescence, these and many of the other lessons of early childhood are apt to be crowded out of the forefront of their minds by all the things that are new and different. What's important is that we've put it there. At this point, we have to work carefully and without seeming to press them to discover where these ideas have been filed. We have to reapply them constantly, usually in a far more mature manner than we've dreamed, and we have to be careful to transform parental pressure (even when it's done nicely, it's still pressure) into more of a mutual-assistance pact. If children continue to lag and mope and groan, or try to duck out from under, it's time for them to learn through more exacting, but prudent, discipline.

⁓

Teach your child to respect work
For instance, we know a girl who would not wear aprons, although it was lovely to have her closet full of clean clothes. She

was also quite willing to admit that clean clothes were equal parts of washing, ironing, and Mother. Reminding made no difference, however, and she continued to forget to wear aprons. Clean clothes never really registered in terms of someone else's work.

Finally it was agreed that if she did not wear aprons, she would wash and iron the soiled dresses herself. So came the day when there was nothing to wear.

"Your dresses are all out in the laundry, dear, waiting to be washed."

"But . . ."

"No buts about it, my darling. We agreed that you would do them yourself if you didn't wear aprons."

It was a long and weary session of washing, hanging, gathering, dampening, and ironing a full line of clothes. But oh, the respect for the work. Now it's socks washed at night, blouses ironed, aprons over skirts (or pay for the cleaning). It's a great lesson to learn before twelve: *work does not do itself.* All our comforts are the result of someone's work. We must learn to respect it, if not the easy way, then the hard.

The thing that's so deadly about much of daily work is the repetition. Children continually pull against this goad, as do their parents. We can help them appreciate the necessity of it if we point out its parallel in the spiritual life. We labor day after day at the same faults (work of another order) and find, after meditating thoroughly on "forgive us our trespasses" that the next day we must battle the same old inclination to bear a grudge. It's the constant picking up where we left off and doing all over again that finally makes for accomplishment. Unless we maintain at least the status quo, we're losing ground. Unless we labor at the venial sins, we're one day going to be so cluttered with them that we won't resist the mortal. So this constant reminding of the importance of repeated daily tasks, and being firm about it, is part of the forming of a child's character. Just as conquering little weaknesses makes us stronger and more able to go on to be giants for God, so forming the habit of doing readily and well the small daily tasks, we're ready to go on to more stimulating challenges.

A far better way than bribery to get a child to do what must be done is to allow him to do more mature work when it's done. Monica has a real talent for cooking and will hurry with her room if she's to be allowed to bake a cake or a batch of cookies. Jamie fairly flew to collect the trash recently because he had been promised a lesson in attaching a plug to the end of an electrical cord. These are real rewards, not just because they're novelties, but because they push the horizon back a step further and give a child a taste of more mature accomplishment, a sense of growing up.

One of the most difficult disciplines of work is respect for tools. This is the despair of all parents. More fathers have come close to dementia because of lost hammers and screwdrivers. More mothers have cracked up for the day at the sight of a sink full of cake-baking paraphernalia. The only cures for these lapses are the painful ones. No more building jalopies. No more baking of cakes. Or no dinner until the tools are found, the pots and pans washed and put away. Or, "You must buy a screwdriver to replace the one you lost." There's nothing new about this; the only trouble is we don't hold firm. If all parents adhered to this discipline with their young, this sort of carelessness would probably disappear off the face of the earth.

❧

Discourage greed in your child

I heard a mother say, "I never allow other people to take advantage of my child. Send *him* on *their* errands!" This is the beginning of "let George do it." Children should be encouraged to do work for others, and not just for pay. We are our brothers' keepers. How else are children to discover what it is to serve Christ in their neighbor? When they're little, they don't even want to be paid. They like to do things for people because it gives them a feeling of usefulness. Pay for such tasks should be primarily satisfaction, perhaps a piece of cake and a glass of milk. Maybe, on rare occasions, a very small amount of money. Too many youngsters overpaid for work in the years of elementary school emerge from high school and face the world with one idea only about work: "How much am I going to get?" There's time enough to earn money, and there are jobs for the high school years that involve real work and a just wage for it. But spoiling a child's opportunity to experience the real satisfaction of working for love of neighbor is doing him a grave injustice, and it's rarely undone.

Overpaid, he will not work well, and he will work only until he has what he set out to get — not until a job is finished. He's a clock watcher in the making, and he will so overrate his worth as a workman that he will never be satisfied to do anything for a just wage. It won't be entirely his fault. Parents of children who work for their neighbors should make it clear they don't want them overpaid. Character training, learning to respect a job for its challenge, is far more valuable than a little extra money.

Paid baby-sitting is another custom that has made great inroads on the doctrine of neighborly charity. Responsible baby-sitters deserve just wages, and there are many who have no other way of earning money that's badly needed. But in the rush to grow up and join the ranks of the wage earners, many young girls are being deprived of their opportunity to serve with love, of even the idea that there are deep rewards in service for love. Mothers are now so frantic for baby-sitters, at whatever wages, that they're on the defensive. It's no longer a privilege to sit with a neighbor's baby; it's an act of condescension, and if — as has happened from time to time in our town — local industries slow down and family wages are reduced, mothers and fathers who are vitally needed members of a PTA or a church society cannot afford to pay baby-sitters and so drop out of organizations in which their talents are needed for the common good.

A better way of breaking in potential baby-sitters (when mothers are timid about accepting service for no pay) is baby-sitting for barter. I have paid baby-sitters with coffee cake, with homemade bread, with drawings, and with baby-sitting myself. (Learn how to make homemade bread: all baby-sitters are dead ducks within sniffing distance of homemade bread.) We have two baby-sitters extraordinaire whom we love with all our hearts, worth every nickel of their pay (and when you baby-sit with seven children, you deserve your pay). They endeared themselves to us for all time this past Christmas. One said, "I'm not going to take any money from my friends for sitting anymore. I get a wage, and I don't need their money, and they have families and more expenses than I." Another gave us a Christmas box with a fat bow and inside a year's baby-sittings "for free." There *is* joy in serving, but only those who try it find out.

⥲

Help your child to find joy in serving God and family
Allowances, when a family can afford them, raise another question. Should children be paid for the week's work, or should they receive it in any case? Our feeling about this is that allowances are, in part, a sign of appreciation for cooperating with the work of the entire family. They're also a token share of the family wealth, when there's any wealth to share.

But there are certain restrictions as to how they may be spent, what portion should go into the Sunday offering at Mass, and so on. Obligations incurred through carelessness, such as the lost screwdriver or a broken window that resulted from playing ball in the house, must be paid for out of allowance money. Children are encouraged to share their allowances with the poor, sending some off to the missions or to some particular family that we know is in need. Such things as second-hand wheels needed for homemade jalopies, material and pattern for a skirt, seeds for planting one's special stand of corn, are bought with allowance money. And, of course, there are weeks when things are very tight, and there's no money for allowances at all; then everyone goes without.

Then there's the problem of the child nearby who doesn't have to do any work. "Why doesn't she, and why do I?" This isn't always easy to handle. In the face of a living example of someone who's quite happy without having to do any work, all the high-minded theory seems to break down. The value of training in work, the joy of service, the serving of God are attractive ideas until someone else is waiting outside to play while you still have to wipe the dishes and feed the baby. But they are the answer, just the same. It's hard to apply them to this situation without seeming to make ignoble comparisons, and we mustn't do that.

We have found the most convincing persuasions to be loyalty to the family cause (we all need to do our share so that the family will be happy and things go smoothly) and using the work for a heroic intention.

"Remember the children in poor countries, who need your prayers and your love. Remember our missionaries, who are trying to do so much with so little. It won't take long to do these few dishes, and then you may play. Do them for the love of children who have no homes to work in, no lovely outdoors where they may play, who don't even have dishes to wash or the food to put on them."

Inviting the guest in to wait, or, if she wishes, to help, often solves the problem. Indeed, children who do not have to work at home frequently discover that it's fun to help at the home of someone who does.

≈

Avoid doing unnecessary
work on Sunday

One of the effects of the war effort[63] was to accustom people who worked odd shifts in factories to doing a full day's work on Sunday, either in the shop or catching up on the laundry and house-cleaning at home. This has carried over into postwar years, so that now we find people *saving* work for Sundays. Nevertheless, if it isn't absolutely necessary to work on Sunday, then it's a violation of the Third Commandment to do so.

But what about the family (ours, for instance) for whom Sunday is the only day the father has free? If we're to have a garden, the largest part of the gardening must be done on Sundays. We know families who can work only on Sundays on the houses they're building. This kind of work, dedicated to a richer family life, with a direct relation to our service of God, seems to me an important means of sanctifying Sunday, *if it's necessary to do it on Sunday*.

But we must not let our children become confused. If we *must* garden or build on Sunday, we can make a special act of dedication, asking God to bless our work, understanding that if it could be done otherwise, it would be.

[63] The author refers to World War II. — ED.

How to Raise Good Catholic Children

⤳

Avoid using work as a punishment

There are two cardinal *don'ts* about children and work: don't ask children to do so much work that they miss their fair share of play; and don't ever use work as a punishment. Children, like adults, will work better between periods of rest or play, and they need a far greater portion of play than grown-ups do. Cheated of play, they easily become embittered about all work; they, too, will decide that work is a curse. It's easy to avoid this abuse if it's understood that such and such is the work to be done, and done well, after which their time is free for play.

To punish a child by making him work is asking for trouble. Then work becomes synonymous with unpleasantness and resentment, and all subsequent sermons on the dignity of work are going to go in one ear and out the other.

⤳

Even young children can pray for
insight into discerning their vocations

Praying for the grace to know his vocation goes hand in hand with teaching a child to work. We can help children send out vocational feelers by watching for signs of gracefulness and enthusiasm with particular types of work. There's something very intriguing about knowing one has a vocation picked out for him by God, and watching to see it unfold. Little girls will want to be nuns one day, mothers the next, and ballet dancers the next. It's utterly reasonable, then, to include in one's prayers, "'Please, Blessed Jesus, help me to know if I am to be a nun, a mother, or a ballet dancer." And the days when they decide it's "mother" they're supposed to be, it's a handy suggestion to be reminded to ask God for help finding the right "father." Other people have wasted their entire lives trying to find their vocations. It isn't too early to begin praying in childhood; and if one's vocation is to be motherhood, then fathers are a most essential part!

Family prayer about vocations helps parents to keep hands off in the matter of following in Father's footsteps, or being a lawyer because "I've always hoped for a son who would be a lawyer." It helps level opposition to the first signs of a religious vocation, or the indication that early marriage is best for this girl or this boy. It helps those who may one day become highly trained professional men and women to respect the more humble occupations of their less-gifted brothers and sisters. Doctors, lawyers, scientists, and engineers could not do their work, for all their gifts and training, without the men and women who make their instruments, string their telephone wires, raise their food, and build their laboratories and offices. And when we remember that Christ chose to be a carpenter, we dare not allow any of our children to cultivate any snobbishness about the unimportance of "workmen."

Perhaps the lesson it takes longest to teach is reverence for work; this is an attitude that comes slowly, with maturity. It's the final ingredient in the making of a good workman. We can begin when the children are little by teaching them to notice the properties of materials, consider their source, think of the intelligence of mind and dexterity of hands that are needed to transform them into beauty and usefulness. As our children watch us work, we can point out these things as symbols of spiritual reality.

For instance, yeast. Yeast is a powerful and mysterious plant, microscopically small yet capable of lifting a mountain of dough. Scald it, and it will die. Chill it, and it's inactive. Mix it with lukewarm water or milk, with the proper amounts of sugar and salt, fat and flour, knead it rhythmically on a floured board, and it springs to life and is the unifying principle of bread. How like grace, which, scalded by passion, will die; chilled by indifference, will remain inactive; accepted with gratitude and love, used by the heart and mind and will, will transform souls into more perfect Christians, bearing more effectively their part in the restoring of society to Christ.

A father and son planting a garden work with the symbols of eternal life. Seeds, like self-love, must be buried and seem to die before they will spring to life and bear fruit. Rain, like grace, must water them. The sun, like God's love, must warm them. Weeds, like sin, must be rooted out. This is how Christ taught. The parables He used to teach His followers are under our very noses. Following His example, teaching with our own parables as well, we slowly communicate reverence, and when finally they've learned this, they will be men and women who know it's not a curse, but a blessing, to work.

Chapter 18

*Let your child learn
and grow through play*

"Now that you children have all those nice things to play with, why don't you go *play?*"

Wouldn't it be nice if they did? All those nice trucks and dolls and checkers and trikes . . . What's the matter with children, not wanting to play?

Nothing is the matter with them. There's simply a difference between what parents think is play and what children think is play, and if play were nothing but what parents think it is, this would be a hopelessly dull existence.

Playing is the best means of all for children to learn, because they don't have to be coaxed to do it. It includes everything within range of their experience, and involves only one qualification: it must be *fun*.

It includes all the feeling pleasures, such as playing with mud, or food, or water. It includes the hearing pleasures, such as banging to make noise, or singing, or saying words over and over. It includes the seeing pleasures, such as looking through amber bread wrappers, or watching rain on windows or ants in anthills. It's the thinking pleasures, such as taking all the nice toys apart and trying to put them back together, or being greedy about looking at all the books there are, and all the pictures. It's the smelling pleasures, such as using your mother's cologne, or crushing mint in your fingers, or sniffing empty chocolate boxes. It's the basketball, base-ball, jumping-on-bed pleasures and more of their kind, and the pummeling-your-brothers-within-an-inch-of-their-life pleasures.

No? Listen to how we react.

"Here, here! Stop playing with your food."

"Now, why do you play in puddles with your shoes on?"

"Do you *have* to play with mud?"

"Why must all your play be so destructive?"

"See here, you boys! Stop playing so rough!"

If Adam and Eve had had Cain and Abel before the first sin, what fun they would have had. Nothing they wanted to do would have been wrong, or out of order, or a nuisance or a bother. But it didn't happen that way, and now, after Original Sin, we have the same problems to cope with in play as we have in everything else. We have to teach our children that the same laws of charity apply to playmates as apply, for instance, to the far-removed (and there-fore easily loved) poor children they pray for nightly. We have to show them that the same obligations of service, consideration, sharing, and respect apply in play as in home and work and school. We have to teach them that play is prayer, and help them develop an awareness of good play, which can be lovely prayer, and bad play, which cannot be prayer at all.

Play relates to the whole child, his whole body, all its members, his senses, his imagination, his will, and in his joy after happy play or his discontent after the unhappy, it touches his soul.

◈

Your child learns through play

There are two kinds of things a child learns from play: the char-acter things and the joy things. Most play, when it's successful, makes joy so predominate over all the other effects that we ought to value it for this alone — because joy is a reflection of our Father who is in Heaven. It's a taste of heavenly joy. Children don't say, "Oh joy!" but "Golly, we had fun!" But it means the same thing. And early childhood is the time to connect play with God and the joys of eternity.

I have a suspicion that certain people aren't convinced that this will work; perhaps it sounds like mealy twaddle. But consider: early childhood is not a time of doubts. When taught very young that God provides, and is the source of all blessings, children simply understand it as true. It's part of their wonderful wisdom.

The other night, one of our boys was watching the fire. When we were alone, he said, "I love watching the fire. I was thinking, God is awful good to give us a nice house with a fireplace so we can have fires in it."

Perhaps he will not think of it in quite that way when he's older. He may think then that a fireplace is a blessing because it invites companionship, and his friends enjoy coming to his house and eating in front of the fire. But he has the right thing first, and when the day comes to reflect as a mature person on the joys of this life, he does not have to discover their Source. He knows it already.

Sharing, which is probably the first and most obvious of the lessons to be learned in play, is difficult and has to be learned painfully. It's learned faster when we take pains to praise sharing when we see it. Not sharing can bring play to a dismal end; we can teach children about it by pointing this out also. Using the same motive as before, we can remind him that playmates are other Christs, and we must be as considerate and gentle with them as we would with the Christ Child Himself. This is very difficult, especially when playmates seem most of the time to be piggish contenders for wagons and balls and blocks or the coveted roles of leader, mother, and queen. But the same principles apply, and it helps children to learn surrender by recalling our Lord's counsel that it's better to act as servant than master, to take the lower place than the higher.

Also, in a nice way, we can help them see overpossessiveness, bossiness, and brutality in play as signs that people don't understand what God wants of them or how He meant them to love. Also — *and this helps immensely* — we can smooth resentment against brutish playmates many times by reminding children to pray for them (privately!). Not only has this smoothed resentment, but it has had a noticeable effect on the playmates. And why not?

No Christian is obliged, however, to stand by and allow his children to be victimized forever by playmates. Up to a certain point, he can learn lessons in Christian graciousness by giving in. Past that point, he can often become badly hurt (physically and spiritually) by becoming a kind of professional scapegoat. It's too much to expect a child to rise to the heights of detachment every time he faces a conflict, and when he's hopelessly outweighed, outvoiced, and pushed around time after time, it's good to remove him and substitute other companions or some other form of play. There are such things as self-respect and discrimination to be learned, as well as justice to be upheld; and we do neither our children nor their playmates any favor by allowing neighborhood tyrants to dominate without any correction.

This teaching of Christian behavior does not stop with our own children. We're supposed to help all men find Christ. Often abuses can be smoothed out and eliminated by plunging to the heart of the matter and reminding the neighborhood bully that he has an obligation in God's sight to protect, not victimize, the smaller members of his society. The drive for security is usually the root of such bullying, and a boy who had to find it by dominating can often find greater satisfaction playing the role of protector. A friend of mine settled such a conflict between two boys by inviting them into her home one day during Lent and reminding them of the meaning of Lent and of Easter. "He did it to teach you how to *love* each other. You have an obligation to Him to try to get along." She helped them sort out their whole altercation, piece by piece, and when they analyzed it, each could see he was partly to blame. An uncomfortable rift between two neighboring families was nicely avoided, and the boys were grateful for her help. "Not that they thanked me in so many words," she says, "but they went out hanging on each other." It takes time and patience and understanding and, most of all, faith to appreciate that the aggressors of this world are such because they're unhappy and haven't tried hard enough to love.

⌒

Help your child develop a right
attitude about winning and losing

When he's playing games to win, or being sullen when he loses, is the time to help a child see the right end of play. "Be a good sport," we call it. But how can you be a good sport if you don't know what it means? Competition is not so healthy as we like to think. It places far too much value on winning and exhibitionism, and underrates the degrees and varieties of gifts, the simple joy of participation. Worst of all, it's such an accepted measure for all forms of activity that no amount of philosophizing will comfort great numbers of people who have discovered they're only second bests.

We can help our children to enjoy play, even when it must take the form of competitive play, and to be "good sports," if we try in the beginning to take the emphasis off competition and put in its place an awareness that success in anything for them is doing as well as they're able to do. It has nothing to do with whether God has equipped someone else to do it better. When a child has reached the limit of his ability, it's time to rest, and if such happens to be the case, give honest praise for the talents of the winner.

If prayer is play, too, then basketball in the backyard can be a prayer — but not if it's spoiled by resentment. Nor can play be any kind of prayer if it isn't honest. Cheating doesn't fool anyone, least of all God, and it belongs in the same category of sins as stealing and lying.

We must also help children to be honest about disappointment. "I don't care" isn't honest when one does care. "I did the best I could, but I wish I could have won," is normal and honest; and until children learn to find their joy in effort alone, this attitude will help ease their disappointment. They will find, too, that disappointment is temporary, not long-lived. Everyone tastes defeat and disappointment sooner or later; learning what to do with it in childhood is a great protection against bitterness in maturity. Disappointment, too, can be offered up as prayer.

≈

Athletics teach the value of teamwork

Children learn speed, grace, coordination, accuracy, and many things from athletic skills. We have to be careful, though, that they do not overestimate their capacity or their talent, and we can do them grave harm by encouraging feats obviously beyond their ability. This applies not only to athletic activities but to creative activity and vocational experiments as well. Few children can get too much praise and encouragement, except when we delude them into believing that they possess talents they do not possess or goad them on to heights they can never attain. Art schools, music schools, and dancing schools are full of students who are pursuing will-o'-the-wisps, whose parents have so overrated their natural gifts that instead of seeking the right end with their talents — how to use them to enrich a useful life — they become the means of gigantic frustrations.

Not all boys who are star pitchers on school teams are called by God to be professional ballplayers. But given no means of fitting such gifts into the whole purpose of life, they become ends in themselves, as a newly signed ballplayer put it recently: "A chance to make as much money as N. and marry a Hollywood star like N." This is not the *end* of the talents of ballplayers, nor the purpose of sports.

The gifts are supposed to give glory to God, from whom they came. If we can teach children that this is the whole point of their play and the use of their talents, it might not be so difficult to keep sports where they belong instead of elevating them to the status of a national religion. The point of games is to *play* them, not to watch them, and the purpose of athletics in schools is frustrated when the majority of youngsters watch a few burn off energies in sport while the majority must find an outlet for their energies somewhere else. Fathers and sons watching televised games participate in only the most barren way in the real joy of sports. It's much more to the point if the fathers turn off the TV set and get out and pitch balls to their sons.

Group play and school athletics are important not only because they are a means of expending youthful energy, but also because they teach the value of teamwork, obvious to us, but not often to children. Instinctively each wants to star. "See what I can do." "Watch me." "I do this best, don't I?" Stars soon learn in group play that they're not stars without support, and those who don't star learn the satisfaction of being good support, and find happiness in being needed.

~

Let your child participate in group activity

Group activity is valuable not only for the lessons in cooperation; when organized regularly by parents in a neighborhood, it can do much to set wholesome patterns for play in childhood and wholesome entertainment later on.

We have on our land a typical New England foothill that we call a mountain. If we were to propose to our children, on a day when there's nothing to do, that it would be fun to climb the mountain, they might very well answer, "But we've already done that." But organized as a mountain climb, with five mothers and fifteen or sixteen children, we had a successful afternoon's "play."

All we did was climb to the top, rest, and climb down again. There were children from four to eleven, and each age group went at it in their own manner. The fours tagged along with the mothers, stopping to examine the pipsissewa, the wintergreen, the crow's foot, and lichens. The sixes and sevens shinnied up trees, scouted for Indians, and watched for deer tracks. The elevens ran ahead of everyone else and explored. When we got down, we ate coffee cake and drank cocoa, and the goodbys were "Oh, thanks. We had the *best* time." Every one of these children was a country child; most had mountains of their own. There was nothing new or novel about climbing our mountain. But doing it together made the big difference.

City families can work out similar activities with trips to the park, the zoo, museums, rides on the ferry, and without spending much more than bus fare and money for ice-cream cones. It isn't novelty or detail that makes these things fun; it's doing them

Let your child learn and grow through play

together. Such a group develops a host of common interests and a loyalty to one another that will serve well when they reach high school. At that time, too, the same parents stand a far better chance of setting curfews for the group that will be observed, as well as establishing norms about use of family cars, dress for parties, and coming back to one home or another for refreshments after dances.

~

Make parties simple and fun

Parties are another form of play that contribute to the development of a child's sense of hospitality and graciousness. There's a saying: "God sends everyone to the door," and the Christian welcoming guests to his party welcomes them in Christ's name. As a child of God, he invites his friends to share the bounty the Lord has bestowed on him, the warmth of his home, the food on his table, and the joy of fellowship.

Just a few things make a good party: something that's fun to do; something that's good to eat; and being together. Simplicity and planning are the secret of successful party-giving. (One caution: children do not have fun in front of an audience, especially a bunch of grown-ups sitting around with a drink in one hand, waiting for the party to be over.) This is almost the only way to establish that pattern of entertaining at home which is such a bulwark of wholesomeness in the high school years.

Parties planned around creative activities are not hard to manage with small groups of children, and young guests have the added pleasure of taking home a drawing, or soap sculpture, or clay figure, or even, for little girls, cookies they helped bake and decorate themselves. Parties for Indians to attend in full war paint are an ideal way of collecting children for a session of wild outdoor play. Flying kites, racing jalopies, dressing dolls — all kinds of quite ordinary play — become wonderful and new when done at a party.

One of the best parties we ever had was a Mad Tea Party. And it was *mad*. We had two Alices and a Mad Hatter in an old top hat, a sleepy dormouse (who, alas, didn't fit in the teapot), a number of White Rabbits, a cardboard watch that we buttered, two unbirthday cakes, two tables with numerous odd cups (to which we moved after yelling "Clean cups! Clean cups!"), and positively no table manners. We even had the *half* cup, happily rescued from the Fergusons' trash as it was about to be thrown into the town dump. A delirious time was had by all, and our children were exceptionally well mannered at the table for days following the sky-high limit for manners at the Mad Tea Party.

Parties to celebrate liturgical feasts are joyous praise and prayer and are lovely revelations to children who haven't yet learned to celebrate them.

～

Help your child develop his senses through games

Then there are the other kinds of play, the joyful use of the senses. Too often we're blind to the real joy children find in the most commonplace accessories to living. A baby will amuse himself for hours, picking up unsanitary curiosities with the wet end of a finger and putting them in his mouth: old coffee grounds, spilled tobacco, even little slivers of glass if he can find them (and he usually can). He's exploring with his tongue and his sense of taste; and whether or not he enjoys what he tastes, this is one of the ways he plays. He will tear things, like library books and the Sunday paper, and enjoy the sound of tearing. He will bang on the windowpane or the piano and shout with joy at the noise he makes, and this is his primitive version of "praising with clanging cymbals." He will bang on the heads of his brothers and shout with joy at the noise *they* make. (This is a corrupt form of the praise with clanging cymbals.)

All mothers know that babies do these things, and most of the time we say they're naughty. Not that we're too stupid to think of them as play. We're just too busy to think most of the time. But we can try to remember they're a form of play, and try to appreciate with more reverence the senses God gave our children, through which He communicates to them so many of the joys of living. We can compose games for them to play that will help them develop, not only the use of these senses, but also reverence for the variety of ways they can give praise.

One day when there's "nothing to do," we can suggest a tasting game: tasting five tastes and tasting them again blindfolded. How does salt taste when you can't see it? And sugar, and molasses, in contrast to honey? How mean we were to let Daddy put salt instead of sugar in his coffee last April Fools' Day! King David wrote, "Taste and see that the Lord is sweet."[64] Sugar is sweet; taste it and see. King David meant that we could grow to love being loved by God just as we grow to love sweet things — but first you have to "taste and see." Another time he wrote, "The judgments of the Lord are . . . sweeter than honey and the honeycomb."[65] And St. Bernard said, "Jesus is honey in the mouth, music in the ear, a shout of gladness in the heart." John the Baptist ate wild honey and probably remembered all the things King David wrote. King David, St. John, and St. Bernard had tongues like ours, and gave praise not only with words, but with tasting. We can do that, too.

[64] Ps. 33:9 (RSV = Ps. 34:8).
[65] Ps. 18:10-11 (RSV = Ps. 19:9-10).

And there are smelling games: smelling five boxes of spices and smelling them again blindfolded. Jamie claims that ginger smells like soap. Mace is easy to guess, because we put it in coffee cake. Clove is sharp and cuts your nose, and anise is strange and different. Cinnamon is easy because of cinnamon toast, and remembering our Lady of the feast of the Assumption: "I gave a sweet smell like cinnamon and aromatic balm."[66]

The same game can be played with touching surface and cloth and the leaves of plants, many things. Close your eyes and touch the potato bag. It feels like the Ninivite sackcloth. How would you like to wear *that* all through Lent! Feel the softness of the baby's fuzz. Our Lord's silky head felt like that when He was a Baby.

And the same game can be played with hearing: sitting in the yard and listening for sounds you would not even notice with your eyes open. A spring night that's all sky and scent and breeze becomes a spring night in terms of sound: frogs, and leaves, and cows cropping grass, dogs barking in different voices, people talking far away. Isn't it strange? When we listen with eyes open, we hear so many annoying sounds, like crunching toast and snuffling, and babies crying, and radiators knocking. The whole universe praises God with its sounds, yet so many times we grumble that there's nothing to praise about. But we can make hearing a praise. We can be still and listen and learn to praise simply, the way creation gives praise.

How strange we are. We all want "a richer life" for our children. We want to "give them the best." But they have more than we could ever give them when they come from the hand of God. They possess Him when they receive Baptism. Can we give them more than that? They have bodies that can learn to skip rope and

[66]Ecclus. 24:20 (RSV = Sir. 24:15).

swim and turn somersaults, and hands that can learn to shoot marbles and throw jacks and dress dolls. They have minds that can learn to contrive riddles and count scores and make jokes, and feet that can learn to play hopscotch and kick balls and skate. We do not have to teach children they must play, only to help them learn *how* to play, and the very least of it is the "nice toys" we think we must buy them. They will play, no matter what, because it's part of their longing for Heaven. It's instinctive in them to seek joy.

"Joy is the echo of God's life in us." Let us teach our children how to play, and help them to play. Then with its joy they can praise. And one day they will realize that their joy is the echo of the Lord's joy.

Chapter 19

⁓

*Give your child opportunities
for creative activity*

To be creative is to be like God. To know how to take the things God has created and extend them further in acts of our own creating, to search out in one's head an idea, and work over it with a mind and hands, selecting this, combining with that, cutting away, discarding, adding, fitting, and finally bringing forth something new — this is how we are made to be creators like our Father.

To use love to create as God creates with His love — that is ours, too. We pray to the creative Spirit of God, "Pour forth Thy Spirit and they shall be created, and Thou shalt renew the face of the earth." Out of this love we create families and friendships, and bind society where it is sick, and heal our enemies with our prayers, and work and pray and sacrifice with Christ so that His Mystical Body may be whole and continue to grow. We serve Him in our fellowman with love, feeding him, clothing him, teaching, nursing, administering, interpreting, comforting, encouraging, and in a thousand other ways. This is the creative work of man, who is given natural and supernatural powers of creativeness which, for all they are minute by comparison, are made in the image and likeness of God. And to create is so necessary to one who is made to be a creator that from the beginning we struggle to create.

Babies begin to create almost before they can walk and talk. It's very clumsy, but it's in the image of God, for all its clumsiness. The first thing a baby does when he's put outdoors to play unpenned is find a little dirt, squat down, and start to make something with it, even if it's just the print of his hand, or a hill he scoops up and pours into his other hand, or mud he shapes into a little cake. When you see it so often with so many babies, you sometimes forget to wonder that he should scoop up earth as God did; make his first *thing* with earth as God made man with it; look at it and crow in his way, "Isn't it good?" as God did: "And He looked on it and saw it was good."[67] Maybe it's just because earth is such a willing element and surrenders so easily. Maybe there's no more to it than that.

But if there is, it shouldn't seem such a phenomenon that a child will create before he has mastered the other arts of living. It should seem more like a confirmation, at the very beginning of life, of the purpose of life. The simplicity of his first creativeness is like the simplicity of his faith, neither questioning nor complex. As he believes, when told, in God who made and loves him, in the same way he sets himself instinctively to being what God has made him to be: a creator.

Creative activity for children is crucially important. It's their discovery of themselves as individuals, different from other individuals, with ideas and the power to form them into something. A small child is so honest and the things he creates so full of integrity that his character can be read from the things he creates. For children growing up with the love and knowledge of God as a part of their daily life, as ever-present as three meals a day and sleeping at night, it would be almost impossible to give them the full measure of God without including creative activity. For, if they are to know God and praise Him for the gifts He has put into them, first they must discover the gifts. They must learn not only to give praise *for*

[67] Cf. Gen. 1:4.

Give your child opportunities for creative activity

them, but to praise *with* them; and this begins the integration of what a child learns with how he lives. To know who you are and the powers God has given you, and to serve and praise Him with them — that is the purpose not only of creativeness but of life.

⁀

Help your child to discover and develop his gifts
Discovery of these gifts almost always begins with art. It's wonderful to hear children tell *why* they create, why they draw or paint or model or cut, because they're so unabashed about explaining how important it is to be known as *someone who can do something:* "Because I like to show people what I can draw." And one little boy we know put all his pictures against the windowpane facing the street. "Or else how can everybody see what I draw?" "Because I make things pretty good out of clay, and when I'm done, I have something I made."

Out of all their impressions and knowledge, their most eloquent summations and delightful visions, in a way far more intelligible to them than any attempt at words, children will set down on paper how the world looks and what it's all about. And when their lives include a knowledge of the supernatural, they will make ever so clear how real spiritual realities are to them.

A five-year-old, hearing a news broadcast about a fire, came to his mother later in the day with a picture of it. This was the house afire, and this is the fire truck; here are the firemen and "the poor whose house burned up." The poor were weeping in the front yard.

"And who is this in back of the house?"

"Oh, that. That's an angel praying for the poor."

Knowing the fiver quite well, I'm sure that a verbal explanation of it would not have included the angel. Alone with his knowledge of calamities and how God sometimes permits them

How to Raise Good Catholic Children

for reasons He alone knows (but always so that some greater good might come), the addition of the angel was inevitable: one of the signs of Divine Love caring for the helpless.

Nor does the five-year-old's wisdom manifest itself only in drawings of the supernatural. He has salty things to say about the natural, too. Like the drawing, on the blackboard, of a man's profile with a lot of scribbles in front of his mouth.

"Talking real loud," he explained.

The grown-ups who heard were rather uncomfortable as they reflected how often they talk "real loud."

All children can draw. Anyone who holds that they cannot, and can demonstrate with a houseful of children where there's not a pencil mark on the wall, might have an argument. But I don't believe there's such a house on the face of the earth. Until the children are older and it's time to determine how much talent they have, how far it should be pursued, all they need to draw and draw and *draw* is lots of praise.

There's a time to praise and a time to criticize. If some attempts are better than others, there's always something good one can honestly say about even the least successful tries: "Nice sun, lovely rain, good idea, bright colors . . ." Something in praise, even if no more than praise that they will to create: "How wonderful, that you can sit down and make so many pictures!"

I know a man who wrote stories all the time as a small child. A zealous adult, anticipating the "constructive criticism" stage by about five years, so discouraged him with well-meant criticism that he gave the whole thing up at the age of eight. Thirty years later, he began to write — thirty years of lost training and practice in the art of self-expression. Not all children will write, or draw, or sing, or dance professionally, but they should be encouraged to explore these fields, and in all probability, if we let them alone

Give your child opportunities for creative activity

while they're little, they will discover for themselves the medium through which they can give their most eloquent expression.

Coloring books, cutting out ready-made paper dolls, are not creative. They're fun and exercise, and technically useful for teaching things other than art, but there's nothing remotely creative about coloring blue where a picture is labeled "Color me blue," or putting scissors to dotted lines labeled "cut here." To be entirely creative, children must invent with simple materials and the ideas in their heads. We must be careful to keep hands off, allowing them to reproduce things as *they* see them, not we, and above all discouraging tracing and copying. There are some cutting and design projects where patterns are needed for tracing and repetition, some illustrating projects where pictures are needed for reference, but, by and large, children will provide and invent all by themselves. It's robbery of the worst sort to allow them to substitute the hackneyed ideas of others, slavishly copied, for the rich and imaginative pictures they have inside.

~

Foster good taste in your child

This does not mean that children shouldn't be exposed to good art, but the motive should be to stimulate and inspire them and to spark their own ideas, push back a bit farther their own horizons. Unless parents know good art, however, they cannot know to what to expose their children. So far, in the struggle between the "knows" and the "know-nots" (the one side deploring, the other defending), I don't think that there's yet a bridge over which the know-nots may cross. It isn't enough to realize that there's such a thing as good art. It has also to be comprehended somehow, or it can't be loved. Byzantine mosaics I love dearly, yet it's entirely understandable to me that someone who has never seen them before may protest, "But they're childish, and unreal, and like dolls — cold and stiff."

I believe that the know-nots secretly *want* to know, and I wish someone would start writing books for *them*: books with good illustration and texts that would do for good Christian art what good biographies have done for the saints.

Until then, the best they can do is visit museums, comb through bookstores in the hope of finding something that will explain rather than merely illustrate, search out magazines, and ask for help. This "best" is, of course, excellent enough. Unless, however, they're helped to see what's great about, for instance, a Giotto, they are quite apt to end up standing in front of all the tonnage in a Rubens and deciding that *this* must be good, because it's in a museum and painted by a famous painter and shows the descent from the Cross.

Children don't come equipped with instinctively good taste. The things they draw themselves are usually good because they're free of sophistication, but usually the things they admire are atrocious (unless they've been surrounded by good art from infancy) because they love all that is gaudy and sentimental and they've been exposed to so much sentimental rubbish that their taste has already been corrupted.

We should also encourage children to draw from models and landscapes and nature. They won't draw what *we* see, but they will enjoy drawing what *they* see, looking at a brother or sister or street or field and putting it down on paper, and it's important that we save examples of the works they create, for reference and encouragement. If we let them alone to create in their own way, they will reveal many things that we're too old and sour to see ever again with our own eyes, and will recapture only now and then, when we see them through the eyes of children.

Give your child opportunities for creative activity

After living in the country for a long time and seeing many hayfields cut, I saw an entirely new pattern of a hayfield at a local exhibit of children's art. One little girl did a lovely thing with the pattern a baler makes as it goes round and round, dropping bales like the checkpoints in a labyrinth. It was exactly as a hayfield looks, but I was no longer simple enough to see it that way.

I've seen many pictures of shepherds receiving with joy the news of the angels at Bethlehem, but never one that explored the glory of the *Gloria* so gloriously as a four-year-old's shepherds staggering down the hills with staves giddily swinging over their heads under rays of starlight that fell from the top of the sky to pierce the very stones, and at their heels *laughing* lambs. It is this ability to make concrete their own vision that is the divine part of the gift of creating.

We help our children become articulate early in life when we encourage them to create. If we help them discover their abilities, we're helping them to know what to do with their lives in maturity. If we teach them further that these things come from God and have a purpose, their early years' creating will discover for them not only what works and skills and arts are *theirs*, but especially how they best speak and serve and praise God.

One child started with drawing, and discovered she had talent not for drawing *pictures*, but for drawing *designs*. She felt her way through modeling and decorating what she modeled, then to making doll clothes with lots of ribbons and beads for ornamentation, then to decorating cookies, and this led to cooking. When asked why she liked cooking best of all the creative arts, she answered, "Because it makes me feel like a woman."

There could be no better end for creative activity for a girl than that it discover for her what womanliness is, and the arts and works that are womanly. She may become a lawyer, a nurse, a teacher, a religious, or a mother, but whatever God wants her to be, if she is to serve well in it, she must be womanly. Our society is by no means lacking in women who are unwomanly, to whom *woman* is synonymous with *sexiness*, not with *womanliness*.

It's the quality of womanliness in a girl, manliness in a boy, governing the talents and expressed through their talents with tenderness, strength, humor, compassion, purity, and so many other ways, that will help these children discover whom God made when He made *them*. The more they discover the things they can do with their heads and hands, with their eyes and ears and minds and bodies, and know that it is by grace they do them — grace freely given with the gift — the less they will be driven to imitate others, go where the crowd goes, do what the crowd does. This is the only alternative for people who never discover the gifts God put in them or how to use them. Alone, they have no feeling of wholeness; they're not *someone*, but *anyone*; and in a frantic effort to identify themselves as someone, they imitate what seems to be integrity in others, in tastes, attitudes, likes, dislikes, opinions, behavior — with nowhere a clue as to what they were meant to be themselves.

⏝

Provide materials for young artists

All a two-year-old needs to have a great time drawing is the want-ad section of the Sunday paper, opened out six or eight sheets thick in the playpen, and a fat, bright crayon. He'll scribble and crumple for maybe half an hour, and that's a long time for a two-year-old. When he's outdoors, all he needs is a pan of water, a spoon, an old pie plate, and the inevitable dirt, and he will sculpture and model and bake and pour in an orgy of creation.

When he's older, he needs big paper, lots of room to swing his arms, bright crayons, and big jars of bright paint. If possible, hide the pencils. Pencils make fists tighten and tend to draw faces close to the paper to see where thin little lines are going. They inhibit the freedom and sweep that are so important to keep children from tightening up inside, becoming fussy too soon about unimportant details.

Suitable smocks, aprons, and something for wiping hands on are very important. No one can have any fun trying to splash around with paint if he has to worry about getting dirty — and this applies especially to finger paints.

Easels are good if they're big and sturdy and don't tip over. Low, flat tables to which paper can be thumbtacked (low enough to let a child paint standing up) are often better than easels because paint doesn't drip down so persistently and turn sunny-day pictures into rainy-day pictures. (What else could one do with the blue drips from a cloudless blue sky?)

Powdered poster paints can be bought in bulk in the primary colors — red, yellow, and blue — and mixed for painting sessions in old jars with screw tops. They're a better investment than children's paint sets, and all the colors but black can be mixed from the three primaries. Good brushes, instead of the waggle-ended monstrosities included in paint sets, are important and not very expensive. For little children (or older ones painting mural projects on large paper, wallboard, or wall surfaces) sash brushes from the five-and-ten do very well. They're narrow enough, they stroke the paint well, and they're supple, yet stiff enough to hold up under the scrubbing with soap and water afterward.

It's good to have mats for framing, as everybody knows what glorious things a frame does for a good picture. These are easy to cut from illustration board with a mat knife. Matted, family art can be displayed seriously on any wall, singly or in groups, or on a bulletin board.

How to Raise Good Catholic Children

A large bulletin board can be the focal point for all these creative activities, as well as for relating displays with school work, catechism lessons, exciting family events, and the continually changing message of the liturgical seasons. A large blackboard is an equally valuable feature of a house with children and the best incentive of all to get children to "draw big." Nailed to the wall, it's an invitation to draw, print, write, number, play games, or scribble for the joy of scribbling — which few children can resist. If there's a smooth, paintable wall, the whole wall may be covered with blackboard paint, which comes in colors, as well as in black.

Brown wrapping paper, shelving paper, newspaper stock, the backs of old wallpaper rolls, large pads of manila, and even tissue paper (which we print with potato block print and use for gift wrappings) lend themselves to experiment with crayon, paint, hard chalks, pastels, colored inks, india ink and lettering pens, and leftover paint from home decorating projects. It's just a step to doing variations of these with pastings, montage techniques, glitter, sequins, tiny beads and buttons, and all sorts of odds and ends families save because "there must be something we can use it for."

Colored construction paper for cutting and pasting projects, gilt papers, aluminum foil, lace paper doilies, designs or multiple figures cut in folded paper, colored felts to cut and appliqué, fabrics to cut and paste and sew — all such treasures as these can be used to illustrate the mysteries and the feast days, to serve as valentines, Christmas and Easter greetings, gifts, to explain lessons in schoolbooks, in catechism.

We're working right now on the catechism lesson about the three theological virtues and the seven gifts of the Holy Spirit — such meaningless mouthfuls when encountered the first time, but easy to learn when the three theological virtues are three yellow knights, cut on a threefold piece of paper so that they stand hand in hand, each one decorated with a symbol of faith or hope or charity (charity has a gold crown because St. Paul said, "and the greatest of these is charity"[68]). The gifts are sevenfold doves cut out the same way, flying wing to wing. A child who carefully letters on one dove after the other the words *wisdom, understanding, counsel, fortitude, knowledge, piety,* and *fear of the Lord* can hardly avoid learning them. Then, if the figures are posted on the bulletin board, they're easier to remember and to explain: "Do you know what those men are? Well, they're three theological virtues — see?"

Then there are the modeling and carving materials. Plasticine, water clays, and soap to carve, salt blocks to sculpture, dough to twist and weave and tie into shapes, plaster of paris and plastic materials to pour into homemade molds, papier-mâché for masks and puppets (made with shredded newspaper and flour paste, wet buckram, gummed brown paper tape), soft woods to whittle, animals to make from vegetables, cookies to cut freehand and decorate — all these and more suggest the variety of media with which children should experiment in order to find which one is particularly *theirs* and says the best the things they want to say. The local library is full of books on how to do all these things.

As the children learn how to use their heads and hands, slowly they begin to understand that it's proper and fitting to *make* rather than merely to *buy.* The little boy who once said, "When I grow up, I'm going to buy a statue factory, so I can give my mother all the nice statues she wants," discovers that making statues requires time, and thought, and love, and that you can do better at this than factories can.

[68] 1 Cor. 13:13.

How to Raise Good Catholic Children

⤸

Rhyming and dancing

Children learn to rhyme easily, with ingenious humor and terrible puns and a galloping appetite for *Nonsense Rhymes*, Gilbert and Sullivan, and *The Hunting of the Snark*. In the process, they come upon intriguing ways with words and meter and the subtle art of turning a phrase.

"Somebody make up a rhyme."

A very small somebody says right away, "Mrs. Horse is very coarse." And a big somebody adds, "Not only coarse, but also hoarse." Groans.

What a joy to discover that you possess a wit and can stuff it into a small space of seven or eight measures and make it come out in rhyme! Round-robin rhymes for the whole family are lots of fun and make dish-wiping and yard-raking and cellar-cleaning go much faster, especially with a foolish story at the end that has everyone laughing to tears. Impromptu rhymes can be far more palatable correction for things like table manners than plain old scoldings:

> *Poor old Peter is a horrible eater.*
> *He'd be such a joy if he'd eat like a boy.*

Appreciating rhymes helps greatly in disposing of the vulgar verses heard in schoolyards and brought home for family edification: "Too bad. God gives people the talent to rhyme, and they have to go and spoil it."

Children should dance, too. *And* their mothers. And fathers? I've seen the father in our house walk in on the mother in our house as she was dancing a Spanish fandango — and flee as if the Devil were after him. Not that our fandangos are that terrible. I've been assured by the children that they're *very* fandango, and as the children constitute my only audience for the performance, what they think is all that counts.

But the important thing about mothers' dancing is that when children see them dance, they will dance, too, whether fandangos or ballet or waltzes or just enacting what the music is saying. That's how children should dance: to spill out the kind of joy music stirs up in them, to tell stories, to invent. It's a real deprivation for children to grow up believing that the few unimaginative variations of what we call social dancing are the sum total of dancing. People have always danced, to show their praise and their joy, to express their sorrow and tell their stories; small children especially want to dance, and should be encouraged to do so.

Mary, the sister of Aaron, danced with the women as a thanksgiving to the Lord for freeing the Jews from Egypt. "Let us sing to the Lord, for He is gloriously magnified; the horse and his rider He hath thrown into the sea."[69] In the last psalm, David calls on all the talent in the temple to praise the Lord, among them the dancers: "Praise Him with timbrel and dance; praise Him with strings and pipe."[70]

Many of the liturgical forms, processions, parts of the Mass, and the lovely winglike movement of the arms of a priest when he gives a blessing, had their beginnings in dignified dance forms. And many of our most common play activities are dance. A little girl said, breathlessly, "I was skipping rope to the *Alleluia*." It was Easter. Is there a more joyous way to sing, "Alleluia" than while skipping rope?

Our children like to compose dances to *Peter and the Wolf* because there are more than enough roles for everyone. We've

[69] Exod. 15:21.
[70] Ps. 150:4.

discovered among our albums music that fits *Le longleur du Notre Dame;* so we have danced to that. Another album has a passage that's like Mary Magdalene walking alone in the garden on Easter morning; so we've invented things for that. A friend (a *real* dancer) once danced for me a beautiful Crusader to some Bach; so now and then, the children try Crusaders to Bach, too. They like to dramatize in a dance-like way the Peter Pan music (with newspaper pirate hats and swords in sashes) and the Pinocchio music (with invisible long noses), and especially the *Tyl Eulenspiegel* music. Peter put a pair of boxer dungarees on his head and said, "This is a Tyl Orange-beagle hat" because the Eichenberg illustrations in the book show Tyl with a hat like that. One day I heard him explain, "This is a St. John Bosco hat — oh no, I mean Tyl Orange-beagle." (St. John Bosco also walked the tightrope as a boy; very easy to see how one could become confused.)

All children love Spanish music because they can use their heels and fingers, and tambourines and castanets (real or invented). Christmas carols make lovely dances, sweet and reverent, with someone cradling the Christ Child and the others bowing in a procession before Him (St. Teresa of Avila once danced with the Christ Child in her arms). They love to improvise to music that tells stories, such as *The Moldau, En Saga, Valse Triste,* and they like to dance to all kinds of folk music, but especially American, since they're learning square dances in school. Dancing to the music from *Hansel and Gretel* calls for singing, too, like "Brother, come and dance with me," and "Susie, little Susie, pray what is the news?" "The geese are running barefoot because they've no shoes." The favorite of the Humperdinck lyrics for singing and acting is "When at night I go to sleep," with the fourteen angels.

Children don't have to go to dancing school to dance. Children *dance.* Yet, today when they're exposed to so much vulgar dancing

Give your child opportunities for creative activity

on TV and in the movies, it's almost impossible to explain about dancing that it's good, but that this dancing, or that, is bad. It wasn't intended when God made people who could dance that only a few should do it to show off before the many. He made us to give praise to Him with our whole bodies, and dancing is one of the ways. If children are encouraged to dance among themselves, artlessly and without any intent to perform, they'll learn with their bodies and their mind, how movements can express joy and praise, and they'll begin to have a criterion to measure which kinds of dance are pure and which are not.

~

Singing and acting

Together with dancing goes singing, about which we as a family know very little except how to sing. We have a modest collection of albums, and we can read music well enough to pick out tunes with one finger on the piano. There's the radio (pretty carefully supervised), and a little sheet music we've bought, and some we've been given. Our friends who go to the Trapp Family Music Camp have sung for us the things they learned, and given us help with our attempt to interpret chant notation. And our school music supervisor, who teaches charming songs at school, gave us a lovely Huron Indian carol (which the neighborhood children are learning for the next carol sing). Then there are the books of Christmas carols and the songs in *Laughing Meadows*, the Grailville song book, and there are many fine American folk songs recorded.

All these things satisfy the appetites of children for good songs, and vastly minimize the temptation to pick up the sophisticated and often very vulgar lyrics of popular music. Even in homes where radio and TV are carefully supervised, it's futile to think children can be kept from hearing these tunes and memorizing the lyrics, but we can help them form judgments about singing in the same way as we can about dancing, by having them sing what is good to please God. Several years ago, a popular recording star had youngsters all over the country singing with her, "Lover, it's immoral, but why quarrel with our bliss?" And we wonder why youth centers with their supervised dances to such music as this don't help as much as we had hoped to keep the barriers to moral danger intact.

A voice is a gift from God, and we can teach our children to listen not only to songs, but with reverent wonder to voices, and to judge whether the voice and the song are reflecting any of the glory due to God, who gave the gift. Listening to fine recordings of great choral music can help them develop a sense of the anonymity which should mark group singing, where soloists are a distraction rather than an addition to all-together singing the praises of God. And we discover now and then that fine operatic recordings communicate to them audibly ideas they have struggled to put into visual form. Such is the *Whistling Aria* from Boito's *Mephistopheles*. After debating which of the pictured forms of the Devil was probably most like him, hearing that eerie whistle dart about so diabolically left no doubt in their minds as to how he sounds and how fast he gets about.

When children sing all their songs for God and sing together often in our families, they're creating, just as surely as when they use their hands to draw or their bodies to dance, and our homes are warmer and more full of love for the harmonies we've created with our voices.

Acting should be part of a child's creative activity, too, because it's such a happy way to learn, to develop his observation of the nature of simple things and explain in a combination of all the arts the many things children want to explain. Little children love to act out spontaneously the things they see around them, like a

Give your child opportunities for creative activity

chair, or a table, or a clock, or a cat; and little boys profit enormously from special occasions for indulging their animal spirits. John does a magnificent imitation of a goat chewing her cud — more goaty than even the goats. When this is his contribution to a session of "What am I?" the screams and howls are lovely satisfaction for the goat in him and he behaves better in public for it — well, for a few days, anyway.

One year on Mardi Gras, we had family charades to describe what fault each one would give up for Lent. This is a good way to make fun of yourself, admit your weakness, and face up seriously to the kind of mortification that would be most important for you. One child came in chewing on a thumb. Another slugged imaginary playmates with such abandon that we were moved to great compassion for the real playmates. Another carried a pillow and a dinner plate, symbols of the two daily chores most repugnant and most successfully avoided. One grown-up came in jawing silently and wagging a finger this way and that, and another grown-up said, "Oh! I was going to do that!" We were properly overcome to see our faults displayed publicly, and as not one act was greeted with any dissent, it was a penitent group who wagged their way to bed that night, well aware that Lent had come just in time.

Charades are never-ending fun for children; I've never heard them say they had too much of them. Puppets they love, too, and they're easy to make and use. Our easiest puppets have been hand puppets, made with stuffed socks, faces painted or embroidered, costumes designed from leftover scraps of material, yarn, beads, buttons — anything that's around. We've had them for liturgical feasts, such as Epiphany, the three elegant Magis with jeweled crowns, oriental hairdos and robes, and for ordinary Punch and Judy shows, and one for Thumbelina, made with a really live thumb. Our stage is an old threefold screen. We took each panel apart, slip-covered it with sprigged yellow calico, cut a square window in the middle panel for the stage and tacked gray flounces with red ball fringe across the top and sides for a curtain. Rehinged so that the wings fold back, it's easily stored away when not in use, and even portable when we want to lend it to other puppeteers. Friends of ours devised a stage with two deep flounces to tack across the top and middle section of a doorway, with a space open in between for the performers.

Even tiny children can maneuver hand puppets, and the illusion is so complete that all they need to do is wag the puppets to a folk song or a Christmas carol in order to carry their part in a family entertainment. One of the reasons puppet shows are especially successful with small children is that they submerge their self-consciousness in the antics of a tiny little person they do not identify with themselves, and the laughter of the audience never seems to be directed *at* them — a puzzlement many small actors find it hard to understand when they appear in person.

Songs such as "Old MacDonald Had a Farm," and "I've Been Working on the Railroad," which the audience can sing with the puppet, are a great success. Graduating from these to reciting nursery rhymes and little poems provides plenty of material for small fries who are not able to memorize lines of plays or carry on dialogues between two puppets at once. Older children can write their own scripts and invent stage business that they're sure is hysterically funny; for these it's especially profitable to suggest tableaux and simple recitatives relating to the liturgical feasts.

❧

Help your child to see design in the tempo of daily life
Working in many art forms, using talent easily and spontaneously, finding that their creations are respected and useful, slowly

children cross the bridge that connects art and work, and bring their sense of creating to bear on the more subtle arts of daily life. They discover that setting a table — or hanging the wash, folding the sheets, planting the garden — can be a design. They discover the rhythm for kneading dough, milking a goat, hammering a nail, rocking the baby. There's a pace for raking, another for sweeping. There's a pattern for scrubbing the floor, another for ironing a dress. Kneeling to comfort a child is a reverence, as genuflecting. Praying out loud together is a harmony, just whispering together while the baby sleeps. Walking with pails of water for the goats is measured and careful; walking back from Holy Communion has another measure.

These things children learn instinctively, but with more alacrity and with willingness to discover the beauty and satisfaction in ordinary acts if they have had many experiences exploring with their own creativeness. No one is really "all thumbs." Everyone has special gifts that set him apart from his fellows and make him a special person. But many times they're never discovered. It's not work that's ugly, nor working that's unendurable, but the wrong work with the wrong person attempting it that can make it seem ugly and unendurable. Creative artists we must have, and God provides them abundantly in every generation, but the others are no less creative for the practicality of their arts. And the gifts given to these are no less special; they must be sought just as carefully.

≈

Creativity can be found in all types of work
We've committed many sins against man's creativeness with our modern snobbery about work. We've accepted a norm for work that's based on reward, approval, and selfish gain rather than on

motive, integrity, and creative service. We've become confused; we esteem work that's *respected* rather than work that's *respectable*.

Horror is the reaction of most parents to whom it's suggested that domestic service is appropriate work and training for a young girl looking forward to marriage. It does not occur to such parents that the creative arts she would practice in so-called menial employment are the same arts she'll practice (with greater grace for her training) when she's a wife and mother. How does sending her to work in a factory, to file papers and stack cards in an office, train her in the art of homemaking?

This is how far we have strayed from the recognition and understanding of creativeness. We respect people for the creativeness of their hobbies, not their lives, and admire the successful fellows who work creatively in wood or paint or whatever on their weekends, more than carpenters, plumbers, and farmers, who work creatively all week along.

For Christian parents who want to help their children find their whole usefulness, how to use their whole lives — not just certain departments — creatively in the service of God, these points need thinking out. People are not haphazardly created with a dash of this and that added for interest by a Creator who dabbles in variations on the same old theme. Each one was made to serve Him in a special way. The discovery of *how* begins when they're very little and learn to make visible and tangible their own ideas, formed by the knowledge of God, His love for them, and the truths Christ teaches.

Chapter 20

*Remember that all
families have difficulties*

One of the great dangers in writing about family unity is that treating the family as a unit, a whole body that's a miniature of the Mystical Body, everything you say will sound good, maybe a bit inspiring, maybe a bit sentimental, but also maybe a bit pat. And looking from the subject treated in the round to *your* family, you're apt to sigh and throw up your hands and say, "Yes, I suppose so, but I just wish it could be that way in *our* family."

Of course, it *is* that way in "our family," no matter who we are, because a family is always a unit even at the times it feels its disunity most painfully, and that ought to be the most comforting thought of all if we could just hang on to it. A family *is* because God wills it, because He made a design for it, because it grows out of a sacrament that makes one person of two, and they bear fruit in the cocreation with God of children who receive their bodies from their parents, their souls from God. And if there are times when the unity does not *feel* like unity, it shouldn't be surprising. In spite of its mystical oneness, a family is made of several — sometimes many — individuals, each one of whom is the most important person in his life, and this makes for great conflict, in spite of the ties of blood and sacramental oneness.

But rather than prove some flaw in the family as a wise design, it only proves its wisdom, because man is a social creature made to live in the world with millions of others like himself, and if he had not this little society for learning in the beginning how to get along, he'd be hopelessly lost once turned out into the world.

Consider the advantages of learning to live as part of a family. Consider, first, how it is with all of us: in spite of our deep love for one another, we remain self-centered, wrapped up in our own desires, ambitions, plans, pains, and sensitivities. The father works hard, and sometimes feels no one appreciates it, that all his work is taken for granted. The mother works as hard and sometimes feels the same way. The children are full of wonder and energy and curiosity, have a thousand discoveries to make every day, and many times feel that any claim on them beyond the most moderate (like washing a bit, eating at the proper time, sleeping some of the time) is unfair and robs them of time for the really important things. On a bad day, when all these injustices are stinging all the members of the family at the same time, the life of this group called family can become a screaming dissonance rather than a harmonious unit.

Yet, let someone come for a visit, and suddenly, like magic, the group springs back to its primal unity. There's an understanding in the minds of each (in his own way — and unspoken): "We're a *family*. We can't let them see us like this!"

Instantly the father is aware that his work has been fruitful in providing *this* house for *these* children, in feeding and clothing them, and it has been done in union with this wife. It's good; he's proud; he wants no thanks. The mother is suddenly immensely proud of *these* children, of *this* husband who supports them all, and her suffering over their faults and failures and ingratitude is evaporated in the warmth of her confidence that the guests will see much to admire in them. And the children are busy greeting and entertaining the guests, or, if they're shy, seeking refuge with *this* father or *this* mother, all eager to show what "we have," what "we've done," and what "we're going to do."

In the discussions that follow, there's much pointing out of the child who has Daddy's eyes, and Mother's hair, the one who is "just like his father — it's really too comical," and the other who does things "just like her mother — it's quite wonderful." There's the one who has done well at school ("we're all so proud"), and the one who has had a struggle ("but we all help, and we're sure things will come along"). And the sense of family burns very bright.

With what marvelously invisible ties divine genius has bound the family together. Its members are so united that when all the outward signs of unity fail — when sharing the same house, eating at the same table, driving in the same car, bearing the same name, all fail to preserve the *sense* of unity — a challenge that might expose the disunity they sometimes suffer will prick them once, and they spring immediately into a full-blown state of unity. Family unity is not and never has been a matter of tangibles *first*. These protect, strengthen, and nourish it; but the unity is because it is first of all from God.

There are more striking examples of the force of these ties. Catastrophe strips them naked, and in times of suffering, one sees the complete annihilation of self in all the members for the sake of the afflicted member. But, of course, the white peak of intense devotion cannot last. The child, the mother, the father recovers, life returns to "normal," and little by little the same old obstacles to perfect harmony emerge.

⤳

Difficulties are part of every family
Gathering together all the times of love and great devotion, and all the times of irritation and misunderstanding, we see God's

wisdom in this sacred thing called family. No one comes into the world knowing anything. That there will be pain and struggle in the learning is the most obvious thing of all. We start from scratch. We have souls upon which He will pour His grace so that we may learn. We have minds we must subject to others so that we may learn. We have instincts, senses, and a great variety of gifts all beautifully ordered and planned by God, but at every step of our learning, we think we've learned enough to be our own masters; because we have not, however, our instincts, our senses, our impetuous minds make of our lives a magnificent hodgepodge. It's part of growing to maturity that we will pass through one stage of hodgepodge after another.

But suppose He had skipped the family, this small and private cell where beginning begins. Suppose we were put to discovering why we are here and how we are to act on it in the middle of a mob! The family by its very nature is private, and even at its largest, it's never a mob.

I remember reading a long time ago about a little girl who told Monsignor Ligutti that she liked living in the country "because nobody can hear us yell at each other." Or did she say, "hear us fight"? No matter; whichever she said, that is a distinct advantage, not only about living in the country, but also about being part of a family, because in all families, no matter how hard they struggle for holiness, there are times when tempers fly, when judgments are not prudent, when selfishness makes ugly claims over all loyalty, and we get fed up. And even if the family doesn't live in the country, at least they can "keep it in the family"!

Obviously these defections are not pleasing to God. But for creatures inheriting Original Sin, weakened by its scar even after it's removed by Baptism, they're almost inevitable. This isn't to imply that our sins are predestined. It's just facing the facts. We've inherited a terrible weakness and God has great compassion for us in our weakness — or else why the Redemption?

Even though He did design the family before sin came (I can hardly tear my mind away from this once I get to wondering what it would be like to raise children untouched by Original Sin!), its pattern is the ideal beginning of life even in a world full of sin. He has combined our obligation as stewards of children who rightfully belong to Him with our own fierce pride in possession, made our children from our own flesh, and planted deep in us strong parental instincts, enclosed us with a sacrament that continually feeds us grace, and in this combination of securities, a new generation begins.

It would certainly seem, then, that somewhere there ought to be a foolproof pattern for raising a Catholic family. Do we not have the law of God reduced to the most careful detail so that we need never guess about the right or wrong of anything? Have we not the Mass, the sacraments, sacramentals, and methods of knowing and meeting God through prayer, work, suffering, and joy? We're even called to be part of the Body of Christ, the Church — which gives our lives motive far beyond even the highest humanitarian reason for being good. We are partakers in divine life, every day, every hour. Having conceived us in His mind without any need for us, after the Fall and the Redemption, He permits us to be needed. To be needed by God puts the highest price on human life. Certainly all this ought to produce a formula for all Catholic parents to apply and thereby achieve the ideal.

It would — if we did not have free wills. Like nicely trained animals, we could be trained and forever after do as we've been trained to do. But added to all the other gifts — and higher than all the others — is the gift of free will. Free will puts us, in one way, almost on a par with God. He made us because He loves us, but He does not force us to love Him back. He has left us free to love Him or not to love Him. The price of the happiness for which He created us is our own love, *freely given*. Nothing could prove better than this how God loves man. Both man and the angels fell when they loved themselves more than God. To define very simply what is the weakness left by Original Sin: it's the ancient inheritance of Adam's self-love.

⁓

Let your love overcome your weaknesses

Thus one can get just so precise, and no more, with a formula for the raising of perfect Christians, for each member of a family is an "original," unlike anyone else; and the formula must be extemporaneously woven of Christian principles warmed by Christian love. No wonder life can be far from serene, sometimes, in even a deeply Christian home. Perfect serenity comes when we achieve perfect love, and that's the work of a lifetime.

It's ideal that the first love of one's life grows out of one's dependence on parents. This is instinctive, born of need, and it creates a relationship ripe for the unfolding of the knowledge of God's love. For we believe those we love and are loved by (this isn't the same love as physical passion), and God waits for the child to come first to parents who love him before His own greater love is revealed to him. The child's love for his parents is so strong, so satisfying, and their love returned is so rewarding, that it covers over a multitude of parental weaknesses and mistakes. There's a saying — a corruption of St. Augustine's famous words, I suppose — that goes, "You can love a child, and do as you please." This does not give any of us license to do as we please with our children, but allays the fear that the destructive power of our weaknesses might be greater than the constructive power of our love.

I remember one time feeling terrible remorse for a scolding delivered in the heat of my own temper. Going to one of the boys that night, I said, "I'm terribly sorry, dear. I was much too cross. What you did was naughty, but not *that* naughty, and I hope you'll forgive my ranting at you."

And he looked at me with that beaming face children turn to the ones they love and said, "Sure I will. What did you say?"

That's the kind of experience that teaches parents more than a thousand books, and we learned a little of humility that night, of how love forgives and forgets. Children forgive, not because they're wise, but because they love. It's the only reason for forgiving. One must love all men — but what a vast order that is! So God begins the lesson in the intimate life of a family, and one step at a time we expand in love, savor what it is to love and be loved, and in this warm security, we learn how God loves us, and how to return His love. Each step brings us closer to the day when we can reach out beyond the fences around our own yard and love those beyond.

⁀

The family is our first teacher

We first learn to serve in the family. We tend and care for those dear to us, work and sacrifice for them, and, struggling to see each member of the family as another Christ, to help our children develop the same vision, we begin to see Him in the members of other families, to see that our community is not just a collection of population figures but many individual "other Christs." Thus, we learn to carry our service of Him beyond the enclosure of *our* family out into society.

We learn to pray together in the family. We pray for our needs, for blessings on our family. And ever so slowly the horizon moves back a bit, and we're able to hold in our minds the first great idea of the Mystical Body. We make our first effort to join our prayers with the prayers of the whole Body, for the souls of all men in dedication to a cause that began on the Cross and will not end until the end of time.

We first learn about sin, also, in the family. And again we must thank God for the privacy where these first rebellions can (if they must) take place in a hidden manner; where we may correct them, encourage the use of grace, habits of prayer, humility in self-knowledge, and the sense of deep contrition. The child who is piggish and steals his brother's lollipop, who slaps his sister, who disobeys his father learns in the simplest terms that it's wrong, that he has offended God and a member of his family, and that apology and retribution are due. How wise God is, knowing we will fall, to permit our first falls to take place at home. How meaningless it would be if they should come in the midst of a faceless society where cheating a mass of workers, say, is cheating a statistic — not a number of particular people who have rights and to whom we're bound to behave in a moral way.

Even the very painful clashes between one member and another teach us much. Christ has said many times to the mystics that human failings followed by true remorse are useful to Him, because He treasures the remorse, which gives Him glory, and because, by our falls, we discover our dependence on Him. So, too, the remorse following periods of trial within the family teaches humility to both the offender and the offended, the one seeing how weak he is, the other recalling that he has been as weak on another occasion. Patience with one another's faults grows because there are faults to be patient with.

Parents, plumbing their own relationship with God, learn to understand the motives for their children's behavior when they see their own behavior mirrored against perfection. I know a child has licked the frosting all around the bottom of the cake because I have been horribly tempted to do the same myself — and sometimes did! I know a child will lie to save face because I have been tempted to do the same myself. I know he's reluctant to apologize because time and time again, I have hated apologizing, have hated to admit I was wrong. I know the ugly, rebellious thoughts in his mind because I've had the same ugliness in my own.

Abroad in the world, our instinct for self-preservation (especially the preservation of our own good opinion of ourselves) prompts us to measure what others do and minimize our own actions, which seem less grave. It's easy: there are so many who are worse than we. But at home, we're few, and each fault stands out to accuse us by its effect on the father, the mother, the brothers, the sisters, and on the very atmosphere of the house in which we live. Our house is less happy for our ugliness, warmer for our love, *and we can see it.*

One day we will mill around with the multitude, and it will all seem to make relatively unimportant the goodness or ugliness of our own acts. After all, who knows — and who cares? But if we have learned in the bosom of the family that sin is sin, that it does affect us, does affect the people around us, does offend God (who both sees *and* cares) we can cross that bridge between private and public life with the conviction that the same rules of behavior apply to each. A sin is not less grave because it offends a number of people whose names and addresses we do not know. It's always a sin, and always an offense against God — but the slow, piece-by-piece integration of this knowledge begins in the hidden daily life of the family. What divine delicacy, to have designed for these needs the privacy of the family!

We've said that it's impossible to arrive at a precise and perfect formula, because each soul is different and the pattern will be different for each one. But the *way* will be the same — for Christ said, "I am the Way."[71] As long as we know, when we fail each other, that we have failed Him, and when we serve each other, that we have served Him, sanctity is within reach. It is Christ who will perfect us — we will not do it ourselves; and it is Christ who will perfect our family life. Christ seen in the person of each member responded to by the other members, all "other Christs." When we acknowledge the divine indwelling of the Father, the Son, and the Holy Spirit, and ask God's help, He will respond, and we will begin to learn.

Do we love one another? It's His love burning in us. Do we try hard? It's His grace that feeds us. Are we slow to learn? He has infinite patience. Are we loyal; do we protect, defend, calm, and comfort? In His great sacrament of Matrimony, He begins the family by making two into one body, sharing the same flesh: "No man hates his own body."[72]

We need to know the ideal. But we must not be discouraged because we fall short of it. The "ideal family" is not the end of all this living. Its end is union with God. This is the essence of the sanctity of the family. It's the womb of sanctity. There's no other beginning for man. He's always born of a mother and father. And the end for which he's created is always God. The family produces the man who is made for God. It's a magnificent thing.

[71] John 14:6.
[72] Cf. Eph. 5:29.

Recommended reading

⁀

Although many of the books recommended here are out of print, used copies may be available in used bookstores, in libraries, and on the Internet.

⁀

Sex Instruction for Children
Parents, Children, and the Facts of Life, by Henry V. Sattler, C.SS.R.
The Difficult Commandment, by C. C. Martindale, S.J. (for boys)

⁀

The Sacraments
The Power of the Sacraments, by George Cardinal Grente
The Eucharist, The Life of the Church, by Dom Bede Lebbe, O.S.B.

⁀

The Mass
Interpreting the Sunday Mass, by W. R. Bonniwell, O.P.
Living the Mass, by François Desplanques, S.J.
The Meaning of the Mass, by Revs. Paul Bussard and Felix Kirsch, O.F.M. Cap.

How to Raise Good Catholic Children

⌒

The Liturgical Year in the Family
The Christmas Book, by Francis X. Weiser, S.J.
The Easter Book, by Francis X. Weiser, S.J.
Cooking for Christ, by Florence Berger
The Week with Christ, by Emeric Lawrence, O.S.B.
The Church's Year of Grace, by Rev. Pius Parsch
Family Life in Christ, by Therese Mueller
Our Children's Year of Grace, by Therese Mueller
The Externals of the Catholic Church, by Msgr. John F. Sullivan
The Story of the Trapp Family Singers, by Maria Augusta Trapp
Yesterday, Today and Forever, by Maria Augusta Trapp
A Candle Is Lighted, by P. Stewart Craig (liturgical customs
   throughout the year)
The Story of the Redemption for Children (chant, with simple
   verses and modern notation)
Trapp Family Book of Christmas Songs, by Maria Augusta Trapp

⌒

Catechism for Parents
The Catholic Faith and *The Catholic Faith Explained* (teaching
   manual), by Felix Kirsch, O.F.M. Cap, and Sister M.
   Brendan, I.H.M.

Sophia Institute Press®